ROOSEVELT
CONFRONTS
HITLER

ROOSEVELT CONFRONTS HITLER

America's Entry into World War II

Patrick J. Hearden

NORTHERN ILLINOIS UNIVERSITY PRESS

DEKALB, ILLINOIS 1987

Library of Congress
Cataloging-in-Publication Data
Hearden, Patrick J., 1942–
Roosevelt confronts Hitler.
Bibliography: p.
Includes index.
1. World War, 1939–1945—Causes.
2. World War, 1939–1945—Diplomatic history.
3. World War, 1939–1945—United States.
4. United States—Foriegn relations—1933–1945.
5. United States—Foreign relations—Germany.
6. Germany—Foreign relations—United States. I. Title.
D742.U5H43 1986   940.53'11   86–23688
ISBN 0–87580–124–2
ISBN 0–87580–538–8 (pbk.)

3   4   5   6   7

For William Appleman Williams

Contents

Preface

THE PURPOSE of this
study is to explain how and why the United States became
involved in the Second World War. While acknowledging that
the Japanese attack against Pearl Harbor determined just when
the United States formally entered the global conflict, my investigation goes beyond the simple issue of historical timing
and grapples with the complex question of underlying causation.
The primary documents clearly reveal that American leaders
regarded the Third Reich as the root of the crisis in international relations during the prewar years. Indeed, President
Franklin D. Roosevelt began maneuvering the United States
into a military confrontation with Adolf Hitler several months
before the Japanese launched their raid on the American naval
base in Hawaii. While broadly concerned about the general nature
of New Deal diplomacy, this work focuses special attention on
American policy toward Nazi Germany between 1933 and 1941.

Although President Roosevelt repeatedly claimed in public
speeches that Hitler was bent upon world conquest, the question of strategic defense was not the primary factor underlying
the American decision to intervene in the epic contest. Military
authorities in Washington discounted the idea that Nazi Germany could successfully invade the Western Hemisphere and
threaten the physical security of the United States. American
military experts pointed out that the United States possessed
naval supremacy in home waters. They also noted that land-
based aircraft could bomb enemy troop ships long before they

could reach American shores. But their arguments extended far beyond considerations of hemispheric defense. American strategic planners advocated a huge rearmament program that would enable the United States to help defeat the German Wehrmacht on the battlefields of Europe.

Although President Roosevelt and his State Department advisers were genuinely concerned about the plight of the Jews inside the Third Reich, this ethical question was even less important than the issue of national security in prompting the preparation for a military showdown with Nazi Germany. American leaders did make minimal efforts to promote an orderly migration of Jewish people who were suffering from Nazi persecution. However, they did not embark upon a military crusade to prevent Hitler and his henchmen from exterminating millions of helpless Jews. The members of the inner circle around Roosevelt had decided to wage war against Germany long before they learned about the Final Solution, which the Nazis began to implement on the eastern front following their invasion of Russia. In addition, they did remarkably little to help rescue European Jews even after the atrocity stories about death camps and gas chambers were confirmed during the course of the war.

The American decision to enter the war was actually based much more upon economic considerations and ideological commitments than on either moral aspirations or military apprehensions. American leaders were primarily concerned about the menace that a triumphant Germany would present to the free enterprise system in the United States. Preoccupied with the fundamental problem of domestic overproduction, government officials and their associates in the business community were terrified by the thought that the world might be closed to American commerce. They feared that, if Hitler and his Axis partners succeeded in carving up the planet into exclusive trade zones, the New Deal planners would have to regulate the American economy to create an internal balance between supply and demand. Convinced that capitalism could not function within the framework of only one country, they chose to fight to keep foreign markets open for surplus American commodities and thereby to preserve entrepreneurial freedom in the United States.

x

Acknowledgments

*W*ILLIAM APPLEMAN
Williams served as my graduate adviser at the University of
Wisconsin some two decades ago. Professor Williams provided
me with a broad conceptual framework and taught me that
historical understanding demands a thorough investigation of
primary documents.

Several other historians have given me the benefit of their
critical judgment and friendly encouragement. Herbert T.
Hoover of the University of South Dakota persuaded me to
undertake this project. Lloyd C. Gardner of Rutgers University,
Michael J. Hogan of Ohio State University, Melvyn P. Leffler
of the University of Virginia, and Robert H. Van Meter of Skid-
more College were all kind enough to share with me their
insights based upon research in related topics. Gerard H. Clar-
field of the University of Missouri and Carl P. Parrini of Northern Illinois University read the entire manuscript and made
valuable suggestions for revising the content. Lester H. Cohen,
Robert A. McDaniel, and John L. Larson of Purdue University
offered useful stylistic comments on different parts of my work.

Thomas J. McCormick of the University of Wisconsin de-
serves special thanks for his generosity and helpfulness. He
spent endless hours with me during warm summer evenings
in Madison discussing the nature of America's policy toward
Nazi Germany. Sometimes William C. Lloyd and J. Michael
Thorn would join in the conversations and force me to rethink
or clarify the ideas that were bouncing back and forth between
McCormick and myself.

Ronny Johnson did a superb job of editing my manuscript, and Mary Lincoln, the director of the Northern Illinois University Press, worked closely with me during the final stages of revision.

Many librarians working in historical depositories scattered across the United States aided me in locating important materials. William R. Emerson and his staff at the Franklin D. Roosevelt Library were particularly helpful in facilitating my examination of the manuscript collections in their vast holdings.

Grants from the Eleanor Roosevelt Institute and the Graduate Council of the University of South Dakota helped finance my research trips.

ROOSEVELT
CONFRONTS
HITLER

one

Introduction: The Crisis
of Capitalism

THE PEOPLE of the
United States basked in the sunshine of wealth and welfare
during the Roaring Twenties. While corporations were reaping
large profits and rewarding investors with handsome dividends,
consumers were enjoying a vast array of new gadgets ranging
from electric refrigerators to Model T Fords. These products of
science and technology not only made life more comfortable
for the American people but also reinforced their steadfast belief in material progress. As businessmen expanded their industrial and commercial operations, moreover, farmers saw
their sons and daughters flock into nearby cities to find jobs
which paid steady wages. Those who were fortunate enough
to join the ranks of the urban middle class were especially
captivated by the prevailing spirit of optimism. They danced
the Charleston, listened to jazz, and frequented speakeasies.
Even less-flamboyant Americans exhibited an abiding faith in
the future. Indeed, Americans from all walks of life felt confident that the United States had entered a New Era of lasting
peace and enduring prosperity.

Herbert C. Hoover personified the liberal ideology as well
as the ebullient mood of the affluent decade. Reared in a Quaker
family and orphaned while still a young boy, he worked hard
and became a millionaire by age forty. Hoover spent the rest
of his life preaching the gospel of economic liberty because he
feared that governmental regulation would stifle individual initiative and undermine entrepreneurial freedom. But while

3

Hoover believed that people should be free to improve their own position in the marketplace, he also thought that they should be willing to join together to promote the common good. As secretary of commerce between 1921 and 1928, he encouraged the formation of trade associations and farm organizations. He likewise urged business executives and union leaders to work with each other to eliminate wasteful labor strikes and to sponsor efficient methods of production. In a similar fashion, Hoover favored persuasion rather than coersion in his efforts to promote harmonious relations between foreign countries. In short, he hoped that the principle of voluntary cooperation would serve as a recipe for achieving both domestic prosperity and world peace.[1]

Hoover was the prophet of the New Era during the Indian Summer of capitalism. While stock prices were soaring toward dizzying heights on Wall Street, he became the Republican candidate for president, and the speculative fever only confirmed his confidence in the free enterprise system. "We in America today," Hoover exclaimed in his acceptance speech in August 1928, "are nearer to the final triumph over poverty than ever before in the history of any land."[2] After his sweeping victory in the presidential election, the new Chief Executive promised that the United States would continue to enjoy the fruits of abundance. "I have no fears for the future of our country," Hoover declared in his inaugural address in March 1929. "It is bright with hope."[3] Yet, as the hours of sunlight grew shorter in October 1929, the Great Crash on Wall Street brought the bull market to an abrupt close. And when stock prices continued to plummet, Hoover's dream of a golden destiny for the American people turned into the nightmare of a global depression. Soon the dual scourges of want and war threatened the very existence of free enterprise everywhere in the world.

The crisis of capitalism had deep roots in agrarian soil. During the First World War, American agriculture had experienced a period of rapid expansion. European demand for food and fiber from the United States dramatically increased, and prices for basic staples like wheat and cotton more than doubled. American farmers responded to the situation by mortgaging their holdings, buying more land and equipment, and

4

expanding their production. As a result, farmers throughout the United States reaped large profits. But the bubble burst shortly after the hostilities ceased and the European demand for American crops declined. Agricultural prices quickly dropped to prewar levels, and American farmers were then forced to pay off the debts which they had negotiated when crop values were inflated. Many could not make their mortgage payments; and, as the number of bankruptcies and foreclosures in the farm belt multiplied, agrarian discontent mounted.[4]

During the decade following the war, the distressed agrarians turned to Washington to obtain relief from their economic troubles. Their representatives in Congress promptly organized the Farm Bloc to secure legislation aimed at ameliorating conditions in the countryside. These politicians from the agricultural states succeeded in enacting a measure which extended liberal federal credits to help farmers meet their financial obligations. But it soon became evident that low-interest loans from the federal government could not remedy the fundamental ills plaguing rural communities. For the fact remained that farmers in the United States were producing much more food than the American people could eat. Convinced that foreign markets were needed to solve the basic problem of domestic overproduction, the Farm Bloc sponsored various schemes calling for the subsidized dumping of agricultural commodities overseas. And although these bills failed to override presidential vetoes, American farmers continued to look abroad for markets to absorb the surplus products of their fields.[5]

It was not long before American manufacturers were likewise wrestling with the question of domestic overproduction. During the 1920s, industrial development in the United States took place at a swift pace while technological innovation and scientific management made factories more efficient and workers more productive. Yet the consequent reduction in manufacturing costs was not translated into lower prices for American consumers. Nor did the actual rise in real wages keep pace with the rapid increase in earnings for big business. And as corporate profits were plowed back into plant construction, the ability of factories in the United States to produce outstripped the capacity of the American people to consume.

Meanwhile, the federal tax policy, which provided relief for the rich but not the poor, reinforced the maldistribution of income and thereby intensified the problem of industrial overproduction in the United States.[6]

As urban centers began to confront the same malady that was undermining the economic health of rural areas, American manufacturers became increasingly interested in obtaining export outlets for their surplus goods. Of course not all industrialists in the United States were prepared to participate in a quest for overseas commerce. Many small manufacturers, particularly those involved in labor-intensive industries, were unable to compete successfully in world markets. In fact, the least efficient producers persistently advocated high tariffs to protect their domestic business. But the larger and more efficient manufacturers, especially those involved in capital-intensive industries, embarked upon a vigorous campaign to penetrate foreign markets. Some industrialists even built branch factories overseas in order to get beyond tariff barriers erected by foreign countries to shield their own manufacturers from stiff American competition. The trade drive produced impressive results. Industrial exports from the United States more than doubled between 1919 and 1929, and as a result, American prosperity became increasingly dependent upon foreign sales.[7]

But the economic consequences of the First World War and the Versailles Peace Conference presented a serious threat to the international market structure. Before the war, Americans borrowed more money than they loaned in their dealings with foreigners, and in line with their traditional debtor status they maintained a favorable balance of trade which enabled them to pay interest on their financial obligations. Then the billions of dollars that Americans loaned the Allies during the conflict transformed the United States into the leading creditor nation in the world. Yet Americans continued to export more goods than they imported in the postwar era. And when the United States refused at Versailles to cancel the Allied war debts, England and France demanded that Germany pay them huge war indemnities. And because the United States was unwilling to join the League of Nations and guarantee the peace settlement,

France began to rearm rapidly in an attempt to achieve security from a possible German attack in the future.[8]

While steering clear of European political entanglements during the 1920s, the United States did become involved in promoting the postwar economic reconstruction of Europe. Policymakers in Washington did not believe that the United States could remain prosperous unless the European countries continued to serve as a vent for surplus American commodities. Neither did they think that Europe could recuperate from the devastating effects of the military ordeal if Germany remained impoverished. American diplomats therefore urged the British and French to reduce their demands for war reparations so that Germany could resume its role as the center of production on the European continent. They also encouraged the former belligerents to work out a disarmament agreement so that heavy military expenditures would not undermine European economic recovery and pave the way for another world war.[9]

Business internationalists in the United States participated in the movement to stimulate the economic rehabilitation of Europe. American financiers extended large loans to the Weimar Republic to help underwrite the Dawes and Young plans designed to scale down war reparations to the capacity of Germany to pay. In addition, the most internationally inclined members of the corporate community advanced schemes to refund the Allied war debts in an attempt to lighten the burden of payment on England and France. But more than anything else, big bankers and large manufacturers interested in foreign commerce advocated a low tariff policy because they realized that high import duties ran counter to the postwar creditor position of the United States. These business executives repeatedly pointed out that trade barriers erected to protect the domestic market made it difficult for European countries to obtain the necessary foreign exchange either to repay their war debts or to purchase American products.[10]

But Republican political leaders, while insisting on collecting the debts that the Allies owed the United States, refused to lower the American tariff and accept payment in European goods. On the contrary, in 1922, they sponsored the Fordney-

7

McCumber Act, which raised import duties to the delight of small manufacturers interested in safeguarding the home market. Rather than supporting a program of tariff reduction, Republican politicians favored a policy of credit extension. American bankers, unencumbered by government regulations on their overseas operations, made large loans to foreign nations with small regard for the soundness of their investments. These American loans permitted European countries to buy more merchandise than they sold when trading with the United States. Such loans likewise enabled Germany to pay the Allies war indemnities which in turn allowed England and France to pay interest on their debts to the United States. Thus, the payment of intergovernmental liabilities as well as the shipment of American commodities across the Atlantic depended upon the continued flow of dollars abroad.[11]

But this situation could not go on forever. As the European countries fell deeper and deeper into debt, the apprehension grew that they would not be able to make good on their financial obligations to the United States. American bankers, fearing that they had been sending good money after bad, began in 1928 to cut back on their overseas investments. And after the debacle on Wall Street in the following year, the export of capital from the United States slowed to a trickle. As the financial arrangement which had buttressed international trade collapsed, foreign outlets for the surplus products of American farms and factories dried up. Soon there were indications that the European nations would default on their debt payments to the United States. The day of reckoning had finally arrived, and the world plunged into a decade of depression.

In his initial response to the Great Depression, President Hoover concentrated on domestic policy. Shortly after the onset of hard times in 1929, he declared that the United States could "make a very large degree of recovery independently of what may happen elsewhere." And in the next year, despite strong criticism from business internationalists, Hoover supported the Hawley-Smoot Act, which raised tariff rates to record levels. The president had convinced himself that Americans could solve their own problems, and he boasted that the United States was "remarkably self-contained."[12] His con-

8

fidence that internal adjustments would be sufficient to restore American prosperity rested upon his faith that enlightened businessmen would put their concern for national welfare before their desire for personal wealth. Hoping to nip the depression in the bud, Hoover optimistically launched a domestic recovery program based upon the principle of voluntary cooperation.

President Hoover placed the major burden for promoting economic recuperation squarely on the shoulders of the business community. In a series of dramatic White House conferences, he secured from corporate leaders pledges not only to maintain production, wages, and employment but also to expand construction to create additional jobs. Then the president directed the Federal Reserve System to loosen its credit requirements in order to make money available for capital investment. In addition, he authorized increased federal spending on public works to complement the anticipated rise in private construction. However, while Hoover exhorted business leaders not to retrench but to expand their operations, they did just the opposite, cutting back production, reducing wages, laying off workers, and curtailing construction. Furthermore, while the Federal Reserve System maintained an easy credit policy, member banks used the additional funds to improve their liquidity and not to make money available for business investment. Thus, Hoover's initial recovery program failed in every detail.[13]

Unwilling to admit failure, President Hoover began to blame Europe for delaying economic rehabilitation in America. A European financial crisis, commencing in April 1931 when Austria's largest bank closed its doors, led to large withdrawals of foreign gold on deposit in the United States. The particularly severe financial problems in Germany, moreover, threatened the stability of the entire American credit system. If German banks defaulted on the huge notes held in the United States, American banks would be even less willing to make loans at home. Striving to isolate the United States from European financial shocks, Hoover proposed a one-year moratorium on all payment of Allied debts and German reparations. "The purpose of this action," he explained in June 1931, "is to give the forthcoming year to the economic recovery of the world and to help free the recuperative forces already in motion in the United States from retarding influences abroad."[14] Although the president blamed European financial disturbances for prolonging the depression, he continued to believe that the restoration of American prosperity need not await European recovery. The United States, Hoover declared in December 1931, could insulate itself from Europe and "make a large measure of recovery independent of the rest of the world." Accordingly, he argued that the "action needed is in the home field and it is urgent."[15]

President Hoover moved quickly on the domestic front to strengthen the country's credit structure. As the number of bank failures reached alarming proportions, he persuaded Wall Street financiers in October 1931 to establish the National Credit Corporation. But when strong banks refused to jeopardize their own position by accepting the slow assets of weak banks, Hoover reluctantly concluded that the government would have to come to the rescue. The Reconstruction Finance Corporation, created in January 1932, was authorized to lend federal funds to railroads, banks, and other financial institutions. The president then pleaded with bankers to extend more credit and with businessmen to borrow more cash to expand their operations. But once again the principle of voluntary cooperation proved inadequate. Although the government made money available, the prevailing pessimism in the business community meant that it would not be used. Hoover was disappointed. "You know," he complained privately, "the only trouble with capitalism is capitalists; they're too damn greedy."[16]

Still, Hoover remained hopeful that a renewal of optimism would provide the psychological incentive necessary for overcoming the depression. He subscribed to the prevailing view that business confidence depended upon a balanced budget. Yet, because spending on public works was increasing while tax collections were decreasing, the federal government had accumulated the largest peacetime deficit in American history. Assuming that fiscal integrity was a prerequisite for economic recovery, Hoover tried to reduce the national debt in 1932 by cutting public works spending and calling for an increase in

10

taxes. But this drive to achieve a balanced budget made it more difficult for Hoover to provide jobs for those without work. His commitment to fiscal orthodoxy also made him more reluctant to reduce the Allied war debts and thereby lose an additional source of revenue for the American government.

Business internationalists, while agreeing with Hoover on the need to balance the budget, argued that the restoration of American prosperity depended upon the revival of foreign commerce. Will Clayton, a leading cotton exporter, put the matter bluntly in April 1930: "It ought to be apparent to every thinking person that the productive capacity of the United States, both in agriculture and in manufactures, is far in excess of domestic requirements."[17] Corporate directors like Clayton advocated a comprehensive program designed to help make European countries become good customers for surplus American commodities. First and foremost, they wanted to lower the tariff wall which was blocking the flow of trade between Europe and the United States. Second, they desired a drastic reduction in intergovernmental payments to help the former European belligerents put their financial houses in order. Third, they wanted to induce European countries to cut the military spending which was contributing to their economic instability. Hoping to achieve these goals, business internationalists called for a reduction in American tariffs and Allied debts in exchange for disarmament agreements, currency stabilization, and trade concessions.

The House of Morgan represented the wishes of the internationalists when in the spring of 1932 it made a major effort to resolve the reparations-debt tangle. Thomas W. Lamont, S. Parker Gilbert, and Russell C. Leffingwell, all Morgan partners, told French officials that if the Allies worked out a reasonable and permanent reparations arrangement with Germany, congressional attitudes toward the debts would probably mellow after the autumn elections.[18] The Morgan partners feared that England and France would use the forthcoming Lausanne Conference to abolish reparations in an attempt to pressure the United States to do the same to their debts. They worried that such a tactic would "harden public opinion in America at the very moment when every proper means should be adopted to soften it."[19] Lamont worked especially hard to deter the British from taking any action that might suggest that the Allies were preparing to repudiate their debts to the United States. "If at Lausanne," he warned, "there should be a complete cancellation of German Reparations the first impression given in America would be that the Governments over here had not attempted to reach the best settlement with Germany that could be arrived at, but simply had addressed themselves to lying down on America to take care of the German default."[20]

Nevertheless, as the Morgan partners had feared, at the Lausanne Conference in June 1932, England and France agreed to terminate reparation demands against Germany on the condition that the United States should similarly renounce its claims regarding war debts. Although disappointed by the British and French, Secretary of State Henry L. Stimson concurred with business leaders like Lamont who believed that a settlement of the question was "of vital importance to our own economy and to any revival of our export trade."[21] Therefore, he thought that the United States should acquiesce in the Allied maneuver to repudiate their financial obligations. But President Hoover disagreed. He complained to Stimson in July 1932 that "the European nations were all in an iniquitous combine against us," and he insisted that "the debts to us could and should be paid." Stimson replied that if he and Hoover differed so fundamentally, he "couldn't give him much good advice" and therefore he "ought not to be his adviser."[22]

This issue remained dormant for several months only to explode like a bombshell in Hoover's face. Almost immediately after the presidential election in November 1932, Great Britain asked the defeated Hoover administration for a suspension of its debt payments, including the installment due in the next month. Other nations soon made similar requests. "The quicker we get these damn debts out of the way," Stimson noted, "in some settlement, in which I hope we may be able to get some *quid pro quo* for our concessions, the better off we will be."[23] He cautioned Hoover that although the United States should try to get the best bargain it could, he "didn't expect that we were going to save much of the debt." Hoover retorted that Stimson was "ten millions of miles away from

12

his position," and reiterated his belief that the debts could be paid because they were "merely a chip on the current of ordinary prosperity."[24] Hoover was adamant because he did not accept the internationalist argument that American recovery depended upon a revival of European trade, which in turn depended on debt cancellation.

During his last months in the White House, however, President Hoover decided to pursue a *quid pro quo* policy. Great Britain had abandoned the gold standard in September 1931, and Hoover feared that cheap European goods would flood the American market if other countries followed England off gold and devalued their currencies. He also worried that the American credit system would be undermined if massive military spending produced a financial collapse in Europe. Desiring to protect American banks and markets from further shocks from abroad, Hoover wanted to trade debt reduction for monetary stabilization and arms limitation. His willingness, in effect, to make the moratorium on intergovernmental payments permanent was consistent with his high tariff position. Both revealed his firm belief that the United States could, if given the chance, pull itself up by its own bootstraps.

Japanese officials, in stark contrast, did not think that their narrow chain of home islands could operate successfully as a self-contained economic unit. During the last third of the nineteenth century, Japan had embarked upon an ambitious modernization program which stimulated visions of imperial grandeur. The swift pace of industrial development enabled Japan to export finished goods in exchange for raw materials and foodstuffs, and the rapid expansion of overseas commerce made it possible for Japan to support a growing urban work force on a limited natural resource base. As the country experienced a dramatic population explosion, it became increasingly dependent upon foreign trade. Japanese leaders, realizing the vital importance of export outlets, soon began casting covetous eyes on the potentially vast markets in the Orient. They hoped, in particular, to obtain exclusive business concessions in China.[25]

But Americans insisted that the Open Door policy should prevail in China. At the beginning of the twentieth century,

13

the United States had induced the leading European and Asian powers to pledge that they would respect the territorial integrity of the Chinese Empire and the principle of equal commercial opportunity in each Chinese province. American businessmen believed that, given a fair field and no favor, they would be able to capture a large share of the China market.[26] But Japanese diplomats, hoping to take advantage of European distresses during the First World War, demanded special economic privileges in China. The United States responded in 1922 by sponsoring the Washington Conference, and the American delegation succeeded in getting the Japanese to renew their promises to abide by the traditional rules of the game in the Orient. And this arrangement remained intact as long as Japan continued to enjoy prosperity within the framework of the Open Door policy.

The onset of global depression and the resurgence of Chinese nationalism, however, presented a serious threat to the Land of the Rising Sun. The hard times caused a drastic decline in western demand for Japanese goods. The United States, which had been the largest consumer of Japanese exports, reduced its purchases from Japan by more than 40 percent between 1929 and 1930. To make matters worse, Europeans joined with Americans in erecting high tariff walls against Japan. The Chinese nationalists, in the meantime, began to boycott Japanese products and to undermine Japanese interests in the province of Manchuria. As a result, the United States actually replaced Japan as the biggest shipper of commodities to China. Japanese leaders, faced with the loss of Oriental as well as Occidental markets, concluded that the principle of equal commercial treatment had failed to meet the needs of their country. After the Japanese army seized Manchuria in September 1931, therefore, civilian authorities in Tokyo decided to set up Manchukuo as a puppet state whose doors would be closed to American trade.[27]

American officials differed in their response to the Japanese move to carve out an exclusive sphere of economic influence in Manchuria. Secretary of State Stimson wanted to suspend trade with Japan. He argued that the Japanese industrial structure would quickly collapse if it were denied access to export markets and raw materials from across the seas. But President Hoover ruled out the option of economic sanctions. He feared that any attempt to badger Japan into withdrawing from Manchuria might lead to a military conflict in the Pacific. In line with his Quaker distaste for violent confrontations, Hoover decided that the United States should employ moral suasion rather than physical coercion against Japan. The president hoped that public condemnation would ultimately persuade the Japanese to cooperate voluntarily with the United States in upholding the principle of nondiscriminatory trade in the Orient. Stimson yielded to Hoover and in January 1932 announced that the United States would not admit the legality of any forceful change in the territorial integrity of China. By refusing to recognize Manchukuo, the Hoover administration reaffirmed American economic interests in Asia without risking war with Japan.[28]

The League of Nations, led by Great Britain, remained equally cautious. Meeting at Geneva in December 1931, the League established a commission under Lord Lytton to investigate the Sino-Japanese conflict, and in March 1932 the powers assembled at Geneva adopted the nonrecognition policy. England refused to go farther and impose sanctions of any kind against Japan. The British were willing to acquiesce in the establishment of Japanese hegemony in Manchuria as long as Japan continued to respect Britain's imperial concerns elsewhere in the Far East. London therefore applauded in October 1932 when the Lytton Commission recommended the creation in Manchuria of an autonomous regime which would remain under China's sovereignty and yet safeguard Japan's special interests. But the Japanese were infuriated when the League endorsed the mild Lytton report, and in February 1933 they withdrew from Geneva. Then the Japanese proceeded to consolidate their position in Manchuria and to extend their control into other provinces in northern China.[29]

Secretary of State Stimson became increasingly concerned about the Japanese menace to American commerce in Asia. Unlike President Hoover, he had never subscribed to the notion that capitalism could work within the confines of a single nation. "Our foreign trade has now become an indispensable cog in the economic machinery of our country," Stimson asserted in November 1932. "It is essential to the successful and profitable functioning of our whole nation."[30] For that reason, he concluded, the American government should exert its influence to keep the door into China open. Stimson reiterated his internationalist outlook a few months later. "Our trade with the Far East has stood the test of the depression more satisfactorily than has our trade with any other region abroad," he declared in March 1933. "It is thus apparent that our policy and action in the Far East are matters of great practical importance to the present and future welfare of the United States."[31]

Stimson had already taken it upon himself to urge President-elect Franklin D. Roosevelt to look after American commercial interests in Asia. During a visit with Roosevelt at his home in Hyde Park in January 1933, the retiring secretary of state spoke at length about the situation in the Orient. Stimson expressed confidence that the Chinese would eventually succeed in resisting the Japanese penetration of their northern provinces. Roosevelt agreed with Stimson that "Japan would ultimately fail through the economic pressure against the job she had undertaken in Manchuria."[32] A week later, Stimson informed the League of Nations that there would be no break in American policy toward the Far East after the new administration took command. Stimson also let it be known in Washington that Roosevelt would support the nonrecognition doctrine when he entered the Whi.. House.

Roosevelt made it clear from the very outset that his administration would sustain the American commitment to the Open Door in China. Some members of the Brains Trust were dismayed. Hoping to promote domestic recovery through internal economic experimentation rather than external commercial expansion, Columbia University professors Rexford Tugwell and Raymond Moley warned Roosevelt in January 1933 that the continuation of the nonrecognition policy toward Manchukuo might result in a war with Japan. Roosevelt admitted the possibility of a military confrontation in the Pacific, but he told Tugwell and Moley that he had no intention of abandoning American interests in China.[33] Neither did Cordell

Hull. After replacing Stimson as secretary of state, Hull told one of his subordinates that "we would fight if Japan tried to tell us that we would not be allowed to trade in China."[34] Thus, while Tugwell and Moley were preparing to launch the New Deal at home, Roosevelt and Hull were looking ahead toward the development of New Frontiers abroad.

FDR more concerned w/ foreign affairs

Secretary Hull and his colleagues in the State Department were determined to establish a liberal capitalist world system based upon the principle of equal commercial opportunity. They believed that the restoration of international trade would enable the United States to overcome the problem of domestic overproduction without resorting to centralized economic planning. They also thought that the revival of world trade would allow other countries to obtain essential foodstuffs and raw materials by engaging in commercial expansion rather than territorial acquisition. Business internationalists supported Hull and his aides in their campaign to remove trade barriers and thereby lay the foundations for a peaceful and prosperous world order. So did President Roosevelt. His administration sometimes seemed confused because he listened to people who did not share his internationalist perspective. But while Roosevelt liked to avoid personal confrontations, he eventually dismissed advisers who continued to advocate a program of economic nationalism. The upshot was that Hull emerged triumphant over his adversaries on the home front.

But the rise of the Third Reich presented a fundamental challenge to Hull's vision of an international capitalist utopia. Shortly after Adolf Hitler became chancellor in January 1933, Nazi authorities in Berlin instituted a system of bilateral barter designed to induce other countries to buy as much as they sold when trading with Germany. The Nazis were able to extract special commercial privileges from various countries by granting them preferential treatment with respect to bond payments, custom quotas, and exchange allocations. As a result of these discriminatory tactics, American exports to Germany declined precipitously, and the United States met with stiff competition in Latin American markets. Nazi Germany, in the meantime, embarked upon a vast rearmament program. Although Hitler repeatedly claimed that his intentions were peaceful, American leaders feared that the rapid arms buildup meant that Germany would ultimately attempt to force a revision in the map of Europe.

State Department officials hoped to promote the collapse of the Nazi regime before Germany could undermine the peace of Europe and the prosperity of America. Believing that Hitler's popularity at home rested upon his ability to provide jobs for factory workers, they aimed to prevent Germany from acquiring overseas materials that were needed for industrial expansion. American diplomats reasoned that, due to a lack of foreign exchange, Germany could not pay for essential natural resources from abroad without obtaining either outside credits or export markets for manufactured goods. Thus, they concluded that the United States should withhold commercial and financial support from the Third Reich in order to create the material conditions for a counterrevolution against national socialism. But while the State Department rejected persistent pleas from Berlin for a trade agreement which would enable Germany to ship a larger quantity of merchandise to the United States, it soon became evident that Hitler would remain in power for an indefinite period.

After failing to inspire a coup against Hitler, the State Department made a concerted effort to reintegrate Germany into a liberal capitalist international community. Secretary Hull and his associates sponsored a campaign to remove barriers to world trade so that Germany could enjoy prosperity without recourse to either bilateral barter or territorial conquest. On the negative side, they feared that the outbreak of a general European war would unleash the forces of social revolution on the continent. On the positive side, they hoped that Hitler would agree to abandon his discriminatory commercial practices and to dismantle his awesome military machine in return for equal access to foreign markets for German products. While some American diplomats insisted that the German dictator would never be satisfied until he achieved mastery over the entire European continent, most believed that the United States had nothing to lose and everything to gain by trying to pacify Hitler at a reasonable price. The State Department therefore embarked upon a program of economic appeasement in

18

hopes of preventing the dogs of war and revolution from ravaging Europe.

Meanwhile, as Germany continued to threaten European security and American prosperity, the Roosevelt administration began to pursue a policy of military intimidation. President Roosevelt and his State Department advisers advocated an extensive rearmament program designed to dissuade Hitler from making any aggressive moves in Europe. They also launched a drive to secure a repeal of the arms embargo so that the American government would be legally free to supply weapons to countries fighting to contain Germany. Roosevelt privately assured Prime Minister Neville Chamberlain that if Hitler started a war, Great Britain would have access to the enormous industrial resources of the United States. The president likewise told King George VI that in the event of hostilities in Europe, the American navy would patrol the Western Atlantic and thereby enable the British to concentrate their fleet on the other side of the ocean. In these ways, the Roosevelt administration was making preparations for an ultimate military showdown with the Third Reich.

not like Hoover (sp?) naïvité

But neither the carrot of economic appeasement nor the club of strategic supremacy could prevent the outbreak of the Second World War. Shortly after Germany concluded a non-aggression pact with Russia in August 1939, Hitler ordered his ferocious Wehrmacht to invade Poland. The British and French immediately declared war on Germany, but they did nothing to help the Poles turn back the Nazi blitzkrieg. After defeating Poland in a matter of weeks, Hitler made plans for a spring offensive, and in May 1940 he launched a vicious attack against the western front. As Nazi panzer divisions raced through Holland and Belgium, the British hurried to evacuate their troops entrapped at Dunkirk, and the French were left alone on the European continent to try to stem the unrelenting German assault. Then Benito Mussolini jumped at the chance to lead Italy into the struggle against England and France, and in June 1940 the beleaguered French asked Germany for an armistice. Already at war with China, the Japanese believed that the German victories in Europe provided them with a golden opportunity to establish a Greater East Asia Co-Prosperity Sphere.

Japanese officials therefore decided to join hands with Hitler and Mussolini, and in September 1940 they announced the formation of the Rome-Berlin-Tokyo Axis.

After the fall of France, American leaders were terrified by the nightmare of a closed world. They feared that if Germany defeated England, Hitler and his Axis partners would partition the planet into exclusive spheres of influence. Government officials and corporate executives were especially alarmed by the prospect of Germany establishing economic hegemony over the entire European continent. They worried that if Hitler emerged triumphant, he would not only close the doors of Europe to American exports but that he would also launch an economic blitzkrieg against the United States in the markets of the world. American leaders realized that the Western Hemisphere contained an ample supply of raw materials which could sustain an expanding industrial structure in the United States. But if Americans could not sell their surplus wares in foreign markets, they reasoned, the federal government would have to intervene in the economy to create a balance between domestic production and home consumption. Thus, they concluded that a German victory in Europe would spell the doom of free enterprise in the United States.

Convinced that capitalism could not survive in one country alone, President Roosevelt and his advisers decided to do everything in their power to assure the defeat of Nazi Germany. Roosevelt realized that England was running low on foreign exchange, and in March 1941 he persuaded Congress to pass the Lend-Lease Act so the United States could ship weapons to Great Britain without receiving payment in dollars. But those closest to the president understood that the British could not defeat Germany by themselves, and during the spring of 1941 they concluded that he should send an American Expeditionary Force to Europe. Meanwhile, the State Department tried to negotiate a settlement with Japan in order to avoid a violent confrontation in the Pacific. At the same time, the military planners in Washington formulated a grand strategy which called for the concentration of American forces in Europe rather than Asia if the United States should become engaged in a two-ocean war. Roosevelt promptly endorsed their plans because he regarded the Third Reich as the root of the crisis in international relations.

But President Roosevelt was left with a difficult dilemma. On the one side, he and his advisers privately agreed that the United States should enter the war against Nazi Germany. On the other side, the overwhelming majority of Americans did not want to have their boys sent to fight on the battlefields of Europe. Roosevelt hoped to resolve his dilemma by provoking Hitler into firing the first shot. Thus, he ordered the American navy to escort convoys carrying munitions toward the British Isles, and then he anxiously waited for German submarines to attack American ships. The president hoped that a dramatic naval incident would not only arouse public opinion in the United States but also give the Japanese an excuse to break away from their Axis connection. In other words, Roosevelt wanted to maneuver the United States into war with Germany through the front door in the Atlantic while keeping Japan from attacking American outposts through the back door in the Pacific. The president was therefore surprised in December 1941 when Japan launched a sudden raid on the American naval base in Hawaii. But he was also relieved, because the Japanese attack at Pearl Harbor provided him with the opportunity to lead a united people into the war against Germany.

Beyond their determination to prevent the Axis powers from dividing the globe into exclusive economic blocs, American leaders hoped that an Allied victory would enable them to establish a liberal capitalist world system after hostilities ceased. Indeed, even before the assault on Pearl Harbor, State Department experts were busy drawing up blueprints for the creation of a postwar international order devoted to the doctrine of equal commercial opportunity. Government officials in Washington and business executives who participated in the decision-making process confidently assumed that the United States would emerge from the military ordeal with a preponderance of power that they could use to run the world in the interests of free enterprise. And they were willing to pay the price of entering the war in order to win the opportunity to lay the foundations for a peaceful and prosperous international community.

two

Hull's Vision of Utopia

THE UNITED STATES stood at a crossroads in March 1933 when Franklin D. Roosevelt entered the White House. The new Chief Executive promised to restore wealth and welfare to the American people, who were suffering from the twin burdens of overproduction and unemployment. But there was a fork in the road to recovery. One path pointed toward economic isolation, with Americans attempting to solve their own problems by making internal adjustments. The other path pointed in an internationalist direction, with Americans trying to remedy their domestic ills by expanding their foreign commerce. The time for decision had come. The choice made by President Roosevelt and his advisers would ultimately determine whether the United States would continue to enjoy the blessings of peace or descend once again into the fires of war.

The United States was in a wretched condition in the months before the Roosevelt administration took office. Thousands of factories across the nation remained silent, and one out of every four industrial workers was jobless. While urban homeowners struggled to make their mortgage payments, hungry masses in the large cities waited in bread lines for their daily handout. Rural life was equally grim. As agricultural prices continued sliding downward, many farmers went bankrupt, and some in the corn belt resorted to violence to protect their property. Agrarian mobs intimidated judges, halted foreclosures, and demanded a moratorium on their debts. And while indigent children in public schools suffered from malnutrition, discouraged farmers frequently destroyed crops which could not be sold for a profit. The bitter irony of poverty amid plenty provoked many Americans to raise searching questions about the rationality and morality of the capitalist system.

The mounting frustrations generated widespread fears of an impending cataclysm in the United States. "Unless something is done for the American farmer," President Edward A. O'Neal of the Farm Bureau Federation warned in January 1933, "we will have revolution in the countryside within less than twelve months."[1] Patience was also running out in the cities, President William Green of the American Federation of Labor cautioned. "The outstanding, transcendent problem at the present moment is to find work for more than ten million workers who have been idle for two or more years," he asserted. "I wonder whether they will continue to sit quietly."[2] Many observers predicted that the unemployed would not remain quiescent. "I can see 'em now," a newspaperman exclaimed, "howling up Fifth Avenue with blood in their eye, howling up Market Street and Beacon Street and Michigan Avenue."[3] Though the man on the street was not yet in a revolutionary mood, more and more Americans in high places worried that danger was fast approaching.

Franklin Roosevelt and his Brains Trust shared these apprehensions. "For the first time," Professor Adolf A. Berle of Columbia University warned in May 1932, "the United States has come within hailing distance of a revolution along continental European lines."[4] Other members of the inner circle were equally alarmed. "No one can live and work in New York this winter without a profound sense of uneasiness," Rexford G. Tugwell wrote in his diary in December 1932. "Never, in modern times, I should think, has there been so widespread unemployment and such moving distress from sheer hunger and cold."[5] In private conversations with Berle and Tugwell and Raymond Moley, Roosevelt repeatedly expressed surprise that the American people had remained tranquil during the ordeal of the past three years. Roosevelt believed that if another president should fail like Hoover had failed, the whole country

23

might erupt in bloodshed. Hence, he was determined to take vigorous action to promote recovery and thereby preserve the political economy of capitalism.[6]

Roosevelt and his advisers believed that they had to stop the devastating price decline in the United States to pave the way for a return to prosperity. They realized that the deflationary tailspin was feeding on itself. The decline in wholesale prices to less than 60 percent of their 1926 level prevented debtors from paying creditors, and the rise in bankruptcies put additional downward pressure on values. At the same time, consumers held their cash in anticipation of lower costs in the future, and the consequent decrease in demand pulled prices further down. Finally, the deflationary spiral stimulated producers to ship their goods to market before values dropped any more, and the increase in supply pushed prices even lower. It was a vicious circle. Business leaders and government officials agreed that the situation needed to be reversed, but they differed over the best way to accomplish that objective. While some hoped to employ internal measures to increase values in the United States, others wanted to revive foreign trade in order to restore prices to their former levels.

The rising tide of economic nationalism, however, militated against the reestablishment of overseas commerce. After the onset of the Great Depression, countries throughout the world engaged in a desperate struggle to protect their business interests both at home and abroad. The United States had led the way in 1930 when the Smoot-Hawley Act elevated the American tariff to an all-time high. Great Britain retaliated in kind. The imperial preference system, organized at Ottawa in 1932, erected a high tariff wall around the entire British Commonwealth. Soon other countries joined in the scramble, and it was not long before the channels of international trade were choked by a vast maze of currency devaluations, exchange controls, clearing agreements, import quotas, and tariff barriers. The virulent economic warfare caused a colossal commercial collapse. The volume of world trade declined 25 percent between 1929 and 1933, and during these same years American exports dropped almost 50 percent in quantity.[7]

Leading internationalists in the Democratic Party hoped

to use the war debt issue to make a bargain designed to reactivate the flow of trade across the Atlantic. They were prepared to scale down the Allied debts to the United States in exchange for agreements which would not only fix the value of world currencies in terms of gold but also lower import duties on overseas commerce. Norman H. Davis, a key Democratic foreign policy adviser, suggested in October 1932 the possibility of lumping debt cancellation, monetary stabilization, and tariff reductions "in a vast game of give-and-take."[8] Roosevelt had to confront the question almost immediately after his victory in November 1932, when England and France requested a postponement of their debt payments due in the very next month. Prominent Democrats such as Colonel Edward M. House and Breckinridge Long wanted Roosevelt to use the debt issue to promote a general settlement calculated to widen the current of commerce between the United States and Western Europe. "We must," Long insisted in December 1932, "use the foreign debts as a potent diplomatic weapon."[9]

But the Brains Trust persuaded Roosevelt that the debt question must be kept separate from the other outstanding issues between the European countries and the United States. Raymond Moley and Rexford Tugwell felt strongly that economic recovery should be sparked through internal means, and they cautioned against taking any immediate international initiatives which might upset Congress and thereby undermine their plans. "Public opinion both at home and abroad was singularly determined, on the one side not to cancel, on the other not to pay," Tugwell explained in January 1933. "This made temporizing necessary. The realities would have their way in the long run, but political considerations had to be taken account of."[10] A few weeks later, while acknowledging that "in time the debts are going to be whittled away to nothing," he reiterated his opposition to a *quid pro quo* strategy.[11] Roosevelt agreed that he should not make any commitments that would jeopardize his future relations with Congress. Consequently, he refused to bind himself on the politically explosive debt issue before he took the oath of office and assumed the reins of power.[12]

Nevertheless, after his inauguration, Roosevelt did attempt to solve the debt problem before the World Economic Conference met in London that June. The president personally assured Prime Minister Ramsay MacDonald in April 1933 that he was willing to ask Congress for full authority to negotiate a final settlement if Great Britain was prepared to make a reasonable compromise. Then Roosevelt presented a tentative formula, worked out by financial adviser James Warburg, which would reduce the debt principal as well as waive the interest payments. But the British rejected the generous Warburg plan and maintained their demands for something close to complete cancellation. They also asked the United States to agree to suspend their installment due on June 15 and to place the debt issue on the agenda of the forthcoming Economic Conference. But Roosevelt refused to take the political risks involved in either immediate suspension or further negotiation.[13] Therefore, he wrote MacDonald in May that in his opinion the major questions confronting the world could "be brought to a satisfactory and mutually advantageous determination at the Conference, without reference to the debts at all, and without their settlement being made in any way contingent upon a debt settlement."[14]

Internationalists in government and business circles looked forward to the establishment of a program for world recovery at the London Economic Conference, hoping that agreements to stabilize exchange rates and to lower tariff barriers would restore international trade and arrest the deflationary spiral. Budget Director Lewis W. Douglas feared that failure at the Economic Conference would mean "intense national economic isolation for all countries."[15] He wrote Roosevelt that he could see no end to the depression "until we face frankly and courageously the fundamental problem of reviving a dead world trade."[16] Former Secretary of State Henry L. Stimson similarly warned the new president that "we could not expect to succeed with economic recovery unless we took up our relations with foreign nations and helped pull everybody out of the trouble."[17] John Foster Dulles of the Sullivan and Cromwell law firm added his voice to the mounting chorus. "There can be no permanent basis for the reestablishment of values which does not include a restoration of the international movement of goods," Dulles insisted. "Otherwise there is a damming up of products in each country and despite efforts at insulation this inevitably affects the world price levels."[18]

The Brains Trust disagreed. Moley and Tugwell wanted to isolate the American economy from the rest of the world and implement their blueprints for domestic recovery. They advocated internal adjustments rather than international arrangements to turn the corner on deflation and to clear the way for a new start at home. They hoped that their price-lifting devices would liquidate the heavy burden of debt in the United States, unfreeze American assets, and stimulate business investment throughout the country. The Brains Trust also had longer range goals. Moley and Tugwell wanted to restructure the American economic system to prevent the recurrence of periods of overproduction and unemployment. They urged the establishment of a business-government partnership which would work to maintain an internal balance between supply and demand. Thus, they did not want the United States to make any commitments at the forthcoming London Conference that might interfere with their recovery plans, which called for a more self-contained economy.[19]

The State Department was filled with anxiety as America stood at the crossroads. Department officials worried that the Brains Trust would lead the country down the left-hand path of national economic planning and thereby abandon the essentials of capitalism. They hoped that instead Roosevelt would steer the United States down the right-hand path of overseas commercial expansion and thus protect the principles of free enterprise. "Either we will eventually revert to the old liberal idea of unrestricted trading," wrote J. Pierrepont Moffat, the chief of the State Department's European Division, "or we will go on in our present direction and create a series of self-supporting, water-tight national units, with Socialistic control."[20] Economic Adviser Herbert Feis likewise expressed fears that a program of economic nationalism would undermine American capitalism. Feis firmly opposed "policies that take account solely of domestic resources" because he believed that "the road to recovery if it is planned in that direction will be arduous to the point of critically testing our ability to maintain the present system."[21] Along with his colleagues in the State Department, Feis waited nervously to see which road the president would choose.

Roosevelt actually favored a middle course. Ideologically committed to private property and free enterprise, he refused to fight the depression with means which would subvert his fundamental aim of preserving the American political economy. Roosevelt basically agreed with the internationalists who regarded foreign markets as vitally important to the successful functioning of corporate capitalism. But he also agreed with the isolationists who worried that the depression might provoke a bloodbath in the United States before world trade could be sufficiently revived. It was a difficult dilemma. The president believed that the sick American economic system needed a quick shot of domestic adrenalin to prevent a cardiac arrest, but after the emergency passed, he intended to prescribe a large dose of foreign commerce to help the patient make a full and enduring recovery. In short, Roosevelt hoped to cure the ills of the country by sponsoring immediate plans for a New Deal at home and by supporting a long-run quest for New Frontiers in the markets of the world.

Amid all the confusion of his first hundred days in the White House, President Roosevelt publicly clarified his position. In his Inaugural Address on March 4, he emphasized the domestic phase of his two-staged strategy for overcoming the crisis confronting the nation. "Our international relations," Roosevelt declared, "though vastly important, are in point of time and necessity, secondary to the establishment of a sound national economy. I favor as a practical policy the putting of first things first. I shall spare no effort to restore world trade by international economic readjustment, but the emergency at home cannot wait on that accomplishment."[22] Then, in a fireside chat on May 7, the president stressed the foreign policy phase of his recovery program. "Hand in hand with the domestic situation which, of course, is our first concern, is the world situation," Roosevelt explained, "and I want to emphasize to you that the domestic situation is inevitably and deeply tied in with the conditions in all of the other nations of the world. In other words, we can get, in all probability, a fair measure of prosperity to return to the United States, but it will not be permanent unless we get a return to prosperity all over the world."[23]

The first major piece of New Deal recovery legislation Roosevelt launched was aimed at helping to solve the problem of agricultural overproduction. He felt that raising crop prices would not only improve conditions in the countryside but also enable farmers to buy more factory goods made in industrial centers. Accordingly, Roosevelt decided to sponsor the domestic allotment plan, which would use funds derived from a processing tax to pay farmers for reducing the acreage they devoted to staple crops. The powerful American Farm Bureau Federation supported the scheme, which would increase agricultural prices by bringing domestic supply in line with home demand, and in May 1933 Congress passed the Agricultural Adjustment Act to provide an incentive for farmers to restrict their output.[24] Yet Roosevelt regarded crop curtailment as a temporary expedient and not as a permanent policy. From the very outset, therefore, he insisted that any proposal for agricultural recovery should "be constituted so that it can be withdrawn whenever the emergency has passed and normal foreign markets have been reestablished."[25]

Secretary of Agriculture Henry A. Wallace agreed. He believed that it would take several years for internationalist policies to combat the depression, and he feared that in the meantime low farm prices would spark a revolt of the rednecks. Wallace advocated the domestic allotment plan as a short-run device to help lift crop values while an internationalist program was being gradually implemented. But he viewed foreign markets rather than scarcity economics as the long-run solution to the problem of agricultural overproduction.[26] Secretary Wallace made his position perfectly clear in his first annual report to the president. "The struggle of the debtor countries for agricultural self-sufficiency, and their natural inclination to buy where they can sell, make it inconceivable that the foreign demand for American agricultural products will expand sufficiently in the near future to absorb our surpluses," he maintained. "The world situation being what it is, our immediate task is to accomplish an emergency adjustment of farm production to demand. This does not mean renouncing foreign trade. It is possible simultaneously to set about adjusting our farm production to the total demand, domestic and foreign, and to work for the removal of unnecessary impediments to international commerce."[27]

The second major piece of New Deal recovery legislation was likewise formulated as a temporary antideflationary measure to meet the emergency at hand. The decline in manufacturing and employment had caused a decrease in consumer demand and industrial prices across the country. The National Industrial Recovery Act, passed in June 1933, was designed to encourage corporate executives to expand production, increase employment, and maintain wages. Roosevelt hoped that businessmen would forgo quick profits and wait for the anticipated rise in purchasing power to propel prices upward.[28] "The aim of this whole effort," the president explained, "is to restore our rich domestic market by raising its vast consuming capacity. If we now inflate prices as fast and as far as we increase wages, the whole project will be set at naught. We cannot hope for the full effect of this plan unless, in those first critical months, and, even at the expense of full initial profits, we defer price increases as long as possible."[29] Roosevelt believed that if businessmen would cooperate, the American people would be able to buy an enlarged total product, and a recovery spiral, once underway, would support itself.

President Roosevelt also hoped that the rush of legislation enacted during the first hundred days would help produce a feeling of confidence and thereby stimulate private investment. "A large majority of the measures passed were regarded as experimental or were specifically designated as temporary," Raymond Moley admitted later. "Underneath all was a determination to achieve a psychological effect upon the country by the appearance of 'action on many fronts.' Roosevelt believed that the very quantity of legislation passed would inspire wonder and confidence. Nearly everyone who participated and knew what was happening realized that these measures *per se* could not promote economic recovery. They would, however, create a climate in which natural forces would assert themselves." Moley concluded his diagnosis of the early

New Deal with a medical metaphor. "Roosevelt's attitude was that if many remedies were tried, some might work and the rest could be scrapped. If the patient could be kept happy, Mother Nature would come to the rescue."[30]

Meanwhile, Roosevelt revealed his internationalist orientation by the way he staffed the State Department and the Foreign Service. Roosevelt asked Senator Cordell Hull of Tennessee to be his secretary of state and Norman H. Davis to serve as America's ambassador at large. A few days after his appointment, Hull publicly stated the basic outlook which would guide his approach to foreign affairs. "This nation," he declared, "henceforth must play its full part in effecting the normal restoration of national economic relationships and in world commercial rehabilitation, from which alone business recovery in satisfactory measure can be hoped for."[31] Those who joined the ranks of the American diplomatic corps and were assigned to the top foreign posts shared his internationalist view. So did every important member of the State Department except one assistant secretary, Brain Truster Raymond Moley. But since Roosevelt had placed Moley in the department to provide him with a salary while he continued to give advice on domestic matters, Moley was responsible only to the president, and he gave little attention to departmental routine. Thus, except for Moley, the State Department and Foreign Service officials provided solid support for Roosevelt's internationalist predilections.[32]

Even before formally taking office, Cordell Hull began to prepare tariff legislation designed to implement his fundamental aim of reviving world commerce. Meeting at his suggestion in February 1933, an interdepartmental group decided to draft a bill authorizing the president to enter into accords with other countries to reduce tariffs without having to submit these treaties to the Senate for approval.[33] Roosevelt told Congress in April 1933 that he would ask for reciprocal trade legislation to help him "break through trade barriers and establish foreign markets for farm and industrial products."[34] Hoping that Congress would grant Roosevelt the power to alter tariff rates by executive order, President Eugene P. Thomas of the National Foreign Trade Council sent Hull a long list of business associations calling for the passage of the reciprocity bill as a preliminary to his participation in the London Economic Conference. "We are heart and soul behind you on this vital issue," Thomas wrote Hull. "Business interests throughout the United States concerned in foreign trade are practically unanimous behind the Administration's policy in this matter."[35]

President Roosevelt encouraged the internationalists in April 1933 by inviting foreign representatives to Washington to prepare for the forthcoming Economic Conference. During these discussions, Hull, Feis, and Warburg tried to work out formulas which would reconcile the economic differences between the United States and other nations. Roosevelt accepted their proposals for the temporary stabilization of exchange rates and a tariff truce for the duration of the London Conference. Following the meetings, he joined with British and French officials in issuing optimistic statements which looked forward to the removal of trade barriers and the reestablishment of monetary stability. These joint communiqués also suggested the need for the major countries to coordinate their domestic recovery programs with a broad international strategy. The president had two things in mind: international accords to restrict the production of certain basic commodities like wheat, and agreements to carry out public works programs in the individual countries. Roosevelt hoped that cooperation on these subjects would help raise prices around the world.[36]

Sometime in May 1933, however, Roosevelt began to perceive potential contradictions between his immediate domestic plans and his ultimate diplomatic objectives. The problem was that prices were rising in the United States but not elsewhere. Thus the architects of the New Deal worried that international agreements to stabilize currencies and reduce tariffs would check the increase in American prices.[37] After securing the approval of the president, Moley delivered a public address on May 20 in an effort to dampen growing expectations of great achievements in London. "Each nation must set its own house in order," Moley warned, "and a meeting of representatives of all nations is useful in large part only to coordinate in some measure these national activities."[38] The internationalists were upset. "Proposals based on the idea of national self-sufficiency appear to be attaining increasing consideration," Feis complained on May 28. He feared that a further decline in American exports "would probably require the American Government to undertake more and more supervision of industry—and probably force the present undertaking in regard to agricultural industries to become permanent rather than temporary."[39]

Nevertheless, on May 31, Secretary of State Hull optimistically set sail for London to sponsor a program of international economic disarmament. He expected that Congress would pass the reciprocal trade agreements bill and thereby enable him to succeed in negotiating tariff reductions. While Hull was aboard ship, however, President Roosevelt informed him that he would not submit the tariff bill to Congress during the present session.[40] Hull was shocked. Upon his arrival in London, he confided to Ambassador Robert W. Bingham that "if he had had the faintest idea that he would not be in a position to deal with the tariff question at this Conference, he would not have come to the Conference at all."[41] Roosevelt had concluded that the New Deal recovery mechanisms needed protection in the immediate future and that tariff legislation would have to be put off until a later congressional session. His decision meant a momentary victory for Moley and the proponents of isolationism over Hull and the advocates of internationalism.

President Roosevelt also decided in June 1933 that proposals for currency stabilization were untimely. The American delegation at London promptly explained his position: "The American Government feels that its efforts to raise prices are the most important contribution that it can make and that anything that would interfere with these efforts and possibly cause a price recession would harm the Conference more than the lack of an immediate agreement for temporary stabilization."[42] When the French insisted upon a stabilization agreement, Roosevelt curtly responded on July 2 with his famous bombshell message. The president repeated his argument that sound internal economies were more important than international monetary arrangements. But he also explained that his long-range goals included "the permanent stabilization of every nation's currency" as well as the "restoration of world trade."[43] So although Roosevelt postponed making any commitments to reduce tariff schedules and stabilize exchange rates, he did intend to make a concerted effort to revive world trade after the New Deal had had sufficient time to start the American economy on the road to recovery.

Roosevelt demonstrated his basic commitment to internationalism in the way he resolved the tension between Hull and Moley. "It was perfectly obvious," Ambassador Bingham observed in London, "that Moley will have to leave the State Department, or that Hull will resign."[44] Roosevelt made his choice without hesitation when the two antagonists returned from the Economic Conference. While the president gave Hull a warm reception at his home in Hyde Park, he gave Moley nothing but a cold shoulder. Roosevelt hoped to get Moley out of the way by sending him to Hawaii to work on criminal justice. Moley refused to leave the country, but Roosevelt did persuade him to accept an appointment with the attorney general to prepare a report on kidnapping and racketeering. When Moley quietly resigned from the State Department at the end of August 1933, his former colleagues welcomed the news. "The State Department," Colonel Edward House reported to Bingham, "is filled with joy over the departure of Moley for new fields."[45] Secretary Hull showed signs of renewed vigor as he savored the sweet taste of revenge. "Henceforth," Pierrepont Moffat rejoiced, "he will be master in his own house."[46]

With Hull now firmly in command at the State Department, the internationalists redoubled their drive for a liberal commercial policy. "I do not think," Ambassador Josephus Daniels wrote from Mexico City in September 1933, "we can have prosperity in the United States unless we can have foreign markets for the surplus products of our farms and factories."[47] Herbert Feis concurred. "The solution of the problems facing various fields of American economic life without some recovery of export markets is very difficult to foresee," he asserted in November 1933. "This condition compels a broad reconsideration of our commercial policy."[48] In his report to the president, Secretary of Agriculture Henry Wallace likewise expressed hope that the United States would "modify its tariff policy so as to permit a larger quantity and value of imports to enter the country" and thereby expand "foreign purchasing power in definite tangible ways."[49] James Warburg agreed. "Complete recovery can only take place on the basis of world recovery," he argued. "This means that all nations must revise their tariff policy."[50]

The constant bombardment helped turn President Roosevelt away from an emphasis on New Deals and toward a commitment to New Frontiers. When Under Secretary of State William Phillips suggested in November 1933 that the conflicting claims of various federal agencies revealed the need for an interdepartmental organization to coordinate foreign trade activities, the president promptly authorized the establishment of the Executive Committee on Commercial Policy under the supervision of Cordell Hull. Then, in December 1933, the White House issued the following statement: "Now the time has come to initiate the second part of the recovery program and to correlate the two parts, the internal adjustments of production with such effective foreign purchasing power as may be developed by reciprocal tariffs, barter, and other international arrangements."[51] Later in the same month, Roosevelt directed the State Department to draft a bill empowering the president to negotiate reciprocal trade treaties which would not have to be submitted to the Senate for ratification.[52]

Secretary of State Hull and his associates immediately began preparing a tariff bill designed to promote international economic cooperation. The final draft, completed in February 1934, would give the president authority to make executive agreements which would increase or decrease any import duty as much as 50 percent in return for adequate compensation from another country. The draftsmen contemplated the negotiation of reciprocal trade agreements embracing the most-favored-nation clause in its unconditional form. This meant that if the United States reduced tariff rates on certain articles imported from a given country, it would automatically lower them on the same items coming from all other nations which gave America equal treatment in regard to tariffs, quotas, and exchange allocation. The authors of the proposed measure hoped that the unconditional most-favored-nation formula would induce statesmen throughout the world to lower their tariffs in order to obtain reduced rates from other countries. In this way, they intended to bring about a universal decrease in commercial restrictions.[53]

President Roosevelt approved the State Department's draft with only one exception. To improve its chances in Congress, Secretary Hull had recommended that the tariff bill be presented as an emergency measure limited to a three-year period. But the president decided to ask for perennial powers to negotiate tariff agreements.[54] In his message to Congress in March 1934, Roosevelt argued that "a full and permanent domestic recovery depends in part upon a revived and strengthened international trade." He added that "American exports cannot be permanently increased without a corresponding increase in imports."[55] The House reacted favorably to the bill, but it amended the measure to the original State Department form, which provided that the new executive power would terminate in three years. Then the Senate passed the revised version in June 1934, and it was with great delight that Hull watched the president sign the Reciprocal Trade Agreements Act. "Each stroke of the pen," he recalled, "seemed to write a message of gladness on my heart."[56]

Secretary Hull realized, however, that the future of the trade agreements program rested upon shaky political foundations. Although Democrats in both legislative branches had given his tariff bill overwhelming support, only two Republicans in the House and only three in the Senate had backed the measure. The partisan nature of the vote worried the State Department. Assistant Secretary Francis B. Sayre therefore informed an Australian emissary in June 1934 that the bitter fight in Congress over the reciprocity bill made it "prudent for the American Government to begin its program of negotiations with countries whose products were not so directly competitive with those of the United States." Despite his caution, Sayre expressed hope that the reciprocal trade program would gain momentum and "enable us to undertake negotiations at a later date with countries whose products were directly competitive."[57] This strategy soon manifested itself in commercial relations between the United States and Latin America. Nations exporting complementary crops like coffee and bananas were the first to feel pressure to negotiate trade agreements, while countries exporting competitive commodities like meat and minerals took a back seat in commercial discussions.[58]

The State Department continued to move cautiously in implementing the Reciprocal Trade Act. Secretary Hull confined negotiations to nations which were the chief exporters of certain commodities to the United States because the resulting commercial concessions would be unconditionally extended to every other country. This principal-supplier tactic was intended not only to maximize America's ability to obtain tariff reductions from other nations but also to minimize the impact of foreign competition in the domestic market. "If the reduction in duty we granted to A were such as not to injure our own producers with whom A was the principal competitor," Hull explained, "it was highly unlikely that our producers would suffer injury from the competition of imports from countries B or C, who were secondary sources of supply."[59] Moreover, despite his belief that foreign nations needed dollar exchange to purchase American products, Hull decided against making an active effort to encourage imports into the United States. Economic Adviser Herbert Feis warned in October 1934 that "the opposition to the whole tariff adjustment program will center on the Department of State." Feis and his superiors therefore thought it advisable to refrain from actively promoting imports in order to avoid "criticism from the protectionist interests in the United States."[60]

Nevertheless, the reciprocal trade program did arouse the wrath of vested interests all across America. The Home Market Club, for example, published warning after warning in 1934 that the importation of cheap foreign goods into the United States would destroy infant industries, drive factory workers from their jobs, and depress agricultural prices.[61] Antagonism toward Hull was particularly acute in the corn belt. A midwestern farm conference held in Iowa in April 1936 demanded the repeal of the Reciprocity Act on the grounds that it was "depriving farmers of the central states of the seaboard markets for cereals and other products."[62] A week later, Secretary of Agriculture Wallace met with about sixty rural editors and tried to convince them that the State Department's commercial policy was in the best interest of American farmers.[63] But the

37

agrarians remained skeptical. "The rank and file of farmers simply don't understand," Wallace complained two years later, "and it is very difficult to get them to understand."[64] Senator George Norris of Nebraska similarly noted that "the trade agreements program was not at all popular in the middlewest."[65]

George N. Peek, the president of the Moline Plow Company, worked zealously to harden rural hostility toward reciprocity. His outspoken opposition to crop curtailment had provoked Wallace to have him dismissed from the Agricultural Adjustment Administration in December 1933, but he was still highly regarded by midwestern farmers. Roosevelt hoped to indulge the pride of the prairie by sending Peek to Czechoslovakia to serve as the American minister with the added appellation of Adviser to the President on Agricultural Imports and Exports with Europe. Roosevelt confided to Under Secretary of State William Phillips that "the additional title was largely to save Peek's face and to induce him to accept the position at Prague."[66] But when Peek refused to take the bait, Roosevelt decided in early December 1933 to put him in charge of a new organization that would be authorized to explore the possibility of extending American trade. The president assured Phillips that the position was only "window dressing" and led him to believe that the appointment would be a "step-out" rather than a "step-in" for Peek.[67] Therefore, Phillips observed, the State Department decided "to sit quietly in the firm belief that things will work out all right and that probably Peek will not be in the game very long."[68]

But it soon became evident that the State Department would not be able to get rid of George Peek without a vehement battle. In his report to the president in late December 1933, Peek proposed the establishment of a Foreign Trade Administration, headed by himself, to replace the Executive Committee on Commercial Policy. He also suggested that the White House should set up a government corporation, under his supervision, to help finance international trade. Phillips thereupon asked the president to delay action on the Peek report until Secretary Hull returned from the Pan American Conference in Montevideo.[69] Roosevelt complied with the request, but the State Department was worried. "Underlying our daily work," Phillips noted in his diary, "is a feeling of uneasiness with respect to the attitude of the president toward the Peek recommendations."[70] Finally, in February 1934, Roosevelt indicated that he would create an Export-Import Bank to be directed by Peek. "This whole thing may develop into another Moley complication," Phillips grumbled. "There is no doubt that Peek is determined to run the whole foreign trade policy of the Government independently of the State Department."[71] Although Roosevelt refused to abolish the Executive Committee, he did agree in March 1934 to make Peek the Special Adviser to the President on Foreign Trade. Hull was shocked. "If Mr. Roosevelt had hit me between the eyes with a sledge hammer," he wrote later, "he could not have stunned me more than by this appointment."[72]

Peek's interest in foreign trade centered on a strong desire to maintain high levels of agricultural production. "I think the farm is like a factory," Peek told a Nebraska congressman. "You should never shut it down until you try to sell the stuff."[73] In like manner, he wrote Senator Cotton Ed Smith of South Carolina that "an ounce of selling effort is worth a pound of crop restriction."[74] Peek advocated commercial expansion abroad as opposed to acreage reduction at home to solve the enduring problem of agricultural surpluses. So did the State Department. "No one has ever assumed that the present restriction of output is anything more than a desperate and temporary expediency," a member of the United States Tariff Commission pointed out. "The recapture of old and the creation of new foreign markets is the goal of the trade agreements program."[75] The real issue between Hull and Peek was not over the wisdom of scarcity economics. "Everyone is agreed we should have foreign trade," Peek admitted. "The question is *what* we shall export—what we shall import—and *how* it can be accomplished."[76]

The Special Adviser to the President was primarily interested in regulating international commerce to enhance the competitive position of American agriculture both at home and abroad. "I have become convinced," he told the head of the Agricultural Adjustment Administration, "that we are getting to a point where we have to control both our exports and our imports. I mean everything, and have selective exports and imports. When we have that we will be in a position to properly look after agricultural exports."[77] Peek wanted to provide food and fiber producers in the United States with "the full benefit of the domestic American market through tariff legislation and other measures shutting down on competitive agricultural imports."[78] He also hoped to negotiate bilateral barter arrangements that would expand the foreign sale of American farm surpluses even if they did not increase the total volume of world trade. "The tactics we plan to use," he explained, "are not so much concerned with reducing the general emphasis on tariff barriers as with promoting specific transactions designed to break through obstructions to trade by relying on the mutual advantages evident on both sides of these transactions."[79]

From this narrow perspective, Peek made a sweeping attack against the whole trade agreements program. He charged that an across-the-board reduction of the American tariff schedule would mean increased agricultural imports and lower farm prices. In other words, the home market would be sacrificed at the expense of the producers and processors of American crops. Peek also challenged the internationalist argument that the anticipated rise in imports resulting from lower tariffs would lead to an increase in agricultural exports. "The foreign purchasing power proceeding from increased imports," he warned the Executive Committee on Commercial Policy, "might be used for the purchase of industrial products rather than agricultural products." The dollar exchange created by expanded imports, he added, "might be used in paying off loans instead of buying products of any kind."[80] In short, Peek claimed that the State Department was neither providing the American farmer with enough protection in the domestic market nor giving him adequate aid in penetrating foreign markets.

Peek repeatedly warned that the consummation of each trade agreement containing an unconditional most-favored-nation clause would progressively diminish America's bargaining power. He believed that the United States should return to the traditional policy of limiting commercial favors to countries offering ample compensation. "There is only one way to do in negotiating," he insisted, "and that is, negotiate with the fellow you want to negotiate with, and not offer the same thing to someone who doesn't give you anything."[81] Uncle Sam should resume the practice of what Peek liked to call good old-fashioned Yankee horse trading. "Foreign nations instead of following our example," he wrote Roosevelt, "have continued and intensified restrictive measures such as high tariffs, administrative restrictions, quota systems, exchange controls, and special exclusive trade agreements from the benefits of which the United States has been barred."[82] In a similar letter to Hull, Peek cited figures which he thought indicated "that the greatest gains in international trade have been made by those countries which have resorted to the employment of special trade agreements and clearing agreements, and that these gains have been made largely at the expense of the United States."[83]

Peek wanted to fight fire with fire. He did not believe that the Department of State would be able to thwart the global drift toward economic nationalism. Not only was he willing to accept the commercial practices prevailing in the world, but he actually hoped to turn them to America's advantage. Peek wanted the United States to set up a system of double-entry bookkeeping in order to achieve a balanced trade relationship with each and every nation around the world. "I think we must approach the problem country by country and commodity by commodity," he wrote a State Department official, "free from the hampering influence of general theses such as the unconditional most-favored-nation principle."[84] Peek advocated exchange restrictions and clearing agreements to establish the basis for bilateral barter.[85] "I believe that much can be accomplished by an aggressive campaign of barter," he asserted, "during the period that foreign commerce is so difficult on account of the control of exchange and other artifices employed by foreign governments."[86] Peek realized that America's economic arsenal included the powerful weapon of dollar diplomacy, and as the president of the Export-Import Bank he hoped to use loans to induce other countries to give the United States preferential commercial treatment.[87]

But Cordell Hull and his aides in the State Department launched a vigorous counterattack against Peek. On the one hand, they argued that trade agreements based upon the principal-supplier formula would neither endanger the domestic market nor destroy America's ability to bargain with foreign nations. On the other hand, they pointed out that an attempt to achieve a balance of payments between pairs of countries would have disastrous economic consequences for the United States. "If we, the country holding the largest gold supplies in the world, went in for direct control of exchanges," Herbert Feis warned, "all countries would apply the same rules to us on a dollar for dollar basis, and our present net export of commodities would disappear."[88] Paul T. Culbertson made the same vital point. "Less than twenty percent of our foreign trade is with countries where our balance of trade is unfavorable," he explained. "If we start restricting exchange, it would, through resulting retaliation, adversely affect the remaining eighty percent of our foreign markets."[89] Hull likewise feared that clearing agreements would undermine "the position of American commerce in many countries which now buy more from us than we buy from them."[90]

State Department officials were even more afraid that bilateral barter would undermine entrepreneurial freedom in the United States. "Such regimentation of foreign trade," Hull warned, "inevitably forces the country that pursues these policies into an extension of internal control over its domestic industries. It leads to classification of imports according to need and to the allotment of raw materials to the various domestic industries on a priority basis. In the final analysis, therefore, it drives inevitably in an ever-widening circle to the regimentation of the whole system of production and ultimately to a regulation of consumption."[91] The same nightmare haunted his associates. "Any direct plan for selective exports and imports means putting the Government into the business of licensing all such movements," Feis cautioned. "My opinion is that an intelligently operated tariff system is a way of directing the channel of exports and imports along nationally beneficial lines without extreme intervention of the government."[92] His colleagues agreed that the trade agreements program provided the only viable alternative to national economic planning.

The State Department received solid support from other government agencies in its battle against George Peek. Both the Treasury Department and the Commerce Department refused to make pertinent commercial data available to the Office of the Special Adviser on Foreign Trade.[93] Treasury Secretary Henry Morgenthau informed Peek that "it should be our ultimate aim to obtain a removal or relaxation of exchange controls in general rather than to participate actively ourselves in a world-wide movement to restrict trade by such controls."[94] Secretary of Agriculture Wallace was in complete agreement, and he became Hull's strongest ally in the fight against bilateral barter. Wallace shared the State Department's apprehension that Peek's approach to foreign trade would necessitate internal as well as external planning. "I doubt very much," Wallace remarked in his diary, "whether Mr. Peek realizes the full implications of his approach."[95]

Nevertheless, even before he became Special Adviser on Foreign Trade in March 1934, Peek began working on a bilateral barter deal with Germany. He was willing to grant the Germans special commercial privileges in the United States to keep them from discriminating against American agricultural products. Peek worked closely with Thomas E. Wilson, a leading Chicago meat packer, to arrange an exchange of midwestern lard for Rhine wine.[96] To help facilitate the transaction, the packers offered to distribute the German wine through their many retail outlets throughout the United States.[97] The meat packers were worried by indications that the Germans intended to cut their import quota on American lard. "It appears that there will be a considerable reduction in the exports of United States lard to Germany," Wilson warned Peek, "unless some mutual concessions can be worked out between our Government and Germany."[98] Peek agreed. "The thing that is on my mind," he replied, "is to try to get these negotiations far enough along so that there is a prospect of real trade between you and the German people providing the respective Governments do the things that are necessary to effectuate the trade."[99] After months of discussion between the Chicago packers and the German authorities, Peek informed the State Department that the project would require intermediate credits advanced by the American government.[100]

The State Department, however, bitterly opposed the extension of credit to underwrite the wine-lard barter proposal. "If the German Government finds that by harsh and discriminatory curtailment of shipments of American goods, it can secure as a consequence special concessions in the American market," Herbert Feis warned in June 1934, "it is almost certain that existing curtailment will be maintained and possibly extended with the German Government asking for special market opportunities or special credits." Worse yet, other European countries might be encouraged to employ similar tactics to extract exceptional commercial concessions from the United States. "The European countries which consider their trade balances with us to be unfavorable," Feis concluded, "are likely to believe that much more can be gained this way than by merely entering into ordinary reciprocal treaties with us."[101] Hull concurred. "The Secretary feels as strongly as we do," Pierrepont Moffat noted in his diary, "that we must not be put in the position of knocking the props out from our intention that the most-favored-nation clauses grant us a right under quotas to our proportionate share of imports. To give in on this essential point to Germany would be inviting similar action against us in every country in Europe."[102]

Although Germany balked at the lard deal, Peek was intent on working out an arrangement with authorities in Berlin for the benefit of American agricultural interests.[103] Germany preferred to make a deal with the United States to obtain raw materials it needed for industrial expansion, and in the autumn of 1934 Peek negotiated a new compact with Germany based upon cotton. The Germans agreed to buy 800,000 bales of the American staple provided that the United States would reciprocate by purchasing subsidized German products.[104] Southern exporting interests flooded the State Department with petitions favoring the proposal. But Brazil, a competitor for the German cotton market, registered sharp objections to the scheme, which would clearly violate the principle of equal commercial treatment. The Brazilian ambassador even threatened to defer signing the pending trade treaty with the United States if the plan went through. The warning struck home. An interdepartmental committee quickly concluded that such a discriminatory accord would "militate seriously against the success of the whole trade agreements program."[105]

Yet, while Secretary Hull was out of town in December 1934, the State Department learned that President Roosevelt had approved Peek's barter agreement with Germany. Realizing that the secretary would be "heartbroken" if the cotton deal went through, William Phillips telephoned the White House and convinced Roosevelt to postpone final word on the matter until Hull returned. "Any such special deals," Phillips complained, "run counter to the Secretary's broad policy of trade agreements and, in fact, undermine some of the very principles on which he has been standing."[106]

Upon his return to Washington, Hull explained the full ramifications of the barter proposal to the president. "The Department has gone forward with its plans to promote a system of reciprocal trade agreements bottomed on equality rather than discrimination," he reminded Roosevelt. "This program and this policy have been constantly thrust in the face of Germany." But if the United States were to give German exports preferential treatment, Hull lectured, other countries would take reprisals against American interests.[107] "No matter how important one tree may be," Pierrepont Moffat concurred, "we have to watch out for the rest of the forest."[108] Persuaded by these arguments, Roosevelt decided to withdraw his approval of the project and, as Moffat was happy to note, "leave it in a comatose condition until it is forgotten and dies of inanition."[109]

But George Peek refused to accept defeat quietly. Frustrated by his failure to shape commercial policy from within the Roosevelt administration, he took his case to the American people. Peek openly attacked the unconditional most-favored-nation principle in published letters and public speeches.[110] Although President Roosevelt became increasingly irritated, he hesitated to fire Peek. "Everyone seems to want to get rid of him," Secretary of Interior Harold L. Ickes explained in May 1935, "but the President is afraid that if he eases him out, Peek, who has a good deal of strength with certain farming elements, might proceed to organize against the Administration."[111] As the political turmoil created by Peek increased, Roosevelt asked Jesse Jones of the Reconstruction Finance Corporation to "get hold of George and tell him he is silly and stupid about the general Foreign Trade policy."[112] Yet Peek continued on the warpath, and in November 1935 Roosevelt finally forced his resignation.

Cordell Hull had won out once again over a dangerous enemy in his campaign to promote a liberal world trading system. The State Department exulted in his victory against George Peek. "The Secretary's methods of dealing with Peek bore a strong resemblance to the method he used in dealing with Moley," a Hull subordinate gloated. "He let him hang himself."[113] Hull was ecstatic. "We have refused to be drawn into a system of bilateral balancing between pairs of countries," he crowed, "because this system is comparatively sterile and requires direct government management of international trade which soon extends to management of domestic production."[114] Henceforth, Hull would be in a strong position to sponsor a policy of reciprocity abroad as opposed to a program of regimentation at home.

Secretary Hull was determined to reverse the global trend toward economic nationalism and to revive world trade. Hull explained to an old friend from Tennessee in August 1935 that his decision to take charge of the State Department had been the result of a strong desire "to restore suitable international relationships as a basis for full and sound business prosperity." The secretary added that he had devoted his whole life to the study of economic factors which "underlie all international relationships at all worth while."[115] In a letter to another acquaintance in February 1936, Hull stated that he was firmly convinced that the "disruption of international trade [had] played an important part in bringing on the depression."[116] Hull repeatedly proclaimed that his paramount objective was to re-establish a liberal capitalist international order based upon the principles of equal commercial opportunity rather than discriminatory trade practices. "We cannot have a peaceful world, we cannot have a prosperous world," he declared in typical fashion, "until we rebuild the international economic structure."[117]

Hull and his associates in the State Department constantly reiterated their belief that the return of domestic prosperity depended upon the revival of foreign commerce. "Our domestic recovery can be neither complete nor durable," Hull asserted in April 1936, "unless our surplus-creating branches of production succeed in regaining at least a substantial portion of their lost foreign markets."[118] Assistant Secretary Sayre agreed. "It is often said that our export trade is unimportant because it comprises less than 10 percent of our total production," he noted. "But general averages in a case like this are seriously misleading. It is not merely that in many of our most important industries and occupations the surpluses which we must sell abroad greatly exceed 10 percent. What is of far more vital consequence is the effect of unsalable surpluses on domestic enterprise. Unsold surpluses, by glutting home markets, demoralize the prices received for that part of the output or crop sold at home, and thereby spread havoc and cause dislocation throughout the industry or occupation. The resulting repercussions are nation-wide and affect producers who themselves do not sell abroad." Such reasoning led Sayre to insist that "international trade is an essential part of our national economy."[119]

President Roosevelt had already come to the same conclusion. In a letter to the president of the Export Managers' Club in March 1934, Roosevelt explained that the promotion of international commerce was "a vital part of our recovery program."[120] He reiterated the point a year later in a message to the president of the National Foreign Trade Council. "Foreign markets must be regained," Roosevelt declared, "if American producers are to rebuild a full and enduring domestic prosperity for our people. There is no other way if we would avoid painful economic dislocation, social readjustments, and unemployment." He noted that international commerce was being throttled by prohibitive tariffs, import quotas, and other restrictive practices. "The growing cost both to the United States and to other nations is becoming intolerable," Roosevelt maintained. "World trade for the profit of all must be liberalized and freed from discriminatory practices. There must be a return to fair and friendly trade methods."[121]

Prominent members of the corporate community, while frequently differing with President Roosevelt on domestic questions, agreed that the American political economy depended upon overseas commercial expansion. They realized that the key problem confronting the country involved the distribution of surplus commodities and not the acquisition of essential materials. Thomas W. Lamont, a senior partner in the J. P. Morgan firm, admitted in May 1935 that the United States "might conceivably work out an existence in time without much reliance upon foreign markets."[122] But Lamont and other business leaders believed that national self-containment would require federal intervention in the economy to create an internal balance between supply and demand. Insisting that control over production decisions must remain in private hands, they were frightened by the very concept of economic self-sufficiency. "Our world trade is very vital," President Alfred P. Sloan of General Motors exclaimed in September 1935, because autarchy would necessitate "adjustments to our national economy appalling to contemplate."[123]

State Department officials likewise warned that a program of economic isolation would undermine entrepreneurial freedom. Assistant Secretary R. Walton Moore wrote an American diplomat in March 1934 that he could not see how to avoid "Government control of all business unless we can widen out our foreign markets."[124] Secretary Hull similarly wrote a friend in December 1935 that if international trade were not restored, the consequences for the United States would be "permanent regimentation on an ever-increasing scale."[125] Francis Sayre was equally concerned about preserving the essence of free enterprise. "If we are to choose the pathway of economic self-sufficiency," he admonished, "we must frankly accept a system of government control over private business enterprise."[126] Sayre warned that such a decision would "sound the death knell of civilization as we know it."[127] Thus, Henry F. Grady of the Trade Agreements Division pointed out that the State Department was doing everything in its power to expand foreign commerce in order to "preserve the capitalist system."[128]

State Department officers also feared that the spread of economic nationalism would sow the seeds of war. "Fierce and unregulated struggles among nations for trade," Hull declared in November 1934, "produce both economic and political disturbances. They are almost certain precursors of war."[129] A few years later, Sayre offered a full explanation of the prevailing view in the State Department. "Industrial nations in these days cannot possibly maintain satisfactory standards of living without importing the foodstuffs and raw materials which they need and exporting to foreign markets the surpluses which they must sell," he lectured. "If access to these through ordinary processes of international trade is seriously obstructed, the pressure to secure necessary raw materials and increased markets through gaining additional territory by conquest and the mailed fist becomes well-nigh irresistible."[130] Sayre concluded that economic nationalism would lead to perpetual warfare. "If goods cannot cross frontiers," he warned, "armies will."[131]

Leading businessmen and bankers in the United States agreed. "Desperate peoples, deprived of trade," Winthrop W. Aldrich of the Chase National Bank warned in December 1936, "feel driven to fight for their outlets and to fight for sources of food and raw materials."[132] The same belief led John Foster Dulles to conclude that "in the long run peace can only be assured under conditions which so open up the world that, irrespective of nationality, equality of opportunity exists in respect of economic conditions."[133] Stirred by such thoughts, President Thomas J. Watson of International Business Machines tirelessly preached the gospel of world peace through world trade. "Agents of trade are missionaries of peace," Watson proclaimed in February 1936.[134] "The more goods we can have flowing back and forth across the borders," he reasoned a few months later, "the less need there is going to be for soldiers marching back and forth across those borders."[135]

American business and government leaders assumed that it was the destiny of their country to occupy the number-one position in a peaceful and prosperous world order. The United States possessed a powerful combination of raw materials, technological skill, and investment capital. Confident that these advantages would enable the country to compete successfully in foreign markets, they simply asked for a fair field and no favor. Their belief in American economic supremacy, in other

49

words, underlaid their desire for a liberal international trading system. "Undoubtedly," Thomas Lamont explained in May 1935, "if it were possible to bring about a moderate lowering of tariffs throughout the world, America would be the country to benefit most by such a move. The reason is that America, with her vastly greater natural resources and with her capacity for economical mass production, would gain far more from her increased foreign sales than she would lose from some trifling falling off of domestic sales."[136]

Business internationalists and government officials alike believed that tariff reform should begin at home. They repeatedly argued that American exports could not be restored until the United States reduced existing barriers to imports from abroad. "If we admit foreign goods into the United States," Henry A. Wallace reasoned in December 1935, "it will provide dollar exchange that other countries can spend."[137] James D. Mooney of General Motors Export Company explained the need for tariff reductions in the same terms. "American exports can only be paid for in dollars," he declared, "and the other countries cannot obtain dollars unless they are able to sell their goods for dollars in America."[138] Alfred Sloan was equally blunt in his assessment of the situation. "To sell," he insisted, "we must buy."[139] Winthrop Aldrich agreed. "We must recognize," he lectured in May 1936, "that exports can, in the last analysis, only be paid for by imports."[140]

The crusade for a more liberal commercial policy came to a climax during the 1936 presidential campaign. Many prominent businessmen who traditionally voted for a Republican candidate were angered by the commitment to high import duties in the platform of the Grand Old Party. Some decided to cast their ballot for the Democratic ticket despite their sharp differences with Roosevelt on many domestic issues. "A vote for President Roosevelt," Will Clayton explained from his perspective as a large cotton exporter, "is a vote to keep Secretary Hull in office, where his work, just beginning to bear fruit, may go forward with infinite benefit to the nation and to the world."[141] Even those who voted Republican were annoyed when Peek published a scathing attack against Hull in a protectionist diatribe entitled *Why Quit Our Own?* George F.

Bauer of the Automobile Manufacturers' Association complained that "Mr. Peek follows the system now employed in Germany."[142] Business internationalists like Bauer and Clayton continued to support Hull and Warren L. Pierson, the handpicked State Department man who had replaced Peek as the president of the Export-Import Bank.

Although Cordell Hull had emerged triumphant over George Peek on the home front, Adolf Hitler loomed large as a far more powerful adversary in the foreign field. As Hitler's challenge to Hull's vision of utopia mounted, Peek argued that the reciprocal trade program could no more maintain international peace than it could restore American prosperity. "The trade agreements," he ridiculed, "will have about as much effect in preserving the peace of the world as they will in driving leprosy out."[143] But even after the American effort to preserve world peace by increasing international trade had failed, Hull still clung to his materialistic interpretation of global affairs. "Yes, war did come, despite the trade agreements," Hull noted after Hitler and his Axis partners were defeated. "But it is a fact that war did not break out between the United States and any country with which we had been able to negotiate a trade agreement. It is also a fact that, with very few exceptions, the countries with which we signed trade agreements joined together in resisting the axis. The political line-up followed the economic line-up."[144]

"Ervine Metzl for FORTUNE Magazine, May 1939"

three

Dr. Schacht's
Frankenstein

THE TREATY of Ver-
sailles, which officially ended the First World War in 1919, set
the stage for the dramatic rise of Adolf Hitler to a position of
supreme power in Germany. During the peace conference, the
victorious Allies demanded that the vanquished Germans
make huge reparation payments as well as surrender valuable
continental and colonial possessions. These harsh terms sowed
the seeds of discontent deep in German soil. Although Hitler
entered the political arena with hopes of reaping the bitter har-
vest, his National Socialist Party failed to attract a large following as long as Germany remained prosperous. But the global
depression beginning in 1929 hit the Weimar Republic with
particular vengeance, and by 1932 one out of every three Germans was unemployed. Most Germans blamed the burdensome
war indemnities for their economic troubles, and many looked
to the charismatic Nazi leader to free them from the shackles
imposed at Versailles. Such were the circumstances which enabled Hitler to become chancellor in January 1933 on the promise that he would provide jobs for the German people and
restore their fatherland to its place in the sun.[1]

The dictator of the Third Reich gave top priority to rearming Germany when he took command. His purposes were two-
fold. In the first place, Hitler aimed to create jobs for those
without work by stimulating heavy industry through a program
of massive military spending. This pump-priming yielded quick
results. The number of unemployed Germans declined from

more than 6 million in January 1933 to about 2½ million by December 1934, and as the German people regained a sense of economic security despite stringent living conditions, they rewarded their führer with widespread support. In the second place, Hitler wanted a rapid arms build-up to provide a powerful instrument for accomplishing his foreign policy goals. He attempted to conceal his desire to dominate Europe by making periodic declarations of peaceful intentions, and some were fooled in the beginning. But the more discerning outside observers recognized that the Nazi rearmament program was designed not only to promote a recovery from the economic collapse in Germany but also to force a revision in the political boundaries of the European continent.[2]

During the decade preceding the Nazi ascendancy in Germany, American diplomats had tried to encourage European disarmament. They feared that large military expenditures would thwart the economic reconstruction of postwar Europe and that an arms race among the former belligerents would culminate in another world war. Americans generally subscribed to the German argument that the Versailles peace settlement was both unworkable and unjust. But while many American officials looked forward to the eventual return of territory taken from Germany, they did not want to see a violent revision of the existing map of Europe.[3] Norman H. Davis, the United States delegate to the Disarmament Conference at Geneva, clearly articulated the prevailing American view. "The real problem that must ultimately be solved," he reasoned in February 1932, "is how to prevent attempts to alter the status quo by force and at the same time remove undue incentive to use force to that end by ample provisions for orderly readjustments which the peace and progress of the world may demand." Davis concluded that "the only two alternatives are disarmament or disaster."[4]

The National Socialist revolution in Germany greatly intensified the American zeal for European disarmament. George S. Messersmith, the American consul general in Berlin, repeatedly warned during the first months of the Nazi regime that Hitler was preparing for hostile actions behind the cloak of peaceful proclamations. "The sincerity of such declarations with regard to the desire for peace over a long period," he cautioned in April 1933, "is inconsistent with the impetus being given in every possible way to extreme militarism among all classes and to the military training of various kinds which is being developed with an extraordinary rapidity even among small children."[5] William C. Bullitt, a foreign policy adviser to President Roosevelt, similarly warned that "the Nazis want five years of peace in order to better prepare for eventual war."[6] Fearing that Hitler was bent on using force to obtain his objectives in Europe, State Department officials stressed their opposition to German rearmament as well as their desire for French disarmament.[7] President Roosevelt shared their views. He therefore asked a German representative in May 1933 to tell Hitler "that the United States will insist that Germany remain in status quo in armament and that we would support every possible effort to have the offensive armament of every other nation brought down to the German level."[8]

American diplomats held diverse opinions with regard to the chances of achieving success at the Geneva Disarmament Conference. Former Secretary of State Henry L. Stimson told Roosevelt in March 1933 that he had become bearish on the subject "in view of the failure of the European nations to do the necessary work of solving the political questions upon which the possibility of a successful disarmament rested."[9] But Norman Davis remained bullish. He hoped that if the French felt safe as a result of a disarmament accord, they would be willing to rectify the settlement inflicted on Germany after the war. "If Germany was not too unreasonable in her demands and inspired confidence in her peaceful intentions," Davis told Hitler in April 1933, "she could thus gain for herself the support of public opinion for such reasonable modifications as may be justified."[10] In short, Davis hoped that the Geneva Conference would lay the groundwork for a pacific revision of the Versailles Treaty.

The Roosevelt administration sought to induce the French to disarm by assuaging their feelings of military insecurity. Though unwilling to guarantee that the United States would defend France in the event of a future German attack, American leaders did offer to relinquish their traditional neutral right to trade with all belligerent nations.[11] Norman Davis formally announced in May 1933 that the United States would not interfere with sanctions imposed by the League of Nations against an aggressor provided the following two conditions were met: if the European powers assembled at Geneva concluded a genuine disarmament agreement; and if the American government concurred with their judgment that the penalized party was guilty of aggression. Roosevelt had already asked Congress for authority to employ an arms embargo against any country he defined as an aggressor, and in April 1933 the House of Representatives passed a resolution giving the president the discretionary power he desired. A few days after the Davis pledge that the United States would not undermine a collective effort to check aggression, however, the Senate Foreign Relations Committee inserted an amendment requiring that any arms embargo must be applied impartially to all participants in a dispute. Refusing to risk a long political battle which might jeopardize his domestic recovery program, Roosevelt decided to postpone a vote on the issue until the next session of Congress.[12]

In the meantime, President Roosevelt and his State Department advisers continued to wrestle with the problem of European disarmament. J. Pierrepont Moffat, the chief of the Western European Affairs Division, was pessimistic. "I do not see an appeasement of the European political situation this early," Moffat wrote in June 1933, "nor do I foresee disarmament without a prior political appeasement."[13] But Roosevelt continued to hope that the French would agree to reduce their military stockpile in return for a German promise not to rearm. "Obviously neither the United States nor Great Britain would want France to disarm if this would mean that Germany would later take advantage of this to seek revenge," the president wrote Davis in August 1933. "Neither do we want to have Germany assert the right to re-arm as a result of failure on the part of the heavily armed nations to take immediate, substantial and constructive steps towards general disarmament."[14] But the French refused to yield to German demands for military equality, and in October 1933, Hitler announced that Germany would withdraw from both the Disarmament Conference and the League of Nations.

The Geneva Conference foundered on the rocks of a fundamental conflict between France and Germany. While the French remained committed to preserving the territorial status quo in Europe, the Germans clung to their revisionist dreams. Allen W. Dulles, serving as an aide to Davis, reported from Geneva that the Nazis were determined to use military intimidation to wrest territorial concessions from France. "Germany has left the Disarmament Conference not primarily because of her dissatisfaction with the work of the Conference, but to indicate her revolt against the entire regime of the Treaty of Versailles," Dulles noted in October 1933. "Germany has now committed herself to a position which carries the implication that she will only give up the rearming issue in connection with the settlement of some of the broader political issues."[15] President Roosevelt, anticipating that the French would try to draw America into the European tangle, immediately telephoned Davis to make it clear that "we are not interested in the political element."[16] A month later, Pierrepont Moffat cautioned American representatives in Geneva against exerting pressure on the French to abandon their insistence on maintaining military superiority. "To go on persuading France or the other armed countries to disarm against their better judgment," he explained, "might well be viewed as an assumption of moral responsibility on our part which public opinion over here will not accept."[17]

The halls of the State Department were filled with anxiety when Hitler bolted from the Disarmament Conference and the League of Nations. "In spite of lip-service to the necessity for reductions for the heavily-armed powers," Minister Hugh R. Wilson warned from Geneva, "the German Government seems more interested in the increase of its own armament."[18] Even Norman Davis began to lose some of his "confidence in the good-faith of the Germans."[19] Distrust of the Nazi regime increased in March 1934 when reports reached the United States that the Reichsbank was giving Hermann Goering first call on foreign exchange to buy airplane parts for the Luftwaffe.[20] Secretary of State Cordell Hull believed that Germany was trying to avoid debt payments to the United States in order "to get the American creditors to finance her rearmament."[21] Pierrepont Moffat agreed. "We don't," he explained to a colleague, "wish our creditors to be put in the position of financing a German re-armament."[22]

Dr. Hjalmar Schacht, the president of the Reichsbank, was already discriminating against American financial interests. Schacht suggested in June 1933 "the possibility of treating various national groups of creditors differently on the basis of the particular balance of trade between Germany and each respective country." He also indicated that the United States was the only principal creditor nation which sold more merchandise than it bought when trading with the Third Reich.[23] Fearing that Germany intended "to use its debt situation as a means of getting trade advantages," Secretary Hull immediately instructed the American embassy in Berlin to demand equal treatment for American bondholders.[24] Dr. Schacht promptly gave the United States definite assurances that he would not sanction a policy of discrimination toward lenders of different countries, but in October 1933 he granted preferential treatment to Swiss creditors because their country agreed to accept additional imports from Germany.[25] Despite American complaints, Schacht quickly negotiated a similar arrangement with Holland.[26] The president and his State Department counselors were "very much incensed," and together they drafted a strong protest demanding that Germany deal with American bondholders on a most-favored-nation basis.[27]

The United States hoped to maintain a common front with Great Britain in order to counter German financial maneuvers. "If every creditor country seeks to secure special advantages in situations where its trade relations give it the opportunity," Under Secretary of State William Phillips explained in January 1934, "the result will be a worldwide contest between creditor governments, which in the final outcome will be expensive to them all."[28] The American desire for Anglo-Saxon economic cooperation deepened each time Dr. Schacht claimed that Germany did not have enough foreign exchange for loan service.[29] But the British, due to their adverse trade balance with Germany, were in a position to extract special financial conces-

Dr. Schacht's Frankenstein

sions from the Reichsbank.[30] And when Schacht announced in June 1934 that he intended to suspend all foreign debt payments, England established a clearing office designed to discharge the German debt by seizing all payments for goods imported from the Third Reich. The threat of retaliation produced quick results. But when the Nazi government promptly agreed to pay full interest to British holders of Dawes and Young bonds which had helped finance the Weimar Republic, American investors felt betrayed.[31] Thomas W. Lamont, speaking for the House of Morgan, expressed his resentment to a banking associate in London. "The American Government," Lamont wrote, "feels very strongly that the American investment community was had, so to speak, and was had at the deliberate urgency of the British."[32]

William E. Dodd, the American ambassador in Germany, gave State Department officials additional reason to become angry. Dodd had been a history professor at the University of Chicago, where he developed a strong bias against big business. Even after he was appointed to his post in Berlin, Dodd complained that many of his associates in the diplomatic corps owned large blocks of DuPont and Standard Oil stocks.[33] Pierrepont Moffat viewed him as "an unfortunate misfit," and Dodd's poor reporting from the field provoked the more irreverent career officers to refer to him as "Ambassador Dud."[34] William Phillips was extremely upset when a partner of J. P. Morgan complained in July 1934 that Dodd was not interested in aiding Americans who possessed Dawes and Young scrip. "This corroborates what we have heard," Phillips observed, "that Dodd dislikes Wall Street and bankers thoroughly and does not realize that the holders of the securities are in large measure innocent Americans, scattered throughout the country. Dodd is showing himself more and more a small town man with no capacity to act as ambassador."[35] On the next day, Dodd cabled from Berlin that instead of pressing the Germans to treat American creditors as favorably as they were treating the British, he had been encouraging Germany to remove the existing discrimination by stopping all payments to England. Cordell Hull was dumbfounded. "We had a council of war in the Secretary's office," Moffat noted in his diary, "and decided to send off a brief telegram to Mr. Dodd saying that we wished to pursue the matter through a positive approach in Berlin rather than through a negative approach in London."[36]

Although Dodd complied with these orders from the State Department, his protest had little impact in Berlin.[37] The American government was in no position to confiscate deposits on German imports because the United States had a favorable trade balance with the Third Reich. "We have no weapon," William Phillips lamented in July 1934, "with which to force Germany to give American holders of German securities equal treatment."[38] Thus, the Nazis refused to cease discriminating against American financial interests unless the State Department agreed to give Germany compensatory commercial concessions. "This country could not possibly acquiesce," Phillips grumbled, "on account of its position as a creditor nation the world over."[39] Finally, in October 1934, Germany announced that it would pay American holders of Dawes coupons only 75 percent of the interest due them, while creditors from all other countries would receive full service. The State Department was outraged. "Could anything," Phillips asked, "be more disgusting?"[40]

German discrimination against American commerce angered the State Department even more. Dr. Schacht inaugurated a system of bilateral barter designed to induce other countries to buy as much from Germany as they sold to the Third Reich. Americans began to feel the effects of the Nazi campaign to balance the books in September 1933, when the German quota on prune imports was altered to favor Yugoslavia at the expense of the United States. "Our whole trade relations with Germany would probably be seriously jeopardized," Hull warned, "if Germany were to embark upon a general policy of customs quotas."[41] His anxiety was not without cause. Authorities in Berlin continued to divert purchases away from the United States and toward countries willing to buy more German goods, and consequently, between 1933 and 1935 American sales to Germany declined by more than 50 percent.[42] The experience of American cotton exports provides a dramatic illustration of the general situation. National Socialist officials pressured German textile manufactures into adapting their spindles and looms to run on cotton grown in Brazil, Egypt, and India. As a result, only 25 percent of the cotton imported into Germany in 1935 came from the United States compared to about 75 percent in 1933.[43]

Despite strong protests from Washington, the German discrimination against American products grew apace. The Reichsbank quickly instituted an exchange control program which penalized countries that had a favorable balance of trade with Germany. Dr. Schacht made sure that the amount of Reichsmarks released to pay for imports from any given nation would correspond with the quantity of German merchandise purchased by that particular country. The State Department was disturbed because the Nazi exchange control policy threatened to curtail drastically the German market for American commodities. In a cable to Berlin in October 1933, Secretary Hull instructed Ambassador Dodd to keep the State Department fully informed about the "use of blocked marks for the encouragement of exports."[44] But Nazi Germany continued to allocate foreign exchange on a basis that discriminated against the United States, and in March 1934 Economic Adviser Herbert Feis wrote Hull that the relationship "that now exists between the two countries is one closely approaching trade warfare."[45]

Against this backdrop, Germany made repeated requests for the opening of commercial negotiations with the United States. Americans were exporting to the Third Reich approximately twice as much as they were importing from Germany, and Nazi authorities were determined to balance their account with the United States. Hans Luther, the German ambassador in Washington, expressed an urgent desire in April 1934 for "trade negotiations permitting Germany to export larger quantities of goods to the United States."[46] The Nazis also wanted to get credit from America so they could purchase raw materials needed for their industrial recovery program. Assistant Secretary of State Francis B. Sayre noted "the great eagerness with which Germany is pressing to obtain an arrangement with the United States whereby Germany would be assured of its supplies of cotton, copper, and other necessary raw materials."[47] But the State Department was in no mood to aid the Nazi regime. "We feel," Pierrepont Moffat explained in June 1934, "that with Germany discriminating against our creditors in the matter of bond payments, against our commerce by means of quotas, and in general showing an unfriendly point of view it is not time to give them the comfort that the announcement of even a small indirect credit would prove to be."[48]

George S. Messersmith led the drive against the economic overtures emanating from the Third Reich. After serving as consul general in Berlin during the first year of the Hitler regime, he became the American minister to Austria. Messersmith insisted again and again in 1934 that the State Department could not expect to conclude a successful trade agreement with Germany as long as the National Socialists continued to run the country. "They do not intend to buy raw stuff from us longer than necessary," he explained. "Raw stuff sources from overseas must gradually be eliminated so as to obviate the danger of being cut off in time of war."[49] To accomplish this, the Nazis aimed both to create domestic substitutes to replace foreign supplies and to establish a large regional economic bloc on the European continent.[50] Even if German authorities did agree to purchase some raw materials from the United States, Messersmith warned, they could not be trusted to keep their word.[51] "These people are so definitely determined not to buy anything that they don't have to," he emphasized, "that if they remain in power no agreement which we might make will be of any use to us."[52] Messersmith believed that the Nazis wanted Uncle Sam "to play the part of Santa Claus" by presenting them with valuable trade concessions.[53] "They have nothing to offer us in exchange," he concluded, "and the bargain they have in mind is too one-sided."[54]

Douglas Miller, the American commercial attaché in Berlin, confirmed these observations. In his monthly economic reviews in 1934, he pointed out that the Nazi drive to concoct ersatz materials through scientific research was motivated by a desire to make Germany less dependent upon natural resources from overseas.[55] Miller also reported that the Nazi leaders were determined to organize the European continent into a *Grossraumwirtschaft* to make Germany economically impregnable if they could not get what they wanted without recourse to war. "The Nazis are not satisfied with the existing map of Europe," he warned. "Germany is to be made the economic center of a self-sustaining territorial block whose dependent nations in Central and Eastern Europe will look to Berlin for leadership. This block is to be so constituted that it can defy wartime blockade and be large enough to give the peoples of it the benefits of free trade now enjoyed by the 48 American states." But Miller hoped to prevent the Nazis from obtaining the outside sources of raw materials they needed to accomplish their ultimate goals. "We should not give financial assistance," he concluded, "we should not initiate trade negotiations."[56]

George Messersmith agreed. Believing that Hitler's popularity at home rested upon the success of his reemployment program, Messersmith wanted the United States to prevent Germany from acquiring natural resources from abroad needed for industrial expansion. "Unless an adequate supply of raw materials is assured," he argued in April 1934, "production and consequently employment in Germany will have to go down."[57] Messersmith reasoned that due to a lack of foreign exchange, Germany could not pay for essential overseas supplies without either credits or exports. "The exchange position of the country is really serious," he reported. "Schacht himself is showing the strain and is at times like an animal in a cage."[58] Messersmith did not want to let him escape. There were only two ways for the Nazis to avoid the impending crisis, he reiterated in August 1934: "They must have credits and they must have trade or they cannot pull through."[59] Seeking to create the material conditions for a counterrevolution against national socialism, Messersmith repeatedly urged the State Department to withhold commercial and financial support from the Third Reich. He hoped that the United States would help topple the Nazi regime so that Germany would no longer present a threat to European peace and American prosperity.[60]

Messersmith envisioned a bright future for American commerce in Germany after the fall of the Third Reich. Anticipating that the Nazis would try to scare "the whole world with the idea that it is either they or Communism in Germany," Messersmith discounted the threat of bolshevism because he did not think that the German people were ready for a radical assault on the institution of private property.[61] "The next phase," he predicted, "will be a conservative government put in by the Reichswehr with the complete elimination of the National Socialist elements."[62] Messersmith argued that following the removal of Hitler and his henchmen, the United States should extend economic aid to the new government "to prevent any drift towards the left in Germany."[63] Noting that "Germany is potentially one of our best customers," Messersmith believed that after the Nazis lost control, Germany would once again purchase large quantities of raw materials from the United States. "The one hope for our markets in Germany," he concluded, "lies in the return of a reasonable government in Germany."[64]

The State Department concurred with Messersmith's analysis. "As long as Germany retains its present agricultural policy and favors its neighbors in purchasing its needed extra food supplies," Pierrepont Moffat asserted in May 1934, "it is going to be pretty hard to see where an agreement can be worked out."[65] Moffat remained skeptical about the possibility of concluding a mutually satisfactory trade pact with the Nazis because he believed that "they wanted the moon and would give nothing in return."[66] Nor did he think that the State Department should allow Germany "to blackmail us through one means or another into negotiating a trade agreement with us on terms satisfactory to her, that is, that we should undertake to buy more German goods."[67] Herbert Feis agreed. "Concessions by this country would probably contribute much towards building up the prestige of the regime and would reinforce it in its policy of strict state control of all foreign trade and its strictly bilateral method of approach," Feis reasoned in June 1934. "A changed regime or policy within Germany might open up a possibility of German concessions to American trade greater than now exist."[68]

Desiring to create the material conditions for a military coup against the Nazi regime, the State Department consistently rejected German pleas for credit and commerce. Thus, Secretary Hull was "somewhat shaken" in the middle of June 1934 when Alanson B. Houghton, the former American ambassador in Berlin, returned from a visit to Germany and reported that the economic situation was not bad enough to weaken Hitler's hold on the country. But Phillips, Moffat, Sayre, and Feis all assured Hull that he was "on the right track."[69] Their optimism grew when the execution of top storm troop officers in the blood purge at the end of June seemed to confirm Messersmith's argument that the Third Reich was on the verge of collapse. "It may well be," Phillips speculated, "that the regular army will now dominate the situation under some form of military government with Hitler only nominally in the saddle."[70] A month later, Hamilton Fish Armstrong of the Council on Foreign Relations urged Hull to discourage American bankers from doing anything which would bolster the Nazi dictatorship. Like Messersmith, Armstrong believed that the whole National Socialist system would disintegrate if deprived of foreign credit to finance raw material imports needed for German industry.[71] "Our ideas," Hull replied, "are in harmony on the particular point which you stress."[72] Moffat likewise reassured Messersmith. "Your comments on the German situation were very interesting," he wrote in August 1934. "We analyzed the situation along very much the same lines."[73]

As it became increasingly evident that Hitler would remain in power for an indefinite period, however, Hull decided that it was time to review American commercial policy toward Germany.[74] A special State Department committee established in October 1934 considered various options open to the Roosevelt administration. Although the group advised against a trade agreement on the grounds that Germany would demand that the United States should make most of the concessions, the members feared that economic retaliation would permanently damage American trade in Germany and provoke the National Socialists to seize American property in Germany. The committee therefore recommended that the United States should continue to let relations drift with the hope that in the future "we may come to an agreement with Germany on terms likely to be much more favorable than seems possible at the present moment."[75] On the very next day, Ambassador Luther gave the required one-year notice that Germany would terminate the 1923 most-favored-nation treaty with the United

States. But Hull and his aides held firm to their position.[76] "If Germany by its discriminatory practices could force us to negotiate figuratively at the point of a pistol," Moffat explained in November 1934, "it would be an invitation to other countries to follow the same path as a lever to obtain concessions from us."[77]

The State Department continued to rebuff German proposals for a new trade pact that would not contain a most-favored-nation clause. "If Germany would accept our thesis of equality of treatment and most-favored-nation," Assistant Secretary Francis B. Sayre informed Luther in April 1935, "we could conclude some sort of agreement overnight."[78] Sayre notified the German embassy later in the same month that the State Department "had completed a new study of the situation but had failed to find a way of reconciling the American system which was based on the most-favored-nation theory and on the reduction of trade barriers with the German system which was based on preferential treatment as a result of bilateral bargaining." While suggesting that the German government might find a way of harmonizing the two antagonistic viewpoints, Sayre insisted that "such a reconciliation would have to be based on the essentials of our program."[79] Sayre thus made it perfectly clear that the State Department would not compromise with Dr. Schacht on basic commercial principles.

The House of Morgan stood firmly behind the Department of State. Some American bankers who were engrossed in protecting their own narrow interests wanted Secretary Hull to back down from his unbending attitude toward Germany. Even President Leon Frazer of the Bank of International Settlements advocated "making arrangements with Germany whereby we would take more of her goods in return for her paying the American holders of the Dawes-Young loans."[80] But the Morgan partners applauded the State Department for refusing to offer the Germans commercial concessions until they stopped discriminating against American trade and finance. "From the very outset of this whole German bond episode," Thomas Lamont complimented Hull in April 1935, "the Department's attitude has, if I may be permitted to say so, been exceptionally fine."[81] At the same time, Lamont warned Dr. Schacht that he must renounce his discriminatory policies "not merely as the first step in restoring Germany to a position of any credit in this country but as a condition of a return to normal commercial relations with the United States."[82] Lamont later urged Schacht to "take the lead in breaking away from this whole system of quotas and clearings and exchange restrictions."[83]

The Nazi exchange control program was the crux of the commercial conflict between Germany and America. Herbert Feis noted in March 1935 that the State Department was preoccupied with the question of how to handle countries "who declare that they will only make such exchange available for the purchase of American goods as may be created by American purchases of their goods."[84] Henry F. Grady, the head of the Trade Agreements Division, suggested that the United States should withhold from such countries any commercial concessions granted in reciprocal treaties with other nations. Feis feared that this approach would be inadequate, but his colleagues were gradually taken by Grady's proposition that "if a country deliberately discriminates against the United States it will not receive the benefit of our unconditional most-favored-nation treatment."[85] During the summer of 1935, Germany did offer to deal with America on an impartial basis with respect to import quotas and customs duties but not with regard to exchange allocation. The State Department, realizing that continued exchange discrimination would render any commercial concessions meaningless, scouted the German proposal.[86] "The most important obstacle to trade negotiations," Francis Sayre explained, "is the lack of ability of the German Government to extend equitable treatment to all American commerce in respect of foreign exchange."[87]

The bitter clash between Hitler and Hull had reached an impasse. Refusing to abandon their preferential trade practices, the National Socialists formally terminated in October 1935 Germany's most-favored-nation treaty with the United States. The Nazis aimed to prod the American government into negotiating a new commercial agreement which would sanction bilateral barter deals based upon discriminatory principles. But the State Department, rather than yielding to the Nazi attempt to extort concessions, responded by placing Germany on a blacklist. In other words, the United States withheld from Germany the commercial benefits which were automatically extended to all other countries under the reciprocal trade program. The ensuing trade war between the two antagonists had a significant impact on the flow of commerce across the Atlantic. Germany took 8.4 percent of America's total exports in 1933 but only 3.8 percent in 1937, whereas in 1933 the United States took 5.4 percent of Germany's exports but in 1937 only 3.7 percent.[88]

In the meantime, the Third Reich intensified its campaign to capture foreign markets for manufactured goods. Possessing neither a continental hinterland nor colonial territory, Germany did not have a natural resource base which was large enough to support its dense metropolitan population. Hitler and his top advisers, despite their strong commitment to centralized planning, knew that national socialism could not function successfully as an isolated economic unit within the existing German borders. Thus, they aimed to export finished products to obtain foreign exchange needed to pay for agricultural supplies and raw materials required for industrial reconstruction and military restoration. Convinced that Germany must either export or die, the Nazis placed the full force of the totalitarian state behind a sustained struggle to penetrate foreign markets. And their discriminatory trade tactics presented a fundamental challenge to the American attempt to establish a liberal capitalist world system based upon the principle of equal commercial opportunity.

In order to lock other countries into bilateral barter arrangements with Germany, Dr. Schacht, the financial mastermind of the Third Reich, invented a special kind of currency called aski marks. Instead of paying for essential imports with regular Reichsmarks, which could be converted into gold and thereby used to obtain other national monetary units like dollars or pounds or francs for the purchase of American or British or French merchandise, Schacht hoped to pay for raw materials and food stuffs with his aski marks, which had no gold value and could be used only to buy specified German products. As the sole purchasing agent for the entire German nation, Schacht was in a strong bargaining position. He planned to offer other countries a large slice of the German market for their surplus commodities, but only on the condition that they would accept aski marks in return. Those countries that agreed to his terms would be forced to buy German goods with the funny money they accumulated. Proud of his financial wizardry, the president of the Reichsbank was eager to employ aski marks to help German exporters outmaneuver their rivals in the markets of the world.

After obtaining Hitler's permission, Dr. Schacht quickly launched a major trade offensive in South America. A German commercial delegation armed with aski marks and export subsidies set sail for Brazil in July 1934, and the emissaries from Berlin drove a hard bargain when they arrived in Rio de Janerio. After threatening to curtail their coffee purchases unless Brazil would agree to buy more German commodities, the Nazi negotiators offered to increase their imports of coffee if Brazil would accept payment in aski marks. American diplomats were worried. Donald Heath of the Division of Latin American Affairs believed that the State Department should do everything possible "to prevent Brazil from concluding a compensation agreement with Germany."[89] Yet, in spite of considerable pressure exerted by Washington against the proposed undertaking, Brazil signed a bilateral accord with the Nazi commercial delegation. So did Argentina, Chile, and Uruguay. As a result, between 1934 and 1936, German exports to Latin America more than doubled.[90]

The Nazi assault on South American markets alarmed business and government leaders in the United States. Herbert Feis warned Cordell Hull in October 1934 that Dr. Schacht might be able "to compel other countries to give Germany terms that may be more favored than those accorded us."[91] Such proved to be the case, and in May 1936, Hull complained to the German chargé d'affairs in Washington that Schacht's commercial practices were "arbitrarily and artificially displacing our Latin American trade."[92] Six months later, Ambassador Dodd wrote from Berlin that Hitler was determined to "crowd the United States out of its position in Latin America."[93] Yankee businessmen were equally vexed. W. T. Moran of the National City Bank lectured the National Foreign Trade Council about the harmful effects of barter deals between Germany and the countries lying south of the Rio Grande. "Quite definitely," Moran concluded in November 1936, "Germany's gain has been our loss in most of the Latin American countries."[94]

Nazi trade methods were even more successful in facilitating the sale of German products down the Danube River to the countries of Southeastern Europe. Writing from his post in Vienna, George Messersmith explained the Nazi strategy for achieving economic hegemony in the Balkans. "Germany has in the last few years proceeded on a definite plan," he reported in June 1936. "She has permitted herself to build up huge debits in practically all of these countries, and through her inability to pay, even if the desire were there, she has forced these states to increase their purchases from her."[95] The results were impressive. Germany's exports to the Danubian region rose 37 percent between 1933 and 1935 while its imports jumped 65 percent.[96] Still not satisfied, Dr. Schacht made a dramatic visit to a number of Balkan countries in June 1936, and he came away from Yugoslavia and Hungary with large orders for German industrial goods.[97] The State Department had much less success when it sent Herbert Feis to several countries in Southeastern Europe to investigate "the possibilities of commercial agreements with them."[98] Messersmith was distressed. "I see insuperable difficulties," he warned Hull in July 1936, "in our being able to do anything with our trade agreement program with these smaller states in this part of the world."[99]

Dr. Schacht had created an economic monster which threatened to undermine Hull's reciprocal trade agreements program. Indeed, with the Reichsbank president serving as the purchasing agent for his entire country, Germany's share of total world exports jumped from 4.3 percent in 1934 up to 8.7 percent in 1936.[100] "The German government," Douglas Miller observed in October 1935, "by controlling its own domestic market and its import and export trade, is able to bring concentrated pressure to bear at any point to secure necessary concessions."[101] A year later, Herbert Feis lamented that "in some situations, American export trade may not be able to sustain itself against this system."[102] James A. Farrell, the former president of United States Steel, was equally worried about totalitarian commercial procedures. "As business men we are not concerned with the forms of government in other countries," Farrell explained in an address before the National Foreign Trade Convention in November 1936, "but we are deeply concerned with any influences that tend to render more difficult our trade relations with the rest of the world."[103]

Meanwhile, the Japanese campaign to establish an exclusive sphere of economic influence in Manchuria gave American businessmen and diplomats additional cause for concern. American petroleum firms were the first large enterprises to suffer from the organization of Japanese monopolies in Manchuria, and they did not hesitate to ask Washington for help. "We feel," the Standard Oil Company of New York wrote Cordell Hull in April 1933, "that the strict maintenance of the 'Open Door' policy is the only hope for the protection of American interests in Manchuria."[104] The State Department promptly dispatched several notes complaining about the discrimination against American business in Manchuria, but these protests had little effect in Tokyo.[105] Maxwell M. Hamilton of the Far Eastern Division concluded in February 1934 that "Japan was determined to limit foreign participation in the trade and commercial development of 'Manchukuo' to commodities and lines of business that Japan itself could not supply."[106] Later in the same year, Pierrepont Moffat noted that the oil monopoly in Manchuria had driven home "the lesson that Japanese superiority in the Far East would definitely mean the closing of the Open Door."[107]

President Roosevelt and his State Department advisers feared that the Japanese would extend their control from Manchuria into other Chinese provinces. Moffat observed in October 1934 that Japan had "clearly shown her hand at desiring only one thing, overlordship in the Far East."[108] Hull had come to the same conclusion, and in March 1935 he sent the president a long memorandum prepared by his subordinates in charge of Far Eastern affairs. "As our own population becomes more and more dense, as the struggle for existence in this country becomes more intense, as we feel increasingly the need of foreign markets," the memorandum argued, "our definite concern for open markets will be more widely felt among our people and our desire for and insistence upon free opportunity to trade with and among the peoples of the Far East will be intensified."[109] Roosevelt concurred. He told Norman Davis in March 1935 that "the American people would not go to war to preserve the integrity of China," but that they would be willing to take up arms to maintain "their right to trade with China."[110]

No group exhibited a greater desire to defend American commercial interests in China than the National Foreign Trade Council. With the blessings of the State Department, this influential business organization dispatched an expedition in 1935 to investigate economic prospects in the Orient. The American Trade Mission, headed by W. Cameron Forbes, returned to the United States with tantalizing stories of a New China embarked upon an ambitious modernization program. Forbes and his associates were particularly impressed by the recent construction of 50,000 miles of roads in China. "We came away convinced that with the utilization of these new means of transportation," Forbes wrote Henry Ford, "China should provide a potential market of incalculable value to the makers of motor vehicles of all sorts."[111] Forbes told the National Foreign Trade Council, in turn, that American trucks and automobiles would transform the new Chinese roads into vital arteries of commerce. Once China became motorized, he concluded, American manufacturers of a wide variety of products would have access to the vast Chinese hinterland.[112]

President Roosevelt was intent on preserving Anglo-American naval supremacy in order to prevent Japan from destroying these dazzling commercial prospects in China. The 5:5:3 ratio regarding capital ships, established by the naval treaty negotiated at the Washington Conference in 1922, permitted the United States and Great Britain to maintain a clear seapower advantage over Japan. But during the ensuing decade the American fleet had remained well below treaty limits, and when Roosevelt took office in March 1933 he found that the United States and Japan possessed approximately equivalent naval forces.[113] The new president quickly issued an executive order which allocated 238 million dollars for the construction of thirty-two warships. And after announcing in January 1934 his intention of bringing the American navy up to full treaty strength, he persuaded Congress to authorize the construction of more than one hundred additional combat vessels.[114] Yet Roosevelt did not want to get into a naval building race with Japan. He hoped instead to negotiate a disarmament accord which would reduce world naval forces by 20 percent without in any way altering the existing ratios governing fleet strength.[115]

The United States and Japan, however, advanced diametrically opposed views concerning naval affairs. On the one hand, Japanese diplomats maintained that the 5:5:3 ratio no longer provided adequate security for their country due to the increased range of ships and planes. They wanted British and American naval forces scaled down to the Japanese level in order to make their own fleet almost invulnerable in Asian waters. On the other hand, American officials claimed that the 1922 ratio provided equality of security for each major seapower. Although their public statements emphasized strategic considerations, the Americans readily admitted in private discussions that the underlying issue involved a conflict in economic objectives.[116] Admiral William H. Standly, the chief of naval operations, pointed out that if Japan achieved naval equality, American commerce would be subject to Japanese discrimination even though the American continent would not be threatened by Japan. In other words, Admiral Standly advocated the maintenance of Anglo-American naval superiority not simply because he wanted to protect the physical security of the United States but largely because he wished to preserve the principle of equal economic opportunity in the Far East.[117]

President Roosevelt hoped to work out an understanding with Great Britain in order to rebuff Japanese demands for naval parity. He therefore instructed Ambassador Robert W. Bingham in February 1934 to promote Anglo-American cooperation with respect to naval matters when he returned to his post in London. If the United States and the United Kingdom acted together and insisted upon maintaining the 5:5:3 ratio, Roosevelt told Bingham, Japan would probably denounce the naval limitation treaties. "Then the British and ourselves," he continued, "could absolutely control the situation by giving the Japanese to understand that every time they built one ship, we would build two."[118] A few months later, the president dispatched Norman Davis to obtain support in London both for a 20 percent reduction in fleet strength and for the continuation of existing naval ratios. But the British had different ideas. They wanted to increase their cruiser strength by at least a third to protect their interests in Europe and Asia. The British Cabinet was even thinking about approaching Japan in hopes of concluding a bilateral nonaggression pact along with an agreement dividing China into spheres of influence.[119]

The president and his close advisers hoped to prevent any rapprochement between England and Japan. Their aims were revealed during an important discussion Roosevelt held in October 1934 with Hull, Moffat, Davis, and Standly about American policy toward the Far East. "It was the consensus of opinion," Moffat recorded, "that in no circumstance should we indicate any intention either to weaken ourselves in the Orient, to indicate an unwillingness to join issue under certain circumstances or a willingness to allow the Japanese to continue pressing forward without protest on our part. Such a policy we felt would throw England and Japan together to a point where they might join forces in attempting to exclude the United States from the Asiatic market."[120] A month later, Roosevelt instructed Davis to warn officials in London that "if Great Britain is even suspected of preferring to play ball with Japan to playing with us," the United States would appeal directly to Canada, Australia, New Zealand, and South Africa "in a definite effort to make these dominions clearly understand that their future security is linked with us."[121]

President Roosevelt succeeded in keeping Great Britain aligned with the United States with regard to Far Eastern diplomacy. Davis was happy when he learned that the British Cabinet had decided against making any separate deals with the Japanese. "The British have come to realize," he reported in December 1934, "that if they are going to induce Japan to 'play ball' they must make her understand that she will have to play on the same team with both of us."[122] But Japan had no intention of playing the game according to American rules. Instead, Japanese officials gave the required two-years' notice that their country would terminate the naval limitation treaty signed in 1922 in Washington. But they could not get Great Britain to side with them. When the London Naval Conference began in December 1935, Davis found that the British group which had formerly favored an accord with Tokyo had been routed. "Whatever tendency there was before to coddle Japan," he wrote Roosevelt, "has disappeared."[123]

Although the American delegates at the London Naval Conference maintained a united front with their British counterparts, they were unable to conclude a naval limitation agreement. The American proposal for a 20 percent reduction in fleet strength got nowhere, and the Japanese withdrew their delegation from London when the United States and Great Britain rejected their demand for naval parity.[124] Consequently, the major seapowers were free to expand their fleets to whatever size they deemed necessary for the protection of their respective interests. President Roosevelt thereupon assured Admiral Standly that the United States would build three warships for every one launched by Japan.[125] The president also made his wishes known on Capitol Hill, and in the spring of 1936, Congress authorized over 500 million dollars for naval expansion. When the Japanese responded by enlarging their own shipbuilding program, Roosevelt and his advisers realized that they had failed to prevent a race between the United States and Japan for naval supremacy in the Pacific.[126]

At the same time, American leaders were faced with the fact that they had also failed to prepare the grounds in Germany for a counter coup against the Third Reich. Apparently blinded by his intense hatred for national socialism, George Messersmith persisted in predicting that the Nazi government was on the brink of collapse. "I still believe that the financial and economic factor will bring this regime to its knees and to defeat," he wrote William Phillips in February 1936. "It all depends upon the pressure from the outside being maintained firmly and unalterably."[127] But reports from Raymond H. Geist of the American embassy in Berlin had convinced Phillips that the idea of toppling Adolf Hitler in the foreseeable future was "utterly out of the question."[128] Douglas Jenkins, the American consul general in Berlin, concurred. "The consensus of well-informed opinion now," he informed the State Department in November 1935, "is that Mr. Hitler and the Nazi regime are firmly established."[129]

President Roosevelt had already begun to explore the possibilities for taking collective action to contain the Third Reich.[130] He suggested to Cordell Hull and Norman Davis in April 1934 that the United States, Great Britain, and France should ask Germany for permission to send a commission to investigate Nazi armament violations of the Versailles Treaty. If Hitler refused, the president argued, the other nations should cut off all trade with Germany. Hull and Davis were sympathetic, but they thought the scheme should be tied to a general European disarmament conference.[131] A month later, Roosevelt told the Belgian ambassador in Washington that the United States would support a boycott against German exports if Hitler declined to take part in efforts to reach a disarmament accord.[132] Then, in October 1934, Roosevelt proposed to William Phillips that America, England, and France should agree not to trade with any nation that invaded a neighbor.[133] Although Pierrepont Moffat immediately pointed out the problems involved in defining the crossing of a frontier as an act of aggression, the president refused to let the matter rest.[134]

Roosevelt soon formulated a new plan designed to enable him to promote collective security through executive action and without legislative restraint. He instructed Ambassador Bingham that at the proper time he should convey to authorities in London the following message: "that in the event the British, French, and Italians should find it necessary to declare an economic boycott against Germany, it would be necessary to have troops at their frontiers in order to prevent smuggling; that if they did put troops there the economic boycott would be military, as well as economic, and that this would enable him to bring our country into such economic boycott by Presidential proclamation without having to secure the approval of Congress."[135] After Hitler announced in March 1935 that Germany would develop a half-million-man army in defiance of the Versailles Treaty, Bingham informed British leaders that the president had authorized him to say that the United States would be willing "to join with other nations in enforcing such a boycott."[136] Roosevelt hoped that the European powers would agree to blockade Germany when they met at Stresa to discuss international problems. "A boycott or sanction would not be recognized by us without Congressional action," Roosevelt reiterated to Colonel Edward M. House, "but a blockade would fall under the Executive's power."[137]

However, the president and his diplomatic advisers did not trust Great Britain. Roosevelt wrote Hull in March 1935 that "the present British Government is not sincere in seeking limitation or reduction of present world armaments or present world trade in warlike weapons."[138] John C. Wiley, the American chargé d'affaires in Moscow, cautioned in the same month that Great Britain might sooner or later acquiesce in German territorial expansion eastward as the price for keeping Hitler from rebuilding German seapower. "The materialization of this possibility," Wiley argued, "is the keynote of German foreign policy."[139] American apprehensions grew when the Stresa Conference in April 1935 produced nothing more than empty gestures condemning German militarization. Foreign Secretary John Simon told Hugh Wilson that Great Britain would "not tolerate any attempt to isolate and surround Germany."[140] Indeed, in June 1935, England tacitly acknowledged Germany's right to rearm in a treaty which approved Hitler's demand for a Nazi navy 35 percent as large as the British fleet. The Anglo-German naval pact only strengthened American suspicions. "From the beginning," Messersmith warned Phillips in July 1935, "it has been National Socialist policy to conciliate England and Hitler has definitely dreamed of actual alliance with England in order to get a free hand on the Continent."[141]

Pierrepont Moffat likewise thought that Hitler aimed to achieve mastery over Europe. He told Henry Stimson in May 1935 that he did not believe in the feasibility of "getting Germany back into the club."[142] Moffat had been pessimistic from the very outset. "In my heart of hearts," he wrote Hugh Wilson in Geneva, "I never felt that disarmament was a possibility until Germany accepted the status quo and ceased pursuing a policy to regain what she had lost."[143] Moffat saw little likelihood in satisfying Hitler's land hunger. "Everything we get from Germany and the surrounding countries indicates that

Germany is definitely determined upon achieving a series of objectives which in effect would give her what she would have gained if she had won the war," he wrote another American diplomat concerned with disarmament. "Stresa and Geneva have been interesting to watch but I cannot see that they have done anything to eradicate the disease from which Europe is suffering and I fear that there will be further outbreaks elsewhere on the body politic."[144]

The same apprehension prompted Thomas Lamont to approach the British government regarding the war debt question. The Johnson Act, which prohibited loans to countries in default to the United States, stood in the way of American financial aid to Great Britain in the event of a European crisis. "If England were ever expecting cooperation from the USA in any direction," Lamont warned Chancellor of the Exchequer Neville Chamberlain in June 1935, "she would not get it unless and until some effort was made to work out a debt settlement."[145] A month later, he told Prime Minister Stanley Baldwin that "the War Debts were like a Greek Chorus which always keeps moving on and off the stage but is always making its presence felt." He assured Baldwin that "so much water had gone over the dam that the American people would be disposed to accept an exceedingly moderate settlement."[146] Lamont was most eager to solve the problem. "The defaulted British Debt to the USA Government constitutes a complete obstacle to any cooperation in world affairs between the British and American people," he noted later. "Lacking such an adjustment some time in the next year or so, England could whistle her head off so far as any American co-operation were concerned in any European mess."[147]

The lack of public support for a discretionary arms embargo provided an additional roadblock against American participation in collective action in Europe. Many Americans had become disillusioned after the First World War when the results did not match the rhetoric that had been used to inspire them to fight. The war had not made the world safe for democracy. Nor had it been a war to end all wars. This disillusionment generated a widespread belief that the United States should never again become involved in a European conflict. But

Roosevelt wished to restrain Hitler by threatening to take sides against any aggressor in a future European war. And when Congress convened in January 1934, he hoped to obtain the legislation he had sought the previous spring enabling him to cooperate with the League of Nations by banning the shipment of weapons to any nation he defined as an aggressor. But the State Department warned the president that Congress might pass an impartial arms embargo which would prohibit Americans from supplying the implements of war to all belligerent nations. Hence, Roosevelt once again decided to let the question lie dormant.[148]

The events of the following year, however, brought the issue to a head. On the one hand, the Senate established a committee under the chairmanship of Gerald P. Nye to investigate the munitions industry. The Nye Committee conducted sensational hearings which convinced many Americans that their country had been drawn into the First World War by big bankers and munitions makers. These disturbing conclusions reinforced desires in Congress for legislation designed to keep the United States out of future European disputes. On the other hand, the German rearmament program sharpened the determination of the Roosevelt administration to deter Hitler from making any aggressive moves. The State Department therefore prepared a draft bill which would empower the president to impose an arms embargo against whatever country he might designate.[149] "The President was definite in his opinion," William Phillips noted in July 1935, "that the President should always be free with regard to the placing of embargoes on the export of arms and ammunition."[150] But Roosevelt did not press the issue after it became apparent that the Senate would defeat any measure which would give him the discretionary authority that he desired. Then, after persuading Congress to limit the mandate to a six-month period, Roosevelt decided in August 1935 to sign a neutrality bill which required him to impose an arms embargo against all parties to a military conflict.

Although Roosevelt was not satisfied with the neutrality law, he realized that the inflexible measure would serve his purposes in the impending war between Italy and Ethiopia. Roosevelt and Hull hoped to hinder Benito Mussolini when he launched his African adventure. In addition to invoking an arms embargo in October 1935, the State Department issued a public statement warning that "any of our people who voluntarily engage in transactions of any character with either of the belligerents do so at their own risk."[151] The admonishment against trade was far more significant than the restriction on arms shipments. A reduction in American commerce with both belligerents would not affect Ethiopia, which had no means of obtaining strategic supplies from abroad, but it would harm Italy, which depended heavily upon the importation of essential raw materials. Roosevelt was delighted when the League of Nations imposed economic sanctions against Italy in order to establish a precedent for future collective action against Germany. "If I may so phrase it," Hugh Wilson reported from Switzerland, "we are attending a dress rehearsal."[152] Norman Davis explained to Wilson in November 1935 that "the Administration does not want to interfere in any way with the efforts of the League to stop the war in Ethiopia."[153] But England and France refused to prohibit oil exports to Italy, and Mussolini's troops advanced toward victory.[154]

The Ethiopian episode, which dramatized the importance of strategic materials, conditioned the ensuing debate over neutrality legislation. Many congressmen who aimed to insulate the United States from European wars wanted a mandatory embargo on raw materials as well as military supplies applied to all belligerent nations. The Roosevelt administration agreed on the question of restricting trade in essential resources, but it demanded that the president should be free to invoke the embargo against the country of his choice.[155] "The crux of the matter lies in the deep question of allowing some discretion to the Chief Executive," Roosevelt wrote William Dodd in December 1935. "I hope that next January I can get an even stronger law, leaving, however, some authority to the President."[156] But the disagreement over mandatory versus discretionary trade restrictions led to an impasse, and in February 1936, Congress simply extended the impartial arms embargo for another year.[157]

A week later, German soldiers marched across the Rhine River and reoccupied the demilitarized area along the western frontier of the Third Reich. The German maneuver, although a flagrant violation of the Versailles Treaty, was not opposed by collective action of any sort. The French refused to employ military force against the Nazi army, and the British ruled out the use of economic sanctions to induce Hitler to withdraw the Wehrmacht from the Rhineland. Consequently, the League of Nations once again was limited to making meaningless condemnations of German behavior. The United States government remained officially aloof from the European affair, but beneath the surface American diplomats reacted in different ways to the German reoccupation of the Rhineland.[158]

Norman Davis responded with optimism. He hoped that the remilitarization of the Rhineland would prompt France to abandon "that old ambition to be the predominant political influence in Europe" and to seek strategic security through an arms limitation accord. "Germany had justice on her side," he asserted in May 1936, "and we were never able to get a disarmament agreement at Geneva, although we came three times within an inch of it, because each time the French backed off." Davis believed that the construction of German fortifications along the French border might be a blessing in disguise. "Now the French are getting very eager to get a disarmament agreement," he explained, "because they know that Germany can build faster than France can, and the French General Staff is in favor of it." Davis thought that the Nazis were also prepared to agree to an arms limitation. "Hitler now says that he is ready to go as far as anybody wants to go on disarmament," he noted. "I believe he will do it."[159]

George Messersmith disagreed. "The German objectives remain unchanged," he warned Hull in July 1936, "and her principle aim now is to gain time and to assure herself of the means to complete that program of preparation which will enable her to brandish the sword over Europe."[160] Messersmith continued to oppose economic concessions to Germany as long as the Nazis remained in power. "One hears more and more that German industry must be given relief if there is to be a stoppage of its rearmament program," he reiterated to Hull. "The relief that Germany needs in the way of markets is real, but it cannot come with safety or be facilitated by anyone until the menace of the present government is removed. Otherwise, all these measures for relief could only result in the feeding of the monster which is out to devour Europe."[161] Messersmith never altered his convictions about the foreign policy of the Third Reich. "There can be no peace in Europe," he admonished once more, "if the present German government remains in power."[162]

Messersmith was not alone in his apprehension about Nazi ambitions. "The catastrophe may be averted for a time," Ambassador John Cudahy wrote from Warsaw in March 1936, "but if the Hitler Government is not overthrown a war in Europe is as certain as the rising sun."[163] Discussions with officials in Berlin likewise convinced Ambassador William Dodd that the Nazis would refuse to disarm until all their territorial aspirations were satisfied. "Hitler and Mussolini intend to control all Europe," he warned Roosevelt in October 1936. "If that be agreed to beforehand, a peace conference is quite possible; but what sort of peace?" [164] A month later, Dodd again discounted the possibility that Germany would participate in a conference designed to preserve peace. "It is my feeling," he wrote Roosevelt, "that Hitler is simply waiting for his best opportunity to seize what he wants."[165]

American leaders were receiving conflicting signals from the Third Reich. On the one hand, Nazi militants gave every indication that they intended to acquire essential raw materials through territorial conquest rather than peaceful commerce.[166] Their preparations for war seemed to be on schedule when at the Nuremberg party rally in September 1936 they announced their Four Year Plan to reduce German dependence upon distant resources.[167] On the other hand, Schacht and his friends repeatedly proclaimed their desire to resume liberal trade relations with the rest of the world. Ambassador Luther told Cordell Hull in August 1935 "that Dr. Schacht and others were definitely of the opinion that the bilateral trade method practiced by Germany for some time had proven hurtful upon the whole rather than helpful, that they were now very strongly behind the economic program which the United States was undertaking to carry forward as it related to international relationships, and that as conditions made it possible his Government would manifest its interest in this program."[168]

The debate in the United States over German aims revolved around assessments of Schacht's ability to influence Hitler. Messersmith warned that Schacht would never succeed in persuading the führer to abandon the Nazi commercial program. "He is a prisoner in his position," Messersmith argued in November 1934, "and must do the best he can although out of sympathy with most everything he does."[169] Many Americans agreed that Schacht could not control the economic monster he had created, but most had not given up all hope of reintegrating Germany into a peaceful international society based upon the doctrine of equal commercial opportunity. "Dr. Schacht subscribed to your ideas completely," a subordinate reported to Hull in June 1936, "and told me how he wished that he might be able to convince Hitler and other Nazi leaders of the desirability of moving toward more normal trade relations."[170] Two months later, Thomas Lamont tried to encourage the Reichsbank president in his attempt to redirect German commercial policy. "I have a feeling that if we could once reestablish foreign trade and get it going," Lamont wrote Schacht, "the political difficulties would righten themselves."[171]

Americans who concerned themselves with foreign affairs hoped that European political troubles could be resolved without recourse to war. Most sympathized with German desires to regain territory lost at Versailles. "Germany's imminent return to former political might on the Continent," Hugh Wilson reasoned in June 1935, "has created an imperious necessity for political readjustment in Europe."[172] Vera Michels Dean of the Foreign Policy Association agreed. She feared that an attempt to preserve the European status quo by encircling Germany would provoke a violent explosion. "If peace is to be assured and security restored," she argued, "organization against aggression must be accompanied by honest efforts to meet the legitimate territorial claims of Germany."[173] Though the United States refused to become entangled in these political problems, American leaders were eager to make an economic contribution to the preservation of European peace.

The Roosevelt administration hoped that the removal of trade barriers would set the stage for a political settlement in Europe. "We may make a mighty contribution to the cause of world peace," Ambassador Bingham declared in March 1935, "by aiding in the economic recovery of Europe through the restoration of world trade."[174] Other American diplomats likewise articulated the widely held belief that the revival of international commerce would "substantially contribute to the prospects of a peaceful adjustment of current international issues."[175] President Roosevelt shared this conviction that the reduction of tariff barriers would be a constructive step in the direction of permanent peace. "We do not maintain that a more liberal international trade will stop war," Roosevelt proclaimed in August 1936, "but we fear that without a more liberal international trade war is a natural sequence."[176]

American business internationalists joined with their European counterparts in this campaign to prevent the outbreak of war by stimulating the flow of commerce. When leading economists from several countries assembled in March 1935 at Chatham House in London to prepare a program to reduce international friction, they issued a series of resolutions urging monetary stabilization, debt settlements, disarmament agreements, and tariff reductions. Both the International Chamber of Commerce and the National Foreign Trade Council endorsed these declarations.[177] Not long after the Chatham House meeting, the Carnegie Endowment for International Peace sent representatives to confer with members of the International Chamber of Commerce in Paris. "The purpose of this meeting," Commerce Secretary Daniel C. Roper informed Roosevelt, "is to discuss ways in which business organizations can cooperate most effectively with peace organizations in order to secure a more adequate and practical economic approach to world peace."[178]

The State Department assumed a position of leadership in this crusade to establish an economic basis for international friendship. "I quite agree with the thought expressed in your letter that lasting peace cannot come unless we first build sound economic foundations," Francis Sayre wrote John Foster Dulles in March 1936. "It is because I feel so strongly convinced of this that I have put my whole heart into our trade agreements program."[179] Herbert Feis similarly explained in November 1936 that he and his associates were making a concerted effort to turn "the people of Central Europe aside from thoughts of conquest to thoughts of prosperity."[180] But no one worked harder to eradicate the economic causes of war than Cordell Hull. "When nations cannot get what they need by the normal processes of trade," he declared in December 1936, "they will continue to resort to the use of force."[181] Hull repeatedly advanced his reciprocal trade program as the essential framework for economic appeasement.

American diplomats hoped that Great Britain would join with the United States in a drive to reestablish an international order based upon liberal commercial principles. They believed that the British imperial preference system, which had been erected at Ottawa in 1932, stood as a major obstacle to their quest for economic appeasement. Pierrepont Moffat gave vent to a growing apprehension in the State Department that Great Britain would provoke a military explosion if it continued to pursue a restrictive commercial policy. "The more it closes the Empire to outsiders," he warned in June 1936, "the more it is driving the 'have-nots' to seek their place in the sun through unorthodox means."[182] In other words, Moffat and his associates wanted the British to lower the high tariff wall surrounding their empire in order to encourage the Germans to opt for commercial expansion rather than territorial acquisition.

While serving as the American consul general in Sydney during 1936, Moffat flooded the State Department with reports about the workings of British commercial policy. The fact that the Australian government was restricting imports from the United States and diverting purchases to the United Kingdom deeply upset him. "I am convinced that Australia would never have moved against our trade had it not been for British pressure," Moffat complained. "Despite heavy Imperial preferences, despite added advantages in the form of lower Primage taxes, calculations of currency for customs purposes, etc., British goods have been slowly giving way to American in this market."[183] Moffat laid bare the basic reason for Great Britain's economic hostility toward the United States. "It is to be found in the realization that in a system based on commercial equality we can drive England out of the market every time, due to our better goods and our better sales methods," he noted. "I have reluctantly reached the conclusion that Britain is using her financial pressure to make preferential bargains, and that despite lip service to the Secretary's ideals, she is really fighting his theory of equality of commercial treatment to the last ditch."[184]

State Department officials realized that two different groups in London were struggling for control over British commercial affairs. One group, headed by the Foreign Office, advocated a less discriminatory trade policy in order to avoid alienating the United States in face of the impending crisis in Europe. Another group, represented by the Treasury and the Board of Trade, remained committed to imperial preferences and immediate profits regardless of the international political consequences.[185] Leo Pasvolsky, a State Department economic expert, believed that the mounting tensions in Europe would give the United States sufficient leverage to compel England to liberalize its commercial policy.[186] Norman Davis agreed. "The right person could sit down with the British and accomplish very much in the right direction," he reasoned in July 1936. "They are particularly eager not to antagonize us."[187] Moffat also hoped that the scales could be tipped in favor of the Foreign Office and against the Treasury in Great Britain. "At present she thinks she can count on our help politically and yet hit us below the belt commercially all over the world," he complained in October 1936. "The Government, sooner or later, will have to decide on which side of the fence it will play and impose its decision on the different Ministries."[188]

Secretary Hull made repeated appeals to secure British cooperation in his drive to restore world trade. Hull complained to Ambassador Ronald Lindsay in February 1936 that the United Kingdom had been "confining its chief attention to the narrow and shortsighted economic view which in the main contemplates purely bilateral bargaining." The time had come for the English-speaking countries to get together behind a movement to reduce international trade barriers, he argued, "unless we were willing to take the great risk of letting the

German nation get ahead of us with a military rampage over Europe."[189] Hull warned Lindsay that the Anglo-Saxon peoples had better promote a liberal trade program before it was too late. "What rational person anywhere," he asked in October 1936, "imagines that the 65 million German population, without enough food or enough clothing or enough materials to work with, will sit there in that state of distress and deterioration indefinitely?" Hull feared that if the Germans were denied access to foreign markets they "would be meandering up and down the earth taking by force what the necessities of their own nationals would require."[190]

four

The Quest for
Economic Appeasement

THE ROOSEVELT admin-
istration continued to regard Nazi Germany as a dangerous
have-not country which threatened both American prosperity
and European tranquility. Dr. Schacht's bilateral trade practices, designed to increase industrial exports to pay for essential
imports, presented a serious menace to the overseas economic
interests of the United States. And Hitler's rearmament program suggested that he intended to conquer adjacent territory
on the European continent in order to expand the resource base
of the Third Reich. The State Department responded to the
Nazi challenge by sponsoring a drive to remove commercial
barriers around the globe so that Germany could acquire an
adequate supply of foodstuffs and minerals to sustain its dense
urban population without recourse to either barter or war. Administration spokesmen and business internationalists hoped
that the Nazis would abandon their totalitarian trade tactics
and dismantle their awesome military machine if given equal
access to foreign markets for their manufactured goods. In
short, American leaders advanced a program of economic appeasement in an effort to reintegrate Germany into a liberal
capitalist world system.

State Department officials believed that American goals
could not be achieved without a fundamental reorientation in
German commercial policy. Under Secretary Sumner Welles
complained in May 1937 that Nazi Germany was compelling
other countries to enter into bilateral arrangements at the ex-

pense of the United States. "Extraordinary competition from German goods," he noted, "has resulted in displacement of American trade even in lines where American products have proven themselves able to hold the field against all ordinary competition."[1] A month later, the Division of Trade Agreements expressed even greater concern about the ill effects of Nazi barter methods: "A general reduction of the obstacles to world commerce depends, more than on any other thing, upon whether Germany can be brought back into a free economic system. Unless and until this is done, important sections of the world—Central and Eastern Europe and many of the American Republics—will be unable to follow liberal policies, and what may be even more serious, the German example and influence may continue to draw other leading countries, notably Italy and Japan, constantly farther away from a liberal commercial system."[2]

American diplomats also believed that the preservation of European peace depended upon a basic transformation in the economic life of Germany. "The whole impulse of the country is war preparation," Ambassador John Cudahy observed in December 1936 from his post in Warsaw. "If this were suddenly stopped, from four to six million people would be thrown out of employment." An enlarged export business, however, would enable German authorities to keep their workers busy making consumer goods rather than military products. "The future looks dismal," Cudahy reasoned, "unless something can be done to relieve the economic conditions of Germany in return for its assurance to stop or diminish its great rearmament program."[3] Leo Pasvolsky concurred. "A resumption of foreign trade," he argued in January 1937, "is the sole constructive way for Germany out of her present difficulties."[4] Later in the year, he explained that "the crux of the problem is whether or not the German economic system can be articulated with a normally functioning world economic system." Pasvolsky concluded that the Nazis "must be convinced of the wisdom of liberal commercial policies if peace is to prevail."[5]

The widespread belief that wars breed revolutions strengthened the desire for peace. The First World War had intensified class antagonisms in several European countries and produced a bloody revolution in Russia. Such challenges to the old order made the aftermath of a second world war appalling for conservatives to contemplate. Another major military conflict in the same generation could conceivably sweep away the existing social structure of the entire European continent. The death and devastation might give credence to the popular notion that wars are always started by the rich but fought by the poor. The suffering and starvation might also lend support to the Marxian argument that modern wars are the inevitable consequence of imperialist rivalries between capitalist nations. Hence the apprehension grew in Europe that another war of attrition would provoke the proletariat and peasantry throughout the continent to rise up in arms against their bourgeois and aristocratic rulers.

This nightmare of revolution frightened observers from the United States. American diplomats stationed in Europe repeatedly warned that a general war on the continent would create the material conditions for a revolt of the masses. "With the social unrest widespread as it is," Ambassador Breckinridge Long wrote from Rome in April 1935, "I can only shudder to think of our social situation a year after another conflict."[6] A year later, Ambassador William E. Dodd warned from Berlin that a long battle would leave Europe "pretty much in ruins and a prey to Bolshevism."[7] The red scare also alarmed Ambassador William C. Bullitt in Paris. "War will mean such horrible suffering," he predicted in December 1936, "that it will end in general revolution."[8]

Americans with business interests in Europe were likewise worried about the prospects for a radical uprising on the continent. "If the last war very nearly ruined the warring nations," the president of General Motors Export Company declared in April 1937, "the next war may do so utterly. Such a debacle could only result in a gigantic and universal social upheaval, with bloody class war and revolution the only possible outcome."[9]

Secretary of State Cordell Hull, horrified by these predictions, embarked upon a vigorous crusade to restore world trade in order to prevent the flames of war and revolution from engulfing Europe. He persistently urged representatives of the leading commercial nations to band together in a movement to eliminate trade restrictions. "The world has sure enough reached a crossroads," he wrote Canadian Prime Minister Mackenzie King in April 1937. "The decision must be made without further delay, whether the civilized nations are to continue down the road leading either to war or to universal economic disaster, or both, or whether they are to choose a way leading to cooperation in the establishment of normal economic relations and the restoration of stable conditions of peace."[10] A few months later, Hull warned the British commercial counselor in Washington that if the channels of international trade remained clogged, it would "not be possible for the British with their navy to prevent 70 million hungry Germans from going on the march when they became sufficiently destitute."[11]

Secretary Hull hoped that the expansion of the reciprocal trade network would open the way for a resolution of European political differences. He reasoned that a revival in world trade might induce German authorities to seek domestic welfare by participating in peaceful commerce rather than by engaging in territorial conquest. As Hull explained to a British Treasury official in September 1937, the trade agreements program aimed at "mobilizing some forty nations behind a definite policy of economic appeasement which in turn would facilitate political appeasement."[12] Hull reiterated his economic approach to the problem of European peace in a letter to Thomas W. Lamont of the J. P. Morgan Company in November 1937. "I really believe that the next four to six months will determine whether this movement for economic rehabilitation," he wrote, "can be advanced and expanded sufficiently to reduce the existing tension in Europe and afford the basis for general or normal international relationships."[13]

Hull insisted that an Anglo-American trade agreement was essential to provide the economic basis for a political settlement in Europe. "The Secretary's underlying idea," Herbert Feis explained in February 1937, "is that if by the joint presentation of the United States and the British Empire a real possibility can be created whereby the countries of Central Europe can be made to hope that their lot can be improved by economic arrangements, and that there is therefore a hopeful alternative to war, that they might be won over towards the making of the necessary political pledges."[14] Hull remained determined to secure an Anglo-American commercial accord. "The Secretary has steadily held the view," Feis again noted in October 1937, "that what must be striven for is an agreement of extensive character and great significance, making both the American and British markets of such increased importance to the world that they would be a very strong magnet, and to secure entry into them on favorable terms would induce the rest of the world to join in a program of lessened restrictions and equality of treatment."[15]

State Department officials, acting on that analysis, bombarded Great Britain with demands for a trade treaty. Norman H. Davis warned Foreign Minister Anthony Eden in April 1937 that "until we can get together on economic policy little headway can be made toward real peace."[16] When Belgian Prime Minister Paul van Zeeland came to Washington in June 1937 to discuss the possibility of reducing obstacles to international commerce, State Department officers urged him to inform the British that "a good Anglo-American trade agreement is the basis from which the broader effort must proceed."[17] Hull himself emphasized in talks with van Zeeland that "the most essential and far-reaching first step that could be taken would be a commercial accord between this country and Great Britain."[18] A month later, Sumner Welles told British Ambassador Ronald Lindsay that "there was no one step today that could be taken that would be more beneficial as a measure moving towards world appeasement than the negotiation of this trade agreement between their two countries."[19]

The House of Morgan worked closely with the State Department in this campaign for Anglo-American economic cooperation. At the request of Secretary Hull, Thomas Lamont talked with several British officials in May 1937 about the need for a commercial pact between the United Kingdom and the United States.[20] He maintained that the American business community thoroughly approved "the idea that with these two great countries taking the lead, the rest of the world would follow, and that thereby one of the basic foundations for the maintenance of world peace would be established."[21] But Lamont soon discovered that some of the experts in the British Treasury were reluctant to abandon their bilateral arrangements, which ran counter to the most-favored-nation principle. "If the British Treasury would force our Treasury to enter into a lot of bilateral agreements of the nature which the British have cultivated," he admonished a member of Parliament in June 1937, "our people, having a far greater range of objects to deal with, could probably beat the British pretty badly at their own game." Lamont also suggested that the United States might stop underwriting British prosperity by purchasing gold if London refused to "enter into an economic alliance with Washington."[22]

State Department officials realized that the Ottawa imperial preference system presented the major roadblock to Anglo-American economic collaboration. "The vital question of whether the whole movement for reduction of trade restrictions is to be extended sufficiently to bring about an expansion and natural development of world trade," Leo Pasvolsky asserted in April 1937, "is in large measure dependent upon the extent to which the British Commonwealth of nations modify their present intra-imperial commercial policies which, in their operation, serve to restrict the possibilities of trade between the Empire nations and non-British countries."[23] In trade negotiations with the United Kingdom, therefore, American diplomats pressed for concessions which cut straight across the Ottawa agreements. "We made it plain," J. Pierrepont Moffat explained in August 1937, "that if payment were demanded by the Dominions before agreeing to a modification of the preferences, such payment must be made by Great Britain and not by the United States. Britain, for instance, could agree to give up certain of her preferences in the Dominions market which would be a *quid pro quo* in that it would enable the Dominions to negotiate further trade agreements."[24]

The State Department hoped that an Anglo-American commercial accord would counter agrarian opposition to the trade agreements program. "There has been a good deal of criticism in agricultural circles," Assistant Secretary Francis B. Sayre explained in April 1937, "that we have heretofore negotiated to a disproportionate extent with agricultural countries and, in consequence, that agriculture has been called upon to make sacrifices in the form of reduced protection in this market for the benefit of industrial exports. If satisfactory concessions can be obtained for our agricultural exports in the important United Kingdom market, it will make it much easier to go forward with negotiations with agricultural countries."[25] Pierrepont Moffat likewise pointed out that domestic political considerations made it necessary to "balance the slate" between urban and rural interests by opening a large foreign market for American farm products.[26] Thus, American diplomats informed Canadian trade representatives in September 1937 that "it will be necessary for us to conclude an agreement with Great Britain before we can undertake further negotiations with agricultural countries."[27]

Trade negotiations with Great Britain, however, proved most difficult. By November 1937, Cordell Hull was in "a positively savage frame of mind about the dilatory tactics of the British." He thought that it was about time "to say to the British that if they did not want to play the game our way they could go to hell and that we would lay down a couple more battleships and withdraw into our shell."[28] Concern about Germany heightened American eagerness for a trade pact with London. Francis Sayre expressed hope in December 1937 that the consumation of negotiations with the British "would practically force Germany to change its commercial policy and also enter into a trade agreement on the basic terms of our trade agreements policy."[29] In a similar fashion, *Business Week* reasoned that the successful completion of a commercial accord with Great Britain would put the United States "in a position to exert pressure on Germany, not to get out of world markets which it can hold legitimately, but to return to accepted methods of trading."[30] Finally, in November 1938, the mounting political tensions in Europe prompted England to acquiesce in American desires for a trade treaty.

Meanwhile, Nazi officials intensified their demands for the return of the colonies which had been taken from Germany at Versailles.[31] Foreign opponents of colonial restoration claimed that Germany could buy an unlimited supply of raw materials in the international marketplace. Reich spokesmen retorted that due to a lack of foreign exchange, Germany needed to purchase natural resources from territories within its own currency system.[32] "It is either silly or cynical, in the face of such facts," Reichsbank President Hjalmar Schacht proclaimed in January 1937, "for foreign commentators to declare that Germany can buy raw materials in the world market at will. No, Germany cannot do that because she does not possess the means of paying for them in foreign currencies; and she does not possess the means because foreign countries do not consume enough of her wares." Schacht found the argument that Germany's former colonies were valueless to be particularly ridiculous. "If the colonies are so bad," he asked his foreign adversaries, "why do you keep them?"[33]

Dr. Schacht repeatedly suggested that President Roosevelt should call a world conference to satisfy Germany's colonial claims.[34] "We can never have a disarmament agreement," he warned Ambassador Dodd in December 1936, "until we get our colonies."[35] A month later, Schacht told Ambassador Joseph E. Davies, who was passing through Berlin on his way to Moscow, that he had been authorized to submit proposals for the stabilization of European boundaries and the discontinuation of military expenditures in return for the restitution of German colonies.[36] French officials had already informed Schacht that they were willing to discuss the colonial question with Germany.[37] They had ideas about creating international consortiums for the development of areas in Africa to provide outlets for the products of German industries.[38] Premier Leon Blum told Ambassador Bullitt in December 1936 that he hoped the United States would actively support French efforts to achieve a reconciliation with Germany based upon an agreement to restore trade and to reduce armaments.[39]

Several American diplomats on duty in Europe, however, were pessimistic about the prospects for economic appeasement. "I remain somewhat skeptical as to Hitler's inclination to accept limitation of armament in return for market outlets," William Bullitt cabled from Paris in January 1937, "as that would seem to mean abandonment of Germany's desire to alter her Polish and Czechoslovakian frontiers."[40] Writing from

Vienna two months later, George Messersmith warned that the Nazi regime was completely committed to the idea of making the Third Reich less dependent upon distant markets. "Germany wishes to acquire territory adjacent to her present frontiers," he argued, "for the purpose of assuring herself of necessary foodstuffs and raw materials found in these envied areas."[41] William Dodd had come to the same conclusion based upon his observations in Berlin. "The German Government," he lamented in March 1937, "is now determined to control and actually annex, neighboring countries."[42]

Nevertheless, President Roosevelt and Secretary Hull decided to send Norman Davis to London in February 1937 to advocate an economic solution to the threat posed by Germany. Before Davis embarked upon his mission, the State Department provided him with a long memorandum which defined the problem confronting Europe in the following way: "Can a compromise be found, or a price paid, which will satisfy the economic necessities of the German people without war, and without making Germany paramount on the continent? If so, there will be no war; if not, war is possible, if not probable." The memorandum reminded Davis that his basic objective was to promote "a general political and economic settlement which would obviate the necessity for Germany to strike out to obtain the sources of raw materials in markets deemed by the German leaders necessary to maintain the standard of living of the German people."[43] A week later, Assistant Secretary R. Walton Moore expressed hope that "the British and French will have enough common sense to meet the demands of Germany for access to sources of raw materials and even for colonies where raw materials may be found."[44]

But the British were unyielding. They rejected the idea of using colonial currency to pay for peace except within the framework of a general settlement with Germany.[45] They also refused to consider a reduction of trade barriers or a limitation of armaments until the Germans were prepared to make political commitments with respect to European boundaries.[46] Foreign Secretary Anthony Eden insisted that the time was not ripe for an international conference. He feared that any move in that direction before the British rearmament program proceeded to a more advanced stage would be construed by the Germans as evidence of British weakness. Eden did not think that Germany possessed sufficient financial resources to compete successfully with Great Britain in the race for military supremacy. Thus, he hoped that the progress of rearmament in his country would have a sobering effect on Germany and thereby enable England to negotiate from a position of strength at a future world conference.[47]

American policymakers were discouraged. They feared that the arms race would cause economic breakdowns in Europe and speed the momentum toward war.[48] Norman Davis did not believe that there could be a political settlement in Europe "without opening up the channels of trade and stopping the suicidal increase in armaments." But the British repeatedly told him that "before any effective step can be taken for economic recovery and disarmament" the Germans would have to make concrete promises regarding their frontiers on the continent. "It is," Davis complained in April 1937, "a vicious circle."[49] President Roosevelt was even more dismayed when he learned that the French were beginning to support the British position.[50] "How do we make progress if England and France say we cannot help Germany and Italy achieve economic security if they continue to arm and threaten," he grumbled in May 1937, "while simultaneously Germany and Italy say we must continue to arm and threaten because they will not give us economic security."[51]

The State Department believed that before the vicious circle could be broken, it would be necessary to remove Ambassador Dodd from his post in Berlin. Dodd had become so hostile to the Nazi regime that he was in no position to help the European powers reach an accommodation. "We should have an understanding Ambassador," William Phillips complained to the president in January 1936, "especially during the next two or three years which were the critical ones for Europe." Roosevelt heartily concurred when Phillips insisted that "it was not right to have our representative practically out of touch with the officials of the Nazi Government."[52] They discussed the possibilities of finding some other work for Dodd outside of government service, and a year later Colonel Edward M.

House suggested that Dodd should be appointed to the Harmsworth professorship at Oxford University.[53] But Dodd was reluctant to resign. "Even if the Germans continue to accept him," Pierrepont Moffat growled in September 1937, "he will be about as useful as a rattlesnake."[54] Finally, Sumner Welles used his influence at the White House to have Dodd recalled, and in November 1937, Dodd was ordered to end his mission before Christmas.[55]

Welles was already at work on a plan for an American peace initiative. In a long memorandum drawn up in October 1937, he urged the president to issue a call on Armistice Day for a world conference to establish norms for international conduct. Welles emphasized the need to reach agreement on "the methods through which all peoples may obtain the right to have access upon equal and effective terms to raw materials and other elements necessary for their economic life." He also suggested the need for a peaceful revision of the Versailles Treaty. "It is possible," he acknowledged, "that before the foundations of a lasting peace can be secured, international adjustments of various kinds may be found in order to remove those inequities which exist by reason of the nature of certain settlements reached at the termination of the Great War." Welles hoped that American cooperation in the removal of trade barriers would set the stage for the European powers to settle their political differences. But while the proposal appealed to Roosevelt, Cordell Hull persuaded the president to shelve the project for the time being.[56]

The Welles plan received new life in January 1938 when Hull gave it his endorsement provided British approval could be secured in advance. Welles was hopeful that an international conference held in Washington would buttress British attempts to appease Hitler. "It is my belief," he explained, "that the proposal in itself will lend support and impetus to the effort of Great Britain, supported by France, to reach the basis for a practical understanding with Germany both on colonies and upon security as well as upon European adjustments." If everything went according to schedule, the United States would collaborate in restoring commerce and restricting armaments, but it would not make any commitments regarding territorial questions. Welles convinced Roosevelt that it was time to act, and on January 11 the president sent a confidential message to Prime Minister Neville Chamberlain outlining the procedure for implementation of the plan.[57]

Chamberlain quickly dismissed the proposal without even consulting Foreign Secretary Eden, who was vacationing abroad. The prime minister cabled Roosevelt on January 14 that any American intervention in the present situation might lead Germany and Italy to make "demands over and above what they would put forward to us if we were in direct negotiation with them." Chamberlain added that his government was prepared to recognize the Italian conquest of Ethiopia, and he asked that the president hold his hand while Great Britain tried to work out an agreement with Hitler and Mussolini.[58] Roosevelt replied on January 17 that he would defer "for a short while" his intention of calling an international conference, but that he opposed recognition of Italian rule in Ethiopia except "as an integral part of measures for world appeasement."[59] Eden then hastily returned to London and insisted that the British government reconsider the entire matter. After a bitter Cabinet debate, Chamberlain cabled Roosevelt on January 21 that Britain would recognize Ethiopia only as part of a general settlement and that Britain would support the proposed diplomatic initiative whenever the president decided to go ahead with it.[60]

Bold strokes taken by Hitler, however, prompted Roosevelt to postpone the project. In a purge which completed the consolidation of Nazi power in Germany, Hitler announced on February 4 that he would be commander in chief of the armed forces and that Joachim von Ribbentrop would replace Konstantin von Neurath as foreign minister. Welles informed the British ambassador on February 9 that the situation in Germany required clarification before it would be wise to go forward, but that the president intended to proceed with his plan in the near future. But while Roosevelt awaited further information, a crisis erupted in Austria. Hitler met with Chancellor Kurt von Schuschnigg at Berchtesgaden on February 12 and made a number of demands designed to undermine the Austrian government. A month later, Nazi troops marched into Vienna, and on March 13, 1938, Hitler incorporated Austria into the Third

Reich. Roosevelt sent word to London on that same day that he had decided to postpone his plan for an indefinite period.[61]

Americans believed that the annexation of Austria would enable Germany to establish economic hegemony over Central and Southeastern Europe. Vienna had been the capital of the old Austro-Hungarian Empire, and it continued to serve as the commercial and financial center for the entire Danubian watershed. "By the acquisition of Vienna," Ambassador Dodd's replacement, Hugh R. Wilson, reported from Berlin, "Germany has acquired a spearhead of the greatest advantage and utility."[62] Douglas Miller, the American commercial attaché in Berlin, likewise pointed out that Germany had obtained "an ideal springboard for the expansion of her foreign trade with Southeastern Europe."[63] Ambassador Anthony Biddle expressed equal concern about the commercial consequences of the *Anschluss*. "Germany's restricted economic system has penetrated into Central and Southeastern Europe with almost unbelievable speed," he observed from Warsaw. "Germany's system is tending to elbow-out trade with those powers which practice a liberal trade policy."[64] As the Nazi commercial invasion of the Balkans continued, *Business Week* noted that "the Reich finds itself in the position of an economic conqueror."[65]

A State Department group headed by Sumner Welles and Assistant Secretary Adolf A. Berle, however, continued to hope that an international conference could preserve peace in Europe.[66] Berle actually welcomed the Austrian annexation. "Whatever can be done by diplomacy," he explained, "does not have to be done later by war."[67] Berle agreed with Ambassador Wilson in Berlin that German expansion eastward would not necessarily present "any very great threat to Western Europe."[68] He therefore suggested that the United States should endeavor to steer the European powers into a conference which would serve to legitimize the *Anschluss* in return for German assent to American desires. "We might work towards an acceptance of the American policy of disarmament, free commercial relations and racial and religious tolerance, in return for frank and generous acceptance of the principle of an enlarged Germany," Berle argued. "If our own doctrines were accepted, indeed, the fear of that enlarged Germany would be in great measure dissipated."[69]

But a different State Department group, led by Cordell Hull and Pierrepont Moffat, believed that the *Anschluss* had destroyed any chance for appeasement in Europe. Some reasoned that Mussolini would do nothing to alienate Hitler now that Nazi soldiers would be stationed at the Brenner Pass. "The Berlin-Rome axis was so strong," Hull argued, "that Italy was not going to make any arrangements with Britain which would endanger that axis."[70] Others feared that Germany would continue on the march. As long as he had served as the chief of the Division of European Affairs, Moffat had never believed that it would be possible to take the Nazis into camp. "Any partial offer of compensation made by Britain and France," he had warned earlier, "would be interpreted as weakness and once swallowed would be followed by new and greater demands."[71] News of the German invasion of Austria prompted Moffat to conclude that Hitler had taken "one more step on the ladder to complete European domination."[72]

The more pessimistic American diplomats, moreover, were already predicting that Japan would join forces with Germany in an attempt to partition the planet into exclusive spheres of economic influence. George Messersmith warned Hull in July 1936 that "Germany feels that Japan will be ready when she is and will be with her."[73] While still occupying his post in Berlin, William Dodd had feared a tripartite division of the world with "Germany dominating Europe, Japan dominating the Far East and the United States dominating both Americas."[74] This nightmare seemed to be materializing after Japanese and Chinese troops exchanged shots in July 1937 at the Marco Polo Bridge. Japan seized upon the skirmish as an excuse for making further conquests on the Asian mainland, and her aggression provoked a determined Chinese resistance. As full-scale fighting ensued, the American dream of a golden market in China began to look like a fleeting mirage on the Gobi desert.

American antagonism toward Tokyo intensified during the autumn of 1937 as Japanese soldiers continued their assault on China. President Roosevelt, while speaking in Chicago on

October 5, suggested that peaceful countries should impose a "quarantine" against aggressor nations to prevent the spread of lawlessness. On the next day, the United States joined with the League of Nations not only in condemning Japan for its military operation in China but also in recommending that an international conference should be held in Brussels to discuss the Far Eastern situation.[75] Some Americans hoped that their government would take punitive action against Japan. Former Secretary of State Henry L. Stimson, for example, regarded moral lectures as ineffective unless accompanied by economic pressure. In a letter to the *New York Times* on October 7, Stimson issued a call for a ban on trade with Japan. He also made a private appeal to the president for an official embargo designed to throttle the Japanese war machine.[76]

Neither the president nor the State Department, however, had any intention of imposing economic sanctions against Japan. A day after his speech in Chicago, Roosevelt told news reporters that he had not meant to imply sanctions when he proposed the idea of a quarantine. Many of his close advisers opposed economic retaliation because they feared that the destruction of Japanese power in the Orient would open the way for the triumph of communism in China. If Japan were completely downed, Pierrepont Moffat warned on October 10, "China would merely fall prey to Russian anarchy and we would have the whole job to do over again and a worse one."[77] Others in the State Department feared that economic reprisals would start the country down a slippery path toward hostilities with Japan. "If sanctions are effective," Hugh Wilson warned on October 18, "they are an act of war and should be recognized as such and we should be ready to embark on war to carry them through."[78]

Most senior officials in the State Department advocated a program of economic appeasement rather than a policy of physical punishment. Japan, like Germany, was perceived as a have-not country that might still be influenced by moderate leaders who wanted to promote domestic prosperity by engaging in peaceful trade relations with the rest of the world. American diplomats therefore responded to Tokyo in much the same way that they would react to Berlin. On the negative side, they supported a huge naval construction program so that the United States would be prepared to wield a big stick in the Pacific. On the positive side, they were ready to offer Japan an economic carrot in order to prevent an ultimate military showdown in the Far East. Their abiding wish was that the Japanese would withdraw their troops from China in return for access to overseas markets and resources.[79]

Hoping to work out an agreement with Japan, the Roosevelt administration curtly dismissed British suggestions that the option of sanctions should be considered at the forthcoming Brussels Conference. In a memorandum sent to the United States on October 19, 1937, Foreign Secretary Anthony Eden argued that economic measures, if generally applied, might be effective in forcing Japan to make peace. The State Department replied that the question of sanctions should not arise in a conference designed to solve the Sino-Japanese conflict by agreement. Despite this American rebuff, Eden reintroduced the issue of sanctions the day before the conference opened on November 3 at Brussels. He told Norman Davis, the head of the American delegation, that Great Britain would be willing to go just as far as the United States in employing physical coercion against Japan.[80] Davis demurred. "We should concentrate every effort on exerting moral pressure," he insisted, "so as to bring about peace by agreement."[81]

Davis made a strenuous effort to achieve American objectives at the Brussels Conference. The delegates from England, France, and Russia asserted at the outset that nothing short of economic pressure would do any good. They also maintained that their respective governments were prepared to employ punitive measures against Japan provided that the United States would cooperate with their collective action. But Davis refused to entertain the question of sanctions and insisted that every effort should be made to bring Japan into negotiations. When the Japanese rejected repeated calls to come to the conference, other representatives tried to bring about a recess. But Davis adhered to the American strategy of prolonging the discussions. He worked to keep the conference in session as long as possible not only to exert moral pressure on Japan but also to convince the American people that their interests were being threatened by events far from their own borders.[82]

A few weeks after the Brussels Conference adjourned, however, Japan began a brutal assault on Nanking, which was under the rule of Chiang Kai-shek and the Kuomintang Nationalists. Japanese bombers roared up the Yangtze River on December 12, sinking the United States gunboat *Panay* and destroying three Standard Oil Company tankers. Although the American naval vessel was clearly marked, the Japanese planes machine-gunned the survivors as they made for shore in small boats. Three Americans were killed. And while the government in Tokyo quickly offered a formal apology and agreed to pay an indemnity for the incident, the Japanese army in China continued to damage American property and mistreat American residents during the siege of Nanking. Most Americans, reacting with caution, believed that their fellow countrymen should be withdrawn from Chinese soil. A State Department study of public sentiment toward the Far Eastern situation in early 1938 concluded that "the controlling feeling in the country was the desire to keep out of war."[83]

But the Roosevelt administration was intent on protecting American economic interests in Asia. Admiral William D. Leahy, the chief of naval operations, wanted to make the American fleet strong enough to take care of any possible difficulties in the Pacific. "It is inconceivable to me," he wrote the president in January 1938, "that we as a nation are going to give up our rights of trading or living in China and confine our activities to our own continental limits."[84] Roosevelt agreed, and a few weeks later he delivered a special message asking Congress for a 20 percent increase in naval construction. But the request aroused those who viewed the projected expansion as a calculated preparation for hostile naval action in the Far East. During congressional committee hearings, Admiral Leahy assured the critics of additional appropriations that the navy was being enlarged strictly for the defense of American shores. His arguments were effective. Despite continued skepticism about the president's intentions, Congress authorized funds for the construction of new warships.[85]

The Japanese army, in the meantime, pushed deep into the Middle Kingdom. Yet Americans took heart when the Communists joined forces with the Kuomintang to challenge the Japanese advance. Upon his return from a visit to the Orient in April 1938, John Foster Dulles praised the Red Army as "the most effective fighting portion and the most patriotic Chinese troops." Dulles concluded that "in all probability Japan could not conquer China."[86] Stanley K. Hornbeck, the senior State Department adviser on Far Eastern affairs, agreed that the growing unity in China would "make Japan's ultimate success unlikely or impossible."[87] Contrary to these optimistic forecasts, however, Japanese forces were able by June 1938 to gain mastery of every important railroad and seaport from northern Manchuria down to the Yangtze River. And the Japanese quickly took advantage of their military campaign by assuming control of all basic industries in North and Central China.[88]

American leaders became increasingly concerned about Japan's attempt to monopolize the China market. The State Department dispatched a series of diplomatic notes to Tokyo protesting the confiscation of American property and the destruction of American business as well as the pernicious treatment of American citizens in China. As the Japanese bombardment of Chinese cities continued in July 1938, Secretary Hull asked American manufacturers and exporters not to sell planes or aeronautical equipment to any nation engaged in air attacks on civil populations.[89] But this "moral embargo" did little to restrain Japan. Indeed, on November 3, 1938, Tokyo boldly announced plans for the creation of a Greater East Asia Co-Prosperity Sphere linking Manchukuo and China with Japan. Foreign Minister Hachiro Arita informed Washington that his government intended to establish a New Order in East Asia for the purpose of assuring Japan the same degree of economic self-sufficiency enjoyed by the United States and the British Empire. Arita also insisted that "the time had passed when Japan could give an unqualified undertaking to respect the Open Door in China."[90]

Treasury Secretary Henry Morgenthau promptly advanced a financial scheme to help the Chinese resist Japan. Morgenthau proposed an immediate twenty-five million dollar credit to China for the shipment of tung oil to be delivered to the United States over a period of years. The State Department opposed the arrangement. Cordell Hull cautioned the president on November 14 that Tokyo would interpret the credit as an effort to strengthen Chinese military resistance rather than as a routine commercial transaction, and he warned that the project might provoke the Japanese to increase their attacks on American economic interests in Asia. But Roosevelt overruled the State Department, and on December 15 the Reconstruction Finance Corporation announced that it would advance the credit to China. The president hoped that the tung oil deal would help Chiang Kai-shek and his Kuomintang government survive after their retreat to Chungking in southwestern China.[91]

Simultaneously, the State Department was considering the larger question of engaging in direct retaliation against Japan. Stanley Hornbeck addressed the issue in a series of memorandums which argued that moral suasion had failed and that the time had arrived to employ material coercion.[92] But most of his colleagues disagreed. They feared that economic sanctions would lead to an armed conflict with Japan and that Great Britain would steer clear and leave the United States to bear the brunt of a battle in the Pacific. "There were many evidences," Pierrepont Moffat warned on November 5, "to the effect that Great Britain would soon consider driving the best bargain she could with Japan irrespective of principle."[93] While a majority in the State Department argued against a comprehensive program of economic reprisals, the senior officials agreed that the doctrine of the Open Door in China must remain intact. Washington therefore dispatched a long note to Tokyo on December 30 denying that the Japanese had any right to establish a New Order in territory not under their sovereignty.[94]

In the meantime, it had become painfully evident that Hitler's land hunger remained unsatiated. Almost immediately after he devoured Austria in March 1938, the führer began casting covetous eyes upon Czechoslovakia. His purposes were well served by the fact that ethnic Germans made up the bulk of the population in the Sudeten area of Czechoslovakia. Arguing that the Versailles Treaty had violated the principle of self-determination, Nazi leaders demanded that the Sudentenland should be reincorporated into the Reich. But France had a moral commitment to defend the territorial integrity of the Czech state, and in May 1938 a war scare swept across Europe. The tension temporarily subsided, however, when it became obvious that neither the French nor the British were willing to fight for the maintenance of the existing Czech boundaries.[95] Their reluctance to stand up to Germany was reinforced by their fear that a military explosion would generate a social revolution and spell the doom of capitalism in Europe. Ambassador Bullitt, echoing apprehensions in Paris, warned that a war to defend Czechoslovakia would result in "the complete destruction of Western Europe and Bolshevism from one end of the continent to the other."[96]

The State Department, alarmed by such dire prospects, stood ready to do whatever it could to prevent war. When the Sudeten crisis came to a climax in September 1938, Assistant Secretary Berle noted that before 1933 liberal thinkers generally viewed the break-up of the Austro-Hungarian Empire as a mistake but that Hitler's methods had generated widespread fears that the absorption of Czechoslovakia would better position Germany for an attack against Western Europe. He thought that the current apprehensions were based upon emotion rather than reason. "We should regard this as merely reconstituting the old system," Berle argued, "undoing the obviously unsound work of Versailles and generally following the line of historical logic."[97] Most of his colleagues were less sanguine about Hitler's ultimate objectives. But they all agreed that it would be "unthinkable" for the British to wage war to protect the Czechs.[98] Like Prime Minister Chamberlain, they feared that a general war in Europe would end in the triumph of communism. "A fight now," Moffat dreaded, "would mean the end of all social structures as we know them."[99]

President Roosevelt agreed with his State Department advisers that America should use its influence to help preserve peace. When word arrived on September 19 that England and France had proposed that Czechoslovakia cede all districts containing a German majority, Roosevelt summoned the British ambassador to a private meeting in the White House. The president said that he would be willing to attend a world conference called by the Western powers to "reorganize all unsatisfactory frontiers on rational lines." If the British and French decided to reject Hitler's demands, he continued, they should merely blockade Germany rather than fight a classical war.[100] A few days later, Berle and Moffat drafted a statement urging negotiations and suggesting that the president would tender his good offices in any effort to work out a peaceful revision of the Versailles Treaty. But Hull had the offer of American mediation deleted from the final draft.[101] Then, on September 26, Roosevelt sent messages to the heads of state in Germany, Czechoslovakia, England, and France urging them to continue negotiations and insisting that their differences could be settled without resort to force.[102]

A day later the State Department held an important meeting to consider what more could be done to promote a pacific resolution of the crisis. "We all agreed," Moffat noted in his diary, "that no stone must be left unturned."[103] But the participants did engage in a tactical debate over the best way to achieve their common objective. Welles and Berle prepared a message for the president to send to Hitler calling for a general European conference and offering to dispatch an American representative to facilitate discussion. Once again Hull demurred, and the promise of American participation was removed from the last draft.[104] In his message cabled to Hitler on September 27, the president reiterated his view that all differences could and should be settled peacefully. Roosevelt also suggested that the current negotiations might need to be supplemented by a conference at some neutral European site.[105] American diplomats, however, were afraid that their efforts would prove inadequate. "The general view here," Berle observed, "is that there is practically no hope of averting war."[106]

News on the very next day that Chamberlain had accepted Hitler's invitation to meet at Munich produced a sense of relief in the United States. The president immediately wired the prime minister a two-word message: "Good man."[107] Roosevelt assumed that all major points had already been agreed upon in principle, because reports from Ambassador Joseph P. Kennedy in London had kept Washington fully informed about England's unwillingness to resist Germany. "From the very first," Moffat congratulated Kennedy, "you seem to have sized up the way the British official mind was running and given us clearly to understand how the crisis would probably end."[108] As was expected, Chamberlain agreed on September 30 to the transfer of the Sudetenland from Czechoslovakia to Germany. American leaders were quick to express their approval of the Munich settlement. "Under all the existing circumstances," Thomas Lamont reasoned, "Chamberlain did the very best job that could possibly have been done."[109] Roosevelt was equally pleased. "I want you to know," he confided to Ambassador William Phillips in Rome, "that I am not one bit upset over the final result."[110] In short, almost everyone rejoiced that war had been avoided.[111]

But it soon became clear that Hitler had taken another step toward the establishment of German economic hegemony in Central and Southeastern Europe. A few days after the Munich agreement, Walther Funk left his office at the Ministry of Economics to make a grand tour of the Danubian region to reap the commercial benefits of Germany's political victory.[112] The Nazi trade mission immediately offered directorships in German business firms to influential political leaders in several Balkan countries. "Every train pulling out of the big Vienna station," *Business Week* reported on October 8, "is filled with sharp-witted German salesmen bound for the Balkans."[113] A week later, Ambassador Biddle wrote from Warsaw that Germany had launched "a reinvigorated trade drive Eastward and Southeastward."[114] Nazi dreams of commercial empire seemed to be materializing as the little countries along the Danube were drawn ever more tightly into the German sphere of influence.[115]

It did not take long for Americans to grasp the economic implications of the agreement at Munich. "There is nothing in the whole area from the Baltic to the Black Sea that Hitler cannot have if he wants it," Douglas Miller warned from Berlin on October 3. "Wherever possible German products may supplant goods now purchased from the United States."[116] A month later, Pierrepont Moffat explained that American commercial interests would suffer because German domination of Central and Eastern Europe would mean "a still further extension of the area under a closed economy."[117] Business spokesmen agreed. Even before the Munich pact was concluded, *Business Week* predicted that the Sudetenland would be incorporated "into the unorthodox barter and exchange system of the Reich."[118] President Eugene P. Thomas of the National Foreign Trade Council pointed out that the economic consequences of Munich would extend far beyond the Czech frontier. "We must envision," he declared on October 31, "the probable creation of an economic *bloc* in Central Europe completely controlled by Germany and subjected to the compensation system of trade."[119]

The Nazi trade offensive in South America also continued to score big gains at the expense of the United States. Germany's share of total Latin American imports increased from 9.5 percent in 1929 to 16.2 percent in 1938, while the figures for the Unites States declined from 38.5 to 33.9 percent.[120] The State Department was disturbed. "The competition is getting keener all the time," Lawrence Duggan, chief of the Division of American Republics, noted in May 1938. "More and more dissatisfaction is being expressed by American exporters."[121] Their complaints centered on the Nazi employment of export subsidies and aski marks, which could be used only for the purchase of German goods. In a similar vein, Moffat explained to his congressman that Germany presented no physical danger in Latin America but that he could expect to see "a commercial competition fought not only with increasing intensity but with illegitimate methods."[122] Business writers made the same point. The continued use of unfair trade tactics, *Fortune* warned in December 1937, would enable Hitler "to go on playing the all but played out game of buying the other man's oil from him and selling him back the gas."[123]

The opportunity for Hitler to play that very game arose in March 1938 when the Mexican government nationalized foreign oil holdings. Hoping for the immediate return of their expropriated properties, the American petroleum companies demanded a cash settlement which was beyond the means of Mexico to pay. They even entertained the idea of financing a revolution in Mexico to produce a new government which would hand back their oil fields.[124] While opposed to such a serious breach of the Good Neighbor policy, the State Department did support a boycott against Mexican oil. But it quickly became apparent that Hitler stood to benefit from the situation. Bernard M. Baruch warned Roosevelt in April 1938 that totalitarian countries might "take the oil from Mexico and supply in return manufactured goods of all kinds, displacing American made goods."[125] His prediction was soon fulfilled. William R. Davis, a maverick American shipper, negotiated a contract in June 1938 to swap Mexican oil for German products.[126]

Ambassador to Mexico Josephus Daniels also feared that the oil controversy would divert Mexican trade from the United States to Nazi Germany. "If the Mexican Government should enter into arrangements to barter petroleum for goods made in Germany," he warned in June 1938, "it will seriously affect the commerce of the United States manufacturers and turn the tide of Mexican purchases from American-made goods to German-made goods."[127] As that process got underway, Daniels became increasingly critical of American oil companies for taking such a hard line toward Mexico. "The oil companies," he complained to Hull in July 1938, "do not seem interested in their country and its commerce enough to concern themselves in the least about it."[128] In short, Daniels charged that the petroleum firms were willing to sacrifice the broad commercial interests of the United States in order to protect their narrow proprietary interests in Mexico.

But the oil dispute was much more complicated than that. Thomas Lamont cautioned Adolf Berle in June 1938 that if the Mexican government were allowed to nationalize foreign petroleum property without paying adequate compensation, "the infection is likely to spread rapidly and disastrously" throughout the entire Western Hemisphere.[129] State Department officials agreed that other countries like Chile and Venezuela might imitate Mexico.[130] Some thought that the disease had been contained. "If the tide of expropriation had not been stopped there," Assistant Secretary George Messersmith explained in November 1938, "it would rapidly have spread all over South America."[131] As the impasse continued, however,

President Roosevelt became increasingly impatient with "the unwillingness of the Standard Oil Company of New Jersey to consider any solution other than the return of the expropriated properties." He gradually reached the conclusion that "the time has come when the two Governments themselves should try to work out a solution to the problem which they believe to be practicable and equitable."[132] Finally, in November 1941, Roosevelt was able to reach a settlement which brought Mexico back into the American economic orbit.

The State Department, in the meantime, had begun to use dollar diplomacy to counter the Nazi assault on markets south of the Rio Grande. President Warren L. Pierson of the Export-Import Bank told Secretary of State Hull in February 1938 that Latin America seemed to be the most promising field for increasing the activities of the institution. And within a year, the Export-Import Bank extended $90,000,000 in loans to facilitate the exportation of commodities from the United States. The financial muscle of Uncle Sam was exercised most effectively in stifling Germany's economic penetration of Brazil. Foreign Minister Oswaldo Aranha came to the United States in February 1939 to negotiate an agreement which strengthened commercial ties between Washington and Rio de Janeiro. The United States promised to provide Brazil with Export-Import Bank credits totalling $19,200,000 in return for pledges of equal treatment with regard to exchange allocation and debt payment.[133] "When I go back to my country I shall propose that we erect a statue to Herr Hitler," Aranha quipped. "For it is Hitler who has at last succeeded in drawing the attention of the United States to Brazil."[134]

Hitler had also succeeded in drawing American attention to the plight of the Jewish people. Almost immediately after coming to power in January 1933, the National Socialists launched a campaign of harrassment and intimidation to spur a Jewish exodus from Germany. Nazi racists employed social segregation, economic discrimination, and political repression to get rid of the Jews. But by December 1937, despite this anti-Semitic movement, only about 25 percent of Germany's Jewish population had left the country. So Hitler decided to shift to terror tactics to get quicker results. Following the annexation of Austria in March 1938, he directed his rabid supporters to resort to extreme persecution in hopes that physical violence would make life unbearable for Jews in the Third Reich. Soon, gangs of fanatic Nazis were roaming the streets attacking Jewish property and beating Jewish people.[135]

The Nazi reign of terror against the Jews coincided with a rapid rise in unemployment in the United States. As the American business cycle began to drop sharply in October 1937, President Roosevelt was besieged with contradictory advice. Fiscal conservatives like Treasury Secretary Henry Morgenthau advocated a balanced budget to restore business confidence.[136] Others, including Marriner S. Eccles, the head of the Federal Reserve Board, urged deficit spending to create purchasing power.[137] The president privately admitted in January 1938 that he "frankly didn't know what the answer was."[138] After six months of floundering, Roosevelt finally opted for a pump-priming program. But economic conditions remained miserable. "The President has begun to age," Adolf Berle observed in May 1938, "and is a little bitter."[139] Although the business cycle gradually turned upward, the New Deal never did solve the basic problem of unemployment. "We have said we would give everybody a job that wanted it," Morgenthau lamented in May 1939. "After eight years of this Administration we have just as much unemployment as when we started."[140]

Such circumstances strongly influenced the way that the American government responded to the Nazi persecution of Jews. During the first eight years of the Great Depression, aliens likely to need public welfare were barred from entering the country. The State Department refused to issue visas to prospective immigrants unless they had enough money to support themselves without a job or unless they had friends or relatives in America who would provide for them. The vicious attack on Jews following the *Anschluss*, however, aroused humanitarian sentiment in the United States. President Roosevelt immediately decided to allow the maximum number of immigrants from Germany and Austria to come into the country under the provisions of the National Origins Quota Act. But widespread concern about unemployment, reinforced by grass-roots nativism and anti-Semitism, kept Roosevelt from doing more to provide a haven for the oppressed in America. In fact, the State Department advised him that any effort to relax the immigration laws might backfire and provoke Congress to tighten existing regulations.[141]

Acting within the constraints imposed by conditions in the United States, Roosevelt issued a call in March 1938 for an international conference to deal with the refugee problem. The president made it clear from the outset that no country would be expected to absorb more immigrants than permitted by existing laws and that no government would be expected to finance resettlement projects.[142] A month later, Roosevelt formed the President's Advisory Committee on Political Refugees to mobilize private organizations which would provide funds for relocating displaced people.[143] And the Intergovernmental Committee on Political Refugees, which met in July 1938 at Evian, began looking in Latin America and Africa for countries which would accept large numbers of Jewish settlers.[144] Beyond his humanitarian desire to aid the victims of racial violence, Roosevelt hoped that a solution to the refugee problem would help set the stage for appeasement in Europe. Vice-Director Robert T. Pell later recalled that the Intergovernmental Committee originated in the hope that "a bridge might be built to the Germans which would enable them to save face and find a road back to the comity of the West."[145]

German commercial imperialists had different ideas. Dr. Schacht's efforts to increase German sales to the United States had been hindered by a boycott against Nazi products sponsored by Jewish organizations protesting anti-Semitism in the Third Reich. But Roosevelt's call for the Evian Conference suggested that the time was ripe to make racial repression pay handsome dividends. After passing laws prohibiting emigrants from taking any property from Germany, therefore, the Nazis intensified their violent attacks against Jews. Then American members of the Intergovernmental Committee on Political Refugees were informed that Schacht was working on a scheme which would allow Jews to take some of their property out of the country if the United States agreed to accept additional imports from Germany. "Boiled down to its simplest terms,"

Pierrepont Moffat observed in August 1938, "the German Government wishes to capitalize on foreign interest in the refugees to obtain an unreasonable competitive advantage in her exports and to artificially deflect the course of international trade. This brings it into head-on collision with Mr. Hull's trade agreement program."[146]

American leaders debated among themselves whether or not to pay Germany ransom in the form of commercial concessions to secure the release of the Jewish hostages. George Rublee, the director of the Intergovernmental Committee, recommended that the United States should help to subsidize an orderly exodus of Jews from the Third Reich by agreeing to purchase extra German goods. "I am convinced that the only method by which Germany can help to finance the Jewish emigration is by increasing her exports," he wrote in September 1938. "And it may be impossible to increase Germany's exports without cheapening their price at the expense of the Jews who are to emigrate."[147] A month later, the State Department considered the question of accepting subsidized German exports to help underwrite the resettlement of Jewish refugees. "It is obvious that the omelet cannot be made without breaking some eggs," Moffat noted. "In other words, that we cannot help the refugees without surrendering some commercial advantages. The question is how much the country is willing to let profits interfere with its emotional desire to be of help."[148] The answer was never in doubt. "We could not afford to give relief to the refugees," Moffat explained, "at the expense of flooding the country with cut-rate goods."[149]

Yet the State Department, after ruling out bribery payments, did attempt to persuade the Nazis to allow Jewish refugees to remove a reasonable percentage of their wealth from the Third Reich. "It is clear that the crux of the negotiation with Germany," Robert Pell explained, "is the question of the transfer of the property in Germany of involuntary emigrants."[150] When Dr. Schacht formally presented his plan in December 1938, the State Department advised George Rublee that "arrangements by which emigrants might take out part of their property in the form of goods should be on an individual basis and not a part of a general agreement in which other

Governments would be asked to participate."[151] Rublee thereupon succeeded in getting the Nazis to drop their demands for an increase in German exports over their usual level. The Rublee plan, signed in February 1939, stipulated that one fourth of the Jewish capital in Germany could be used to purchase German equipment to facilitate overseas settlements. The agreement also called for the creation of an outside organization to raise funds from private sources to help finance immigration projects.[152]

Myron C. Taylor, the chairman of the American delegation to the Intergovernmental Committee, set out immediately to encourage the establishment of an international corporation to implement the Rublee plan. Taylor appealed to Jewish bankers in New York and London to take the lead in funding the proposed foundation. He insisted that "the greatest burden must be borne by the Jews as it was largely their problem and their people who were in the greatest danger."[153] But the Jewish leaders in London refused to contribute any more than nominal amounts to fund settlement projects. Max Warburg said that "there was no reason why the Jewish community should bear the burden of a situation which it had not created."[154] Jewish financiers in New York were also reluctant to provide a substantial amount of money to help relocate refugees. Taylor worked hard to convince influential Jews of the importance of organizing a funding corporation without delay. "There is danger that lacking such responsive action in the outside countries," he admonished in March 1939, "the German Government may cancel its plans for orderly emigration."[155]

President Roosevelt and the State Department agreed that haste was essential. George L. Warren, the executive secretary of the President's Advisory Committee, warned in April 1939 that failure to take immediate action in setting up an international corporation might "result in the transfer of control of emigration and conditions of living to the extremists with possible solutions by annihilation."[156] Raymond H. Geist, the American consul general in Berlin, likewise reported that "unless places of settlement were opened up very shortly the radicals would again gain control in Germany and try to solve the Jewish problem in their own way."[157] The Roosevelt administration became increasingly impatient as Jewish bankers continued to balk at making any significant financial contributions.[158] Sumner Welles wrote Myron Taylor in June 1939 that "the President feels—as you and I do—that the long delay in the accomplishment of anything concrete by these individuals and organizations that are supposedly most interested in furthering an orderly emigration of Jews from Germany to new homes has obviously placed the German authorities in a position where they can sit back and smile and say that the people who are most vocal in their protests against the German treatment of the Jews have been entirely unwilling to do anything of a practical nature to assist the Jewish refugees."[159]

Government officials in the United States had no more success in inducing other countries to accept large numbers of Jewish refugees than they had in persuading private sources to provide sufficient funds for settlement projects: many countries, particularly in Latin America, actually tightened their immigration restrictions. By July 1939, the idea of finding a haven for the oppressed was all but dead. Time would soon run out for the Roosevelt administration to promote an orderly migration of Jewish refugees from Nazi Germany before Europe erupted in warfare.

Meanwhile, Americans pondered the significance of the Munich Conference. Some agreed with George Messersmith that the Nazis could never be trusted to keep their promise not to extend their frontiers beyond the Sudetenland. *Business Week* warned in September 1938 that Hitler aimed to acquire "the rich oil lands of Rumania, the vast grain fields of the Ukraine, the teaming markets of the East."[160] Ambassador Josephus Daniels similarly believed that the Nazis would carry out their long-planned *Drang nach Osten*. "Hitler's demand that all Germans come under the Reich," Daniels wrote Roosevelt in October 1938, "was only a show-window for his program of Berlin to Bagdad."[161] Others thought that Nazi troops would continue goose-stepping across Europe until the entire continent came under the shadow of the swastika. "I have a fear now," J. P. Morgan gloomily foreboded, "that the Germans are going to play their old trick and are going to demand more than they consented to at Munich."[162]

. . . . Unless <u>Goods</u> can cross
international boundaries . . . .

From *Foreign Trade and Domestic Welfare, A Graphic Outline of the Basic Elements Underlying a Choice Between a Liberal Interchange of Goods or Economic Isolation* (New York: National Foreign Trade Council, Inc., n.d.). In the George N. Peek Papers, 1911–1947, held at the University of Missouri by the Western Historical Manuscript Collection—Columbia.

. . . . Soldiers may cross
those boundaries . . . .

In the month following the Munich Conference, however, most business internationalists remained hopeful that economic appeasement would prepare the way for lasting peace. James D. Mooney, the president of General Motors Export Company, advocated increased trade opportunities for Germany in western markets to turn Hitler away from territorial conquests in Eastern Europe. "If Germany is not to move east politically," he argued, "she must move west economically."[163] Others, like Thomas J. Watson of International Business Machines and Winthrop W. Aldrich of the Chase National Bank, also continued to preach the gospel of world peace through world trade.[164] "It is of paramount importance," Aldrich declared in an address before the National Foreign Trade Convention, "that the efforts of the diplomats and of the heads of governments should speedily be reinforced by measures of economic appeasement."[165] Thomas Lamont agreed that the work done at Munich should be supplemented by the removal of commercial barriers. "I do think," he wrote Cordell Hull, "that now there is a chance to work gradually for a broader peace settlement in Europe."[166]

The group in the State Department headed by Sumner Welles and Adolf Berle also believed that the Munich agreement provided an opportunity to advance the cause of peace. Berle continued his search for a way of taming Hitler and thereby "translating the Nietzschean Ubermensch into a pacific animal."[167] On the very day that Chamberlain handed the Sudentenland over to Hitler, Berle suggested to Hull that the time was ripe for the United States to host a world conference to settle all outstanding questions. "It seems to me," he wrote, "that we might consider whether, after the lapse of a brief period of time, the President might not send a new circular message pointing out that a substantial victory for peace had been won; that this could be made permanent only through general settlement implemented by disarmament."[168] In a national radio broadcast three days later, Welles proclaimed that the time had come to establish "a new world order based upon justice and upon law."[169]

But President Roosevelt and some of his other advisers were less optimistic about the meaning of Munich. "I cannot help but feel that unless very soon Europe as a whole takes up important changes in two companion directions—reduction of armaments and lowering of trade barriers—a new crisis will come," Roosevelt wrote shortly after the Munich meeting. "If Hitler means what he said so definitely, he will have to go along and if he did not mean what he said he will not go along. That thought may be a childishly simple one but I think it expresses the immediate test."[170] Hugh Wilson agreed. "Hitler has declared publically and privately that he has no points of conflict with the West and that, with the settlement of the Sudeten question, Germany is a satisfied power as far as the continent is concerned," Wilson observed from his post in Berlin. "If by his subsequent acts he proves that his assurances were made only to gain immediate objectives, and were veils only of his wider intentions, then he will prove himself beyond question a menace to international society."[171]

Hitler tipped his hand in January 1939 when he fired Dr. Schacht from his position as president of the Reichsbank. Schacht had been persistently advocating the use of foreign exchange to obtain raw materials for export industries rather than for military production.[172] He repeatedly expressed his opinion that Germany would be able to solve its economic problems through the resumption of peaceful trade with the rest of the world.[173] But Hitler had different ideas. The führer believed that once Germany was fully armed it would be strong enough to take by force all the natural resources it needed from its neighbors. Thus, he discharged Schacht and ordered his replacement to put the financial assets of the entire nation behind the rearmament program.[174] Outside observers interpreted Schacht's dismissal to mean that the Nazis would continue to engage in bilateral barter and territorial aggrandizement.[175] "The removal of Schacht from the Reichsbank places the radical elements in complete control of the financial and economic structure of Germany," Messersmith warned. "There cannot be any hope of any moderation by the German Government in any internal or external policy."[176]

American diplomats increasingly concluded that the Munich settlement had merely provided for a short interlude between aggressive Nazi moves. "The State Department is very blue," Berle recorded in his diary in January 1939. "The whole situation is dominated by the probable beginning of a general struggle in Europe."[177] Despite the growing pessimism about German aims, no one knew where the Nazis would strike next. Ambassador Biddle wrote from Warsaw that he believed that Hitler would take advantage of the first opportunity which he perceived. "Past events indicate that, in preparing the ground for his expansion program, Hitler has made a scientific study of the potential weak spots in the European political arena," Biddle observed in March 1939. "Hitler has up his sleeve his formulae applicable to each potential opening in the international field. Hence, I believe we may look for him to approach his immediate objectives as a quarterback ready to direct his play through whatever opening in the line he discerns."[178]

five

The Carrot and the Club

I_N *THE* months following
the capitulation at Munich in October 1938, the Roosevelt administration became increasingly concerned about the threat
of a general European war. Although they still hoped that the
Nazi regime would agree to a peaceful settlement of all remaining continental issues in return for an open door to overseas markets, American policymakers believed that the time
had come to make preparations for an ultimate showdown with
the German Wehrmacht. They now sought to prevent the
dreaded holocaust by practicing the dual diplomacy of material
inducement and military intimidation. President Roosevelt
and his State Department advisers advocated a vast rearmament program designed to dissuade Adolf Hitler from taking
any more steps that might precipitate a war in Europe. They also
sponsored a drive to secure a revision in the neutrality laws so
that the United States would be able to supply weapons to
countries fighting to contain the Third Reich. Thus the American government, while continuing to offer the carrot of economic appeasement, began to forge a club of strategic
supremacy.

Public opinion in the United States, however, stood as a
rigid obstacle to American intervention in the impending European cataclysm. Reflecting the deep-seated desire of the
American people to avoid being drawn into future wars, Congress had passed in April 1937 a Neutrality Act which included
a mandatory embargo on the shipment of arms to any

belligerent nations.[1] The grass-roots determination to insulate the country from any military involvements was also revealed by the vigorous debate which surrounded a proposal to restrict the authority of Congress to declare war. Representative Louis Ludlow of Indiana introduced a House resolution calling for a constitutional amendment that would require a popular referendum before the United States could wage war. Despite a strong effort by the Roosevelt administration to mobilize opposition against it, the Ludlow resolution was barely defeated in the House of Representatives in January 1938 by a narrow margin of 209 to 188.[2] As the international scene grew more ominous, most Americans did express sympathy for England and France as opposed to Germany, but the Gallup polls taken in the spring of 1939 continued to show an almost unanimous sentiment against American participation in a foreign war.[3]

Ever sensitive to the popular mood, President Roosevelt conveyed mixed messages in his public statements. On the positive side, he launched a psychological offensive against Germany designed to make the Nazis fear that in the event of further aggression the United States would use its enormous resources to turn the tide of battle in favor of England and France. On the negative side, Roosevelt assured the American people that he would not lead the country into a European conflict. But the president pointed out in his annual address to Congress in January 1939 that there were "many methods short of war" by which the United States might assist the victims of aggression. Then he suggested that at the very least Congress should repeal the arms embargo. On the next day, Roosevelt requested a 1.3 billion dollar military budget, and a week later he asked for a supplementary appropriation of 500 million dollars for army and navy planes. The president stressed the purely defensive aspect of his call for huge military expenditures and insisted that he did not have "any thought of taking part in another war on European soil."[4]

President Roosevelt was no doubt sincere when he said that he wanted a powerful American air force to make the Western Hemisphere impregnable. "Troop ships, supply ships, and early concentrations on shore are extremely vulnerable to air attack," Major General Frank M. Andrews explained in a lecture at the Army War College in October 1938. "Airplane carriers which venture within range of shore-based aviation are taking long chances."[5] A month later, during an important military conference held at the White House, Roosevelt asserted that the United States needed an air force of 20,000 planes and an annual production of 20,000 planes. "We must," he insisted, "have a sufficiently large air force to deter anyone from landing in either North or South America."[6] Hanson W. Baldwin, the eminent military analyst, concluded in April 1939 that the proposed rearmament program would make the United States invincible. "Any invasion of our borders in force, even by a combination of Powers," he declared, "becomes virtually impossible in the forseeable future."[7]

But President Roosevelt had aims that extended far beyond the range of either national or hemispheric defense. During a private conversation in October 1938, Roosevelt asked a well-connected English aristocrat to assure Prime Minister Neville Chamberlain that in case of hostilities in Europe, he "would have the industrial resources of the American nation behind him."[8] Roosevelt explained that although the Neutrality Act prohibited the sale of American weapons to all belligerents, he could circumvent the arms embargo by exporting the basic components of war planes to assembly plants in Canada and England.[9] A month later, the president told War Department officials that he wanted a large air force to deter Germany from making any aggressive moves in Europe. "When I write to foreign countries," he explained, "I must have something to back up my words."[10] The more perceptive outside observers were quick to grasp the implications of the preparedness campaign. "In any realistic appraisal of the American military program as a whole, it should be openly admitted that the armed forces represent an essential element in the pursuit of power politics," a member of the Foreign Policy Association noted in May 1939. "The very existence of forces of the magnitude now planned makes possible their use in overseas conflicts, should the diplomacy they support prove unsuccessful."[11]

The State Department contained several shades of opinion concerning the proper role for America to play in the unfolding European drama. "Highly pleased over the President's decision to rearm in a drastic fashion," Cordell Hull hoped that a display of American military power would discourage Hitler from going on the warpath.[12] Norman Davis and George Messersmith were in a far more belligerent frame of mind. They believed that the United States should provide military aid to democratic countries even at the risk of becoming involved in another European war. But Pierrepont Moffat pointed out the inconsistency in their attitude. "Advocating a policy which was very much not the wish of the people," he noted, "could hardly be reconciled with a belief in the superiority of a democracy as a governmental force."[13] While agreeing with Moffat that the United States should steer clear of any European conflict, Sumner Welles and Adolf Berle still hoped that the president would be able to promote an international conference which would preserve peace on the European continent.[14]

But prospects for a peaceful settlement in Europe grew darker in March 1939 when Germany suddenly dismantled Czechoslovakia. The absorption of Bohemia and Moravia into the Third Reich demonstrated that Nazi ambitions were not limited to bringing about the unification of Germanic people. "In annexing 7,200,000 Czechs," a Foreign Policy Association researcher observed, "Hitler has abandoned even formal adherence to the policy of creating a purely German Reich and has committed himself to the century-old German nationalist dream of a unified German people dominating, as its *Lebensraum*, all Central and Eastern Europe."[15] The dismemberment of Czechoslovakia not only ran counter to the principle of self-determination which the Nazis had used to justify their acquisition of the Sudetenland, but it also violated the solemn pledges Hitler had made at Munich that he would make no more demands on the Czech people. American leaders concluded that Hitler could not be trusted to keep his word and that the Nazis would continue their drive eastward. "More and more the comparison with what is going on now and what went on in the Napoleonic era is becoming apt," Moffat grumbled, "only it looks as though Hitler were more successful even than Napoleon."[16]

American leaders realized that Germany's *Drang nach Osten* would undermine their commercial interests. "The break-up of Czechoslovakia," *Business Week* warned on March 18, "will affect the United States chiefly through a further diminution of the free world trade market."[17] As the editors had anticipated, Germany immediately set out to readjust Czechoslovakian production to meet the economic requirements of the Third Reich. Then, on March 23, Berlin extracted a trade agreement from Bucharest which was designed to keep Rumania on the agricultural half of an imperial relationship with industrial Germany. "This treaty is an important step toward a German-controlled *Grossraumwirtschaft* in Southeastern Europe," a Foreign Policy Association commentator observed. "Rumanian production will, so far as possible, be directed into channels useful to Germany."[18] As Czechoslovakia and Rumania became economic satellites of the Third Reich, Harry Dexter White of the Treasury Department pointed out that German expansion on the European continent presented an indirect as well as a direct menace to American trade. "The elimination of third countries from a part of the European market," he explained, "will later tend to cut down United States exports in the remaining open markets."[19]

The liquidation of Czechoslovakia brought the State Department to the "boiling point."[20] The question of breaking diplomatic relations with Germany was immediately laid on the table for full consideration. "George Messersmith, his eyes aglow, favored any move directed against the Nazis."[21] But most participants in the discussion agreed with Pierrepont Moffat that severing all ties with the Hitler regime "would be like pushing off a toboggan which would lead down a long slope towards eventual war."[22] Although they ruled out a complete break with Germany, they did issue a public statement condemning the Nazi seizure of Bohemia and Moravia.[23] State Department officials also decided that the time had come to exert economic pressure on the Third Reich. They had for several months resisted Treasury Department proposals to retaliate against Germany for shipping subsidized goods to the United States. But as soon as Hitler obliterated Czechoslovakia, they told Secretary Henry Morgenthau that he should go ahead and impose countervailing duties on imports from Germany.[24]

Neither the White House nor the State Department,

however, had abandoned hope for a peaceful settlement in Europe. Assuming that Hitler would be less inclined to risk war without Italian support, President Roosevelt sought to convince Mussolini that Italy had more to lose than to gain by backing Germany. Roosevelt warned the Italian ambassador on March 22 that the United States would assist the victims of aggression and suggested that if Mussolini used his influence to avert war, Italy would have a chance to obtain concessions at the conference table.[25] A few days later, the State Department considered sounding out the British "to see whether they would be interested in a constructive world move towards economic rehabilitation as an alternative to a purely military approach to the present disintegrating world picture."[26] But the British, like the French, were in no mood for conciliation. Premier Edouard Daladier, speaking over the radio on March 29, rejected any thought that France would make substantial concessions to Italy. Two days later, Prime Minister Chamberlain publicly announced that England would defend Poland against any attack.[27] The British guarantee of Polish borders provoked *Barron's* to warn that if the European powers fought another war, they might find that they had "ploughed the ground for Communism."[28]

These same apprehensions of war and revolution prompted Washington to hold out the olive branch to Rome and Berlin. President Roosevelt and his State Department counselors drafted a proposal for a world conference based upon the formula which had been advanced by Sumner Welles more than a year earlier.[29] The president appealed directly to Hitler and Mussolini on April 14, asking them to pledge not to attack any neighboring countries for at least ten years. Roosevelt promised that in return the American government would be willing to participate in discussions aimed at scaling down armaments and "opening up avenues of international trade to the end that every nation of the earth may be enabled to buy and sell on equal terms in the world market." He also suggested that simultaneously the European powers "could undertake such political discussions as they may consider necessary or desirable."[30] Roosevelt hoped for a favorable reply. "Keep your fingers crossed!" he exclaimed to Henry Morgenthau. "There is one chance in five. It had to be done."[31] But Hitler and Mussolini both responded to the American overture with scornful speeches.

The State Department, however, still clung to the policy of economic appeasement as the best hope of averting a European war. "The lowering or removing of barriers to international trade and the application of the principle of equality of commercial treatment," Secretary Hull declared before the World's Fair in May 1939, "would be an inevitable prelude to permanent peace."[32] But there were indications that the British desired commercial warfare rather than economic disarmament. Robert S. Hudson of the British Board of Trade secretly proposed in May 1939 the formation of an Anglo-American cartel to defeat German exporters in world markets. The State Department immediately rejected this suggestion that Great Britain and the United States should resort to Nazi commercial practices in an effort to beat the Germans at their own game. Assistant Secretary Francis B. Sayre explained to Hudson that the American government still hoped "that before too long the Germans would find it harder and harder and more and more costly to extend the scope of their present system, and that the way would then be opened for some general negotiation which would bring about fundamental and general revision of their trade methods."[33]

Business internationalists continued to endorse the State Department's position. "The totalitarian foreign trade policies depend for their success upon the complete regimentation of both foreign and domestic trade," warned Percy W. Bidwell, the director of studies for the Council on Foreign Relations. "As long as we are unwilling to abandon private enterprise, we could not expect to succeed in our efforts to imitate the German trade methods." Rather than resorting to bilateral barter practices to outmaneuver Germany in foreign markets, Bidwell argued, the United States should retain the reciprocal trade agreements program as the basis for "economic appeasement."[34] Thomas J. Watson, the president of International Business Machines, likewise advocated the removal of trade barriers to enable Germany to achieve prosperity through commercial expansion rather than territorial acquisition. "I do not believe,"

Watson lectured the Carnegie Endowment for International Peace in May 1939, "that we can ever keep any country peace-minded so long as economic forces are working against them to such an extent that they can't feed their people."[35]

But President Roosevelt and his advisers in the State Department were becoming increasingly pessimistic about the prospects for peace. Adolf Berle feared in June 1939 that the Nazis were "beginning to beat the tom-toms for a final work-up to a war psychology" and that the European powers were "heading into the coda that leads to the final crash cord."[36] As Germany continued to spend vast sums on armaments, Roosevelt likewise worried that Hitler was bent on war. "If Germany visualizes a peaceful working out of the political and economic problems," he reasoned, "common sense would require the starting of conversations as soon as possible in order to avoid an even worse financial situation."[37] In fact, Roosevelt had already begun thinking about how he could help assure the defeat of Germany if Hitler unleashed his military forces in Europe. The president told King George VI in June 1939 that in case of war he planned to have the American navy patrol the Western Atlantic so that the British could concentrate their fleet on the other side of the ocean. A few weeks later, Roosevelt secretly proposed to Great Britain that the United States should establish "a patrol over the waters of the Western Atlantic with a view of denying them to the German Navy in the event of war."[38]

In the meantime, the Roosevelt administration made a strenuous effort to secure the repeal of the arms embargo. The inner circle in Washington surmised that Hitler might hesitate to order his troops to march if he knew in advance that his adversaries would have full access to American military supplies.[39] Ambassador William C. Bullitt cabled from Paris in May 1939 that the German foreign minister was trying to persuade Hitler that he could risk war because England and France would not be able to obtain weapons from the United States. Bullitt added that the British and French hoped for a modification of the Neutrality Act in the near future.[40] A week later, Roosevelt committed his administration to an all-out campaign to convince Congress to abrogate the arms embargo without delay.

But the president's spokesmen disguised his true objectives. Denying that he had any intention of amending the Neutrality Act in order to aid England and France, they claimed that his sole purpose was to keep the United States out of war.[41]

Many senators and representatives, however, objected to a revision of the neutrality legislation because they fundamentally distrusted Roosevelt. Pierrepont Moffat noted in May 1939 that the congressional opposition could be boiled down to a single emotion: "the fear that the President would wish to line up this country in a war if England and France should become involved in hostilities."[42] As a result, the House of Representatives voted in June 1939 to retain the arms embargo, and the Senate Foreign Relations Committee voted a few weeks later to postpone consideration of the neutrality question until the next session of Congress. Still, Roosevelt refused to abandon the battle. Instead, he invited a group of leading senators to the White House in July 1939 and urged them to repeal the restrictive aspects of the neutrality law. After canvassing the assembled senators, Vice-President John N. Garner gave Roosevelt the bad news: "Well, Captain, we may as well face the facts. You haven't got the votes, and that's all there is to it."[43] The president was disappointed, but the American people seemed satisfied. A Gallup poll taken in August 1939 indicated that a majority of those questioned believed that Congress was right in retaining the arms embargo.[44]

Despite his failure to escape from the confines of the Neutrality Act, President Roosevelt hoped that the establishment of a strong alliance linking England and France with Russia would deter Hitler from aggression. Joseph E. Davies, the former American ambassador to Moscow, provided Roosevelt with a wealth of information about conditions in the Soviet Union and with astute observations about Russian foreign policy. Davies lamented the fact that the purges conducted by Premier Joseph V. Stalin had weakened British and French confidence in the strength of the Red Army. "It is my judgment," he wrote Roosevelt in January 1939, "that both the Soviet government and its army are a great deal stronger than is generally recognized in certain European quarters."[45] In line with this estimate, Davis concluded that the only real hope for peace was a defensive alliance between the Western European powers and the Soviet Union. He repeatedly warned that if the Kremlin were put off by England and France, Russia might make a separate deal with Germany. "Hitler is making a desperate effort to alienate Stalin from France and Britain," Davies wrote in March 1939. "If he does, he can turn his attention to western Europe without any concern as to an attack from behind."[46]

But the prime minister of Great Britain opposed an alliance with the Soviet Union. Chamberlain believed not only that Russia was incapable of maintaining an effective military offensive but also that an attempt to encircle Germany could provoke Hitler to launch an immediate attack. He hoped to prevent war by postponing a military confrontation with the führer until the completion of the British and French defense system ruled out the possibility of a quick German victory. Chamberlain intended to make political and economic concessions to Hitler once the Nazi dictator realized that he could obtain more at the conference table than on the battlefield.[47] "Chamberlain's idea," Ambassador Joseph P. Kennedy reported from London in February 1939, "is that he is going to go along, preparing and arming all the time, but assuming that he can do business with Hitler."[48] Although many English leaders concluded that an agreement with Berlin was no longer feasible and although the British Cabinet insisted on negotiations with Moscow, Chamberlain showed little interest in communicating with the Kremlin.[49] Thus, Kennedy concluded in March 1939 that the British obviously did not expect the Soviets "to make any substantial contribution to the problem of common security."[50]

Both the Americans and the French became increasingly impatient with Chamberlain's attitude toward Russia. Premier Daladier and Foreign Minister Georges Bonnet reasoned that a pact with the Kremlin was essential to check Hitler.[51] "If the Soviet Union could now be brought into the circuit," Daladier told Ambassador Bullitt in May 1939, "there was a considerable chance of preserving peace. If on the other hand the Russians should withdraw into complete isolation the situation would become tragic and untenable since all resistance to Hitler in eastern Europe would collapse."[52] Joseph Davies was in complete agreement. He warned Roosevelt in June 1939 that the Russian bear was getting tired of being cuffed around by the British lion and that as a result Stalin might make a deal with Hitler to protect his country from a German invasion. "It is perfectly amazing to me that the power and strength of the Soviet Government and Army is not accepted in spite of the overwhelming evidence that is at hand," Davies exclaimed. "When the house is burning, it seems so silly to be fearful of bringing in the Fire Department because the water might get your feet wet."[53]

Prompted by that analysis of the situation, President Roosevelt finally decided to approach the Soviets himself in an effort to bring Russia together with England and France. Roosevelt was fully cognizant of the German efforts to strike a bargain with the Kremlin. In fact, certain members of the German embassy in Moscow were providing Washington with complete and accurate reports about the secret negotiations going on between Germany and the Soviet Union.[54] When Ambassador Constantine Oumansky was preparing to return to Moscow in July 1939, therefore, the president asked him to tell Stalin that "if his government joined up with Hitler, it was as certain as that the night followed the day that as soon as Hitler had conquered France, he would turn on Russia, and it would be the Soviet's turn next."[55] Two weeks later, Sumner Welles instructed Ambassador Laurence A. Steinhardt in Moscow to reiterate to Foreign Commissar Vyacheslav Molotov the president's belief that if Russia reached a satisfactory agreement against aggression with England and France, "it would prove to have a decidedly stabilizing effect in the interests of world peace."[56]

The American appeals had little impact in Moscow, however, and on August 22, Berlin announced that Germany and Russia would conclude a nonaggression pact. The two powers agreed, in a secret protocol, to divide Eastern Europe into spheres of influence. On the Russian side, the deal enabled Stalin to postpone a clash with Germany and to secure strategic territory which would strengthen the Soviet Union against any Nazi attack in the future. It also meant that Russia could not be maneuvered into the disastrous position of having to fight the German Wehrmacht alone.[57] On the German side, the arrangement freed Hitler to invade Poland without risking a two-front war. The führer envisioned several favorable scenarios. First, the British and French, with no prospect of Soviet support, might force the Poles to hand over Danzig and the Corridor to Germany. Second, even if the western powers intervened, they would probably be unable to prevent a German victory. Third, after Germany liquidated Poland, the British and French might accept the accomplished fact rather than embark upon a long fight to the death.[58]

The announcement of the Nazi-Soviet pact provoked immediate reactions in Paris and London. Premier Daladier told Ambassador Bullitt on August 22 that without help from Russia the Poles would be defeated in short order. France confronted a terrible choice, he said: either fight at once in a war of doubtful outcome or abandon Poland only to face later the onslaught of a stronger Germany controlling the resources of Eastern Europe. Daladier hoped that President Roosevelt "would issue a declaration stating that war seemed imminent and summoning all the nations of the earth to send delegates immediately to Washington to try to work out a pacific solution."[59] The next day, a close adviser to Chamberlain briefed Ambassador Kennedy on British desires. "The British wanted one thing of us and one thing only," Kennedy reported, "namely that we put pressure on the Poles." But American policymakers scouted the British suggestion that the United States should urge Poland to make concessions to Germany. "As we saw it here," Pierrepont Moffat observed, "it merely meant that they wanted us to assume the responsibility of a new Munich and to do their dirty work for them. This idea received short shrift from the President, the Secretary, and Sumner Welles down."[60]

Nevertheless, Roosevelt decided to make a final effort to avert war through economic appeasement. In a message to King Victor Emmanuel on August 23, the president suggested that the Italian government propose "that no armed forces should attack or invade the territory of any other independent nation, and that this being assured, discussions be undertaken to seek progressive relief from the burden of armaments and to open avenues of international trade including sources of raw materials necessary to the peaceful economic life of each nation." On the next day, Roosevelt sent similar messages to Hitler and President Ignacy Moscicki of Poland. Roosevelt not only reiterated his willingness to participate in discussions aimed at reducing military stockpiles and restoring world commerce, but he also appealed to the two leaders to settle their differences by negotiation, arbitration, or conciliation. The president hoped that even if his last-minute attempts to prevent war failed, they would at least place the burden of guilt on Germany. "I don't think that anyone felt there was more than one chance in a thousand that such messages would affect events," Moffat noted in his diary, "but it seemed that the chance should be taken and above all that the record should be abundantly clear."[61]

Hitler responded to Roosevelt on September 1 by ordering the Wehrmacht to invade Poland. The führer still wished that Chamberlain and Daladier would renege on their promises to defend Poland, but after hesitating briefly, England and France declared war on Germany. Armageddon had arrived. Although the Allies were committed to aiding the Poles, words alone could not stop the Nazi military machine from sweeping across the plains of Poland. Fighter planes and dive bombers roared through the skies, whole divisions of tanks raced forward over fields and across streams, and motorized infantry units rolled down the roads and highways. A vast pincer movement closed around Warsaw with incredible speed, and before the month ended, German soldiers had crushed all Polish resistance. The blitzkrieg was a smashing success, and Russia promptly sent troops into Poland to share in the spoils of victory.

Shortly after the Poles surrendered, Hitler launched a peace offensive in hopes that the Allies would accept German domination of Poland and Czechoslovakia rather than engage in a prolonged conflict. However, the British and the French rejected Hitler's proposals for a peace settlement which would leave Germany in control of Central Europe. They believed that a Nazi assault on the Maginot Line along the French border would fail and that Germany did not have enough resources to win a long war. Assuming that time was on their side, the Allies intended to pursue a defensive strategy rather than fight a battle of blood and steel. They hoped that an Anglo-French blockade would produce an economic collapse in Germany and cause the downfall of the Nazi regime. "The way to win the war," Chamberlain insisted in September 1939, "is to convince the Germans that they cannot win." The British and the French therefore opposed any peace movement until the German people had suffered enough to became disenchanted with their leaders. "I have always been more afraid of a peace offer than of an air raid," Chamberlain explained in October 1939. The Allies hoped that the German people, after realizing that victory was beyond their reach, would remove Hitler from power and accept terms which would guarantee a lasting peace.[62]

Although less sanguine about the prospects for an Allied victory, the Roosevelt administration turned aside German suggestions that the United States should initiate peace talks. Serving as a go-between for Field Marshal Hermann Goering, William R. Davis, who had been purchasing Mexican oil for Germany, asked Roosevelt in September 1939 whether he would act as a mediator in bringing the war to an end. The president told Davis that he would consider the task of mediation if the German government officially requested his services as a peacemaker and if Hitler set forth reasonable proposals for a settlement.[63] But it soon became apparent that Berlin was unwilling to offer peace terms which would be acceptable to London and Paris. After thoroughly examining the situation in October 1939, the State Department concluded that the time was not ripe for the president to try his hand at mediation. "The consensus of the meeting," Assistant Secretary Berle noted, "was that while peace ought to be made, now was not the time."[64] So advised, Roosevelt decided to defer taking any action in hopes that a more opportune moment for peace negotiations would come in the near future.

American diplomats, in the meantime, held differing opinions about the strength of the Nazi-Soviet pact. One school of thought regarded the arrangement as a marriage of convenience which would ultimately end in divorce due to an inherent conflict of interest between the two parties. Joseph Davies, reasoning along these lines, viewed the Soviet advance into eastern Poland as an attempt to establish a security perimeter against a possible Nazi attack in the future. "I doubt it very much," he wrote Hull in October 1939, "that Russia has agreed to give military aid to Germany in the West."[65] The other school of thought feared that Stalin and Hitler would bury their differences and split the European continent into permanent spheres of influence. Adolf Berle, reflecting in this vein, was haunted by visions of a Teutonic-Slavic monster dominating the entire European landscape. "If this nightmare proves real," he concluded in September 1939, "you will have two men able to rule from Manchuria to the Rhine, much as Genghis Khan once ruled."[66]

President Roosevelt and his State Department advisers greatly feared the economic consequences of such a complete totalitarian triumph. A day after Nazi soldiers commenced their assault on Poland, Secretary Hull expressed anxiety that Germany and Russia would win the war and "prevent any Europeans from trading with us except on conditions which Berlin lays down."[67] Economic Adviser Herbert Feis was equally alarmed about the commercial future of the United States. "Hitler has become so decisive a factor in determining what lies ahead of every producer in this country," he warned in October 1939, "that the economist simply cannot think in terms of steady, ordinary development."[68] Just prior to his appointment as assistant secretary, Breckinridge Long likewise worried that Nazi Germany, aided by raw materials from the Soviet Union, would overrun every country in Europe and "exclude us from practically all of those markets."[69] The president shared these apprehensions about the economic repercussions of a Nazi-Soviet victory. "Our world trade," Roosevelt warned in December 1939, "would be at the mercy of the combine."[70]

American diplomats believed that Germany, if victorious, would not only establish economic hegemony in Europe but also intensify its drive to capture South American markets. A few foreign policy advisers, including George Messersmith and William Bullitt, even thought that the Nazis intended to launch a military attack on the Western Hemisphere. "It is absolutely certain," Bullitt wrote hysterically from Paris in September 1939, "that if France and England should be unable to defeat Hitler, we shall have to fight him some day in the Americas."[71]

But the cooler heads in the State Department regarded Germany as an economic threat rather than a military menace in Latin America. Even if Hitler eventually mopped up Europe, Breckinridge Long reasoned in March 1940, "our Fleet would be able to take care of any two Fleets Germany could muster."[72] In the same month, Adolf Berle succinctly defined the problem: "Our real defense lies in the fact that the cost of a Russo-German success, though it may leave them to dominate the field, will leave them so weakened that they need not be feared; in which case our great test will be economic: can we maintain enough economic life for this hemisphere so that one country after another country in South America will not be forced by trade relations to fall into the Berlin orbit?"[73]

Worried about the possibility of a Nazi victory, the Roosevelt administration immediately began preparations for the economic defense of the Western Hemisphere. Business internationalists believed that if the United States would absorb a larger proportion of South American exports, the Latin countries would be not only less likely to make bilateral barter arrangements with Germany but also more able to obtain dollars needed to pay for Yankee merchandise. The National Foreign Trade Council therefore recommended in October 1939 that a study should be made "to determine the means of increasing Latin American production for profitable marketing in the United States and to provide dollar exchange to pay for our exports."[74] This suggestion did not fall on deaf ears in Washington. The Department of Commerce, in cooperation with import merchants, promptly encouraged Latin American producers to commence manufacturing certain items like glassware, linens, and leather gloves for shipment to the United States.[75] The Department of Agriculture likewise tried to help countries south of the Rio Grande expand their production of tropical and semitropical commodities which were in demand in the United States.[76]

The Roosevelt administration also supported from the very outset the Allied attempt to put an economic stranglehold on the Third Reich. Although the British blockade interfered with American trade, the State Department abstained from making any strong protests against Allied violations of international law.[77] At an important conference held in Panama City, moreover, Sumner Welles persuaded the Latin American republics to join with the United States in establishing a "neutrality" zone around the Western Hemisphere. The Declaration of Panama, announced in September 1939, asserted that an area ranging from three hundred to one thousand miles off the Atlantic coast south of the Canadian border should be free from hostile acts by any non-American belligerent. The president immediately ordered the United States fleet to patrol the restricted zone and inform the British admiralty about the movements of Nazi warships. While publicly justifying the naval patrol as a way of keeping war away from the Western Hemisphere, Roosevelt privately hoped that it would help the British subdue Germany through their blockade strategy.[78]

The president believed that the United States could make an even greater contribution to the Allied war of attrition by repealing the arms embargo. On the same day that Nazi soldiers began storming into Poland, Roosevelt informed his Cabinet that he intended to call a special session of Congress to secure a revision in the Neutrality Act. He hoped that England and France would be able to defeat Germany if they had free access to American airplanes and munitions. His decision to seek once again the repeal of the arms embargo was reinforced by pleas from the Allies. "If we are to win this war," Daladier told Ambassador Bullitt in early September 1939, "we shall have to win it on supplies of every kind from the United States."[79] Chamberlain concurred. "If the embargo is repealed this month," he wrote Roosevelt in early October 1939, "I am convinced that the effect on German morale will be devastating."[80]

But President Roosevelt had to move cautiously to avoid arousing suspicions that he would involve the United States in the war. Public-opinion surveys suggested that any indication of a White House willingness to aid the Allies at the risk of war would provoke strong opposition to any alteration in the neutrality laws.[81] Therefore, Thomas W. Lamont counseled Roosevelt on September 16 that "he could not declare too often or too emphatically that he was going to do everything he could to keep the country out of war."[82] The president acted on that advice when he addressed Congress on September 21 in an

139

effort to win bipartisan support for lifting the arms embargo. Nowhere in his message did he mention his desire to assist the Allies. Rather, he asserted that "our acts must be guided by one single hard-headed thought—keeping America out of war." Roosevelt was especially concerned about dispelling charges that an annulment of the arms embargo would constitute the first step on the road toward American participation in the European conflict. "The simple truth," he proclaimed in a radio address on October 26, "is that no person in any responsible place in the national administration in Washington, or in any state Government, or in any city Government, or in any county Government, has ever suggested in any shape, manner or form the remotest possibility of sending the boys of American mothers to fight on the battlefields of Europe."[83]

These public pronouncements set the tone for the congressional debate over the question of revising the Neutrality Act. Administration spokesmen constantly avoided any implication that their purpose was to enable England and France to obtain weapons from the United States. Although their opponents repeatedly claimed that neutrality revision would lead to American entry into war, the administration forces on the floor of Congress carried the day. The new Neutrality Act, signed by the president on November 4, 1939, repealed the arms embargo while retaining the cash and carry provisions of the old law. American ships were not allowed to carry freight to belligerent ports, and American citizens were prohibited from traveling on belligerent vessels. The legislation revealed the ambivalent mood of the American people. They strongly favored the Allied cause, yet they did not want to risk American involvement in the European war. Roosevelt was less reluctant to court danger. But while he would have preferred the elimination of the entire neutrality law, he had succeeded in accomplishing his major objective.[84]

Officials in Washington, though not assuming that the repeal of the arms embargo would automatically assure an Allied success, doubted that the Germans would be able to break through the Maginot Line and score a quick victory. American military authorities believed that "the French possess the finest army in the world, being superior to the Germans in their

High Command, their staff officers, and their regimental and company officers."[85] Admiral Harold R. Stark, the chief of naval operations, reported to Roosevelt in March 1940 that "a successful attack by either belligerent on the fortified Western Front is considered highly improbable."[86] The president himself believed that the Allies would have time on their side in a protracted struggle because "the French and English have more stamina than the Germans."[87] Many others in the administration thought that the Third Reich lacked the raw materials necessary to withstand the siege tactics of the Allies. "All of us have had the sneaking hope," Interior Secretary Harold L. Ickes noted in his diary in May 1940, "that the facade of Germany was a false one behind which the economy would sooner or later break down."[88]

State Department officials, however, did fear that a prolonged military conflict would provoke social revolutions throughout Europe. Breckinridge Long worried in October 1939 that both sides would become so weak that "they could no longer resist the influences of Communism, which would spring not from without but from within the ranks of the hungry, discouraged people in each country."[89] R. Walton Moore was equally concerned about the social and political consequences of a protracted military struggle in Europe. "My own fear is that a war lasting a year or two years, or which may run on for even a longer time," he wrote a colleague in February 1940, "will place the people of Europe in such a terrible position as to produce revolutionary movements looking towards communistic policies."[90] Along with the rest of his associates in the State Department, Pierrepont Moffat was filled with anxiety about "the probability of ultimate Bolshevism."[91]

American business internationalists likewise worried that a prolonged war would provide fertile soil for revolutionary upheavals in Europe. "We fear the social and political explosions that may come," the foreign news editor of the *Wall Street Journal* explained in January 1940, "if undernourished, inadequately clothed and physically exhausted people reach the limits of human endurance and demand the right to something better of life than mere animal existence."[92] John Foster Dulles expressed similar apprehension that "a social revolution" would grow out of a lengthy military ordeal and "sweep a large part of Europe."[93] James D. Mooney, the president of General Motors Export Company, warned in March 1940 that the social consequences of the present European struggle might prove far more disastrous than the last great conflict for two reasons: "First, the techniques of slaughtering and maiming great masses of people have been multiplied during the past twenty years in horror and effectiveness. Second, Europe began the war of 1914–1918 with some economic fat on its bones. Europe begins this war with scarcely economic skin on its bones."[94]

The business internationalists who participated in the Fortune Round Table discussions also feared that an extended war, even one resulting in an Allied victory, would have harmful commercial consequences for the United States. "Although England and France have clung to the capitalist system, the outbreak of war has obliged them to regiment internal production and foreign trade to a large extent," the Fortune group lamented in January 1940. "There is a real danger, therefore, that as a result of a long war all the belligerent powers will permanently accept some form of state-directed economic system."[95] The members of the Round Table reiterated their apprehension that the Allies as well as the Nazis would continue to employ totalitarian commercial methods after the war ended. "To rebuild foreign markets," they warned in April 1940, "the belligerents might resort not only to poorly paid labor but to desperate measures of price control, export bounties, and exchange manipulation. 'Aski' pounds and 'Aski' francs might demoralize competitive trading, as much as, if not more than, Aski marks."[96]

The National Policy Committee had already begun thinking that the United States might have to enter the war in order to promote liberal commercial policies at the peace conference. During an important meeting held at Annapolis in February 1940, the committee members gave vent to the widespread apprehension that the Allies, if they won the war, would exclude American products from areas under their control. "Franco-British economic collaboration," they warned, "is likely to continue into the peace." Most members feared that if the United States did not become involved in the actual fighting it would suffer from a drastic decline in foreign trade after the hostilities ended, but they also felt that if the country participated in the European conflict it would be in a position to apply considerable leverage in determining the nature of the postwar world. "If the United States takes part in the war," they concluded, "she should do so on certain well-understood conditions, rather than give *carte blanche* to the Allies, as she did last time, only to find, with the revelation of the secret treaties, that the democracies are also imperial powers."[97]

A majority in the corporate community, however, believed that the United States should stay out of the European tangle. *Business Week* noted in November 1939 that its readers had responded with overwhelming approval to its recent editorial against American involvement in the armed conflict.[98] "Since we are determined to keep out of war," the National Association of Manufacturers declared in January 1940, "we must be equally determined to refrain from any act that might lead us into it."[99] Business executives feared that entrance into the fight against totalitarianism abroad would inevitably undermine capitalism at home. The president of the Iron and Steel Institute, for example, warned that "in the event of war we can expect a degree of regimentation and control by Government that is now unthinkable."[100] Thomas Lamont was terrified by the same specter. "I believe that if we get in the war, we should find ourselves before we got out of it so regimented that we should never again have the same America," he wrote a friend in February 1940. "I am more afraid of Hitlerizing America than I am of Hitler himself."[101]

Not only did State Department officials agree with business leaders that the United States should avoid hostilities, but they also shared their worries about the possible consequences of a fight to the finish. American diplomats feared that one of the belligerents would emerge triumphant and extend its discriminatory trade tactics or that a prolonged conflict would generate radical social revolutions all across the European continent. Neither of these anticipated results boded well for American commercial interests. But the long hiatus in military operations during the winter of 1939–1940 provided an opportunity for the United States to try to bring the war to an end before full-scale fighting resumed in the spring. After rejecting the idea of American mediation in October 1939, Adolf Berle and Sumner Welles began thinking in December that the president should summon a general peace conference. They hoped that the ultimate settlement would reduce the probability of international friction and increase the volume of American trade.[102]

Under Secretary of State Welles quickly developed a new edition of his earlier plan for an American peace initiative. He contemplated the formation of a congress of neutrals which would serve as a mechanism for sponsoring a European settlement before the expected spring offensive broke the silence on the western front. Welles was optimistic. He told his State Department colleagues in January 1940 that he thought it was highly possible that a critical time would arrive within the next few months when an organization of neutrals might offer a peace proposal.[103] His associates agreed that the president should call a meeting of neutrals for the ostensible purpose of considering methods of maintaining their commercial rights during the war. "But the real and inevitable discussion," Berle noted in his diary, "would be whether mediation could not be proposed, together with possible peace terms, and with an insistence that the neutrals sit at the peace table with equal right."[104]

The State Department thereupon established the Advisory Committee on Problems of Foreign Relations to draw up blueprints for the postwar world which the neutrals could advance at a peace conference. The group, with Welles acting as chairman, commenced formulating plans in January 1940 for a new international order devoted to the doctrine of equal commercial opportunity. Economic expert Leo Pasvolsky emphasized that the United States should direct the process of global reconstruction into channels which "would lead to the establishment of a system of peaceful international economic relations rather than to a period of economic warfare after the cessation of the armed conflict."[105] The other members of the special committee agreed that the principles underlying the reciprocal trade program should form the nucleus of the postwar international structure. "The thought pervading the general discussion," Breckinridge Long observed, "was that it would be necessary to develop some world-wide economic cooperation as the only basis to secure a peace."[106]

In an attempt to end the war before the bloodbath began in the spring, President Roosevelt initiated four parallel diplomatic moves in January and February 1940. First, he asked James D. Mooney of General Motors to find out if the authorities in Berlin were interested in creating an international framework that would assure all countries, including Germany, equal access to world markets after the war. Mooney also informed Hitler that the president would be happy to act as the moderator for peace negotiations if the belligerents requested his assistance.[107] Second, Roosevelt appointed Myron C. Taylor, formerly the chairman of United States Steel, as his personal representative to the Vatican. Immediately upon his arrival in Rome, Taylor asked Pope Pius XII if he thought the time was ripe for the president to offer his services as a mediator.[108] Third, Roosevelt sent forty-two neutral nations messages proposing an exchange of views concerning the establishment of a solid foundation for world peace. The document specifically called attention to the need for reducing armaments and expanding commerce.[109] Fourth, and most significant, Roosevelt dispatched Under Secretary of State Welles on a special mission to Rome, Berlin, Paris, and London to ascertain the attitudes in the four capitals toward the possibility of concluding a peace settlement.[110]

The Welles mission represented the final American effort to promote peace in Europe through the familiar formula of economic appeasement. Though Welles had not been authorized to make any commitment that would bind his government, he was empowered to discuss the need for economic disarmament as well as military security.[111] The under secretary carried to Rome and Berlin a memorandum outlining American desires for the establishment of an international order dedicated to the unconditional most-favored-nation principle. Welles reminded Mussolini and Hitler that if the basis for a just political settlement could be found, the United States would be willing to participate in discussions aimed at limiting offensive weapons and lowering trade barriers. Mussolini assured Welles that he favored liberal commercial relations, but Hitler replied that unrestricted trade could not cure every material problem in the world. The führer also insisted that Germany must maintain its preferential economic position in Central and Southeastern Europe.[112]

In terms of peace negotiations, the Welles mission had in fact been doomed from the very outset. Even before the American representative started discussions in Berlin, Hitler had issued a secret order for all German officials to refrain from showing any interest in exploring the possibilities of peace. The directive stressed that Welles was not to be left "in the slightest doubt that Germany is determined to conclude this war victoriously." The führer personally told Welles that there could be no peace until the German army had crushed the will of the Allies to destroy national socialism. Under Secretary Welles found that British and French leaders were equally convinced that they would have to achieve a decisive military victory in order to accomplish their objectives. Though Daladier and Chamberlain expressed willingness to negotiate with the Nazi regime, neither believed that Hitler would offer a practical plan that would guarantee the future safety of France and England.[113] Nevertheless, Welles still clung to the hope that the moment might arrive for the United States to make a peace move. "I believe there is a slight chance for the negotiation of a lasting peace," he wrote Roosevelt in March 1940, "if the attack for peace is made upon the issue of security."[114]

As dark clouds gathered over Europe, therefore, the State Department continued to prepare for an American peace initiative. The United States obtained promises from Allied representatives in March 1940 that England and France would discontinue their restrictive trade practices at the earliest possible moment.[115] In the same month, Washington received positive responses from most of the neutral governments regarding the American proposal for consultation about postwar reconstruction.[116] So the Advisory Committee on Problems of Foreign Relations quickly drafted a broad statement defining the American position on international trade for communication to the neutral countries. The twelve-point memorandum, completed on April 2, succinctly outlined the American dream of a golden era of peace and prosperity based upon liberal commercial principles.[117] But events overtook the vision. The spring offensive began, and the American peace plan was never delivered. "There literally is not a neutral in Europe," Hugh R. Wilson of the Advisory Committee explained on May 20, "which can or will consult with us now."[118]

During the months preceding the Nazi attack on the western front, American officials feared that Mussolini would ally himself with Hitler in hopes of recreating the old Roman Empire. "Mussolini's position remains that of a turkey buzzard soaring and peering and hoping for something dead to eat," Ambassador Bullitt cabled from Paris in January 1940. "I am entirely certain that he still hopes that Germany will be victorious and that Italy will obtain North Africa and Syria as carrion. England and France cannot offer Italy a comparable meal."[119] During his discussions in Rome, Sumner Welles tried to discourage the Fascist leader from intervening in the conflict. Myron Taylor similarly worked with the Vatican to keep Mussolini from declaring war against the Allies. After Nazi forces occupied Norway and Denmark in April 1940, however, the White House grew increasingly pessimistic about the chances of staying the Duce's hand. Roosevelt believed that Mussolini, assuming that Germany would win, was "waiting until the last minute to get into the war so that he can collect after the peace to the utmost but with minimum risk and loss during the war."[120]

Nevertheless, as Nazi troops made rapid advances toward Paris, the president decided to appeal directly to Mussolini in a desperate attempt to dissuade him from joining forces with Hitler. On April 29 and again on May 14, Roosevelt sent the Duce personal messages containing thinly veiled threats of American intervention if hostilities spread into the Mediterranean region. Neither communication evoked a favorable response. As the German blitzkrieg continued, however, the British and French proposed that Roosevelt should make an overture to Mussolini along the following lines: that the Allied governments were disposed to consider Italian claims with a view to satisfying them after the war; and that the United States would do its utmost to make sure that any agreements reached would be carried out provided that Italy refrained from entering the war against England and France. The president, acting on the Allied request, wrote Mussolini on May 26 that he would be willing to guarantee an appeasement agreement. Despite the Duce's negative reply, Roosevelt sent Mussolini a final message on May 30 warning that Italian participation in the conflict would provoke the United States to increase its rearmament program and to redouble its efforts to ship military supplies to the Allies. But Mussolini was resolved to share in the spoils of a German victory, and on June 10, 1940, Italy declared war on England and France.[121]

The play for position in Europe had a profound impact on developments in Asia. Before launching his attack against Poland, Hitler had attempted to bring Tokyo into the Rome-Berlin Axis. He hoped that the prospect of a conflict with Japan in the Far East would not only neutralize England and France but also discourage the United States from interfering in European affairs. The Japanese for their part desired an accord aimed at the Soviet Union, yet they refused to enter into a firm military alliance directed against any and all powers. Hitler then made an abrupt about-face. After failing in his efforts to court Japan, the führer decided upon a marriage with Russia in order to strengthen his strategic position in Europe. The Nazi-Soviet nonaggression pact, announced in August 1939, caused deep distress in Tokyo. At the time, the Japanese were engaged in bitter hostilities along the Manchurian border with their traditional Russian enemies.[122] Sumner Welles anticipated forthwith that London would attempt to capitalize on the shock felt in Tokyo by offering to "sell out the Chinese completely to the Japanese in return for an Anglo-Japanese understanding."[123]

Great Britain and the United States differed in their reaction to the Nazi-Soviet pact. The British, fearing that Japan might join forces with Germany and Russia, were eager to work out an agreement with Tokyo. As the crisis in Europe moved toward a climax in late August 1939, Great Britain suggested that the United States should use its influence to mediate a settlement of the war in China that would satisfy Japan. The State Department immediately rebuffed the British proposal. American diplomats believed that the accord between Berlin and Moscow would enable the Russians to pay less attention to their western borders and more attention to their eastern frontiers. Few thought that the Japanese would be able to reach an agreement with the Kremlin which would remove the danger of Soviet intervention in the Orient.[124] Adolf Berle, reflecting the general view, predicted that the German-Russian deal would "jar Japan entirely loose from the whole axis situation."[125] Rather than embarking upon a policy of appeasement, therefore, the State Department remained firm in opposing Japanese plans for the creation of a Greater East Asia Co-Prosperity Sphere.

The State Department was determined to prevent Japan from taking advantage of the onset of war in Europe to drive the western powers out of Asia. When Tokyo proposed on September 5 that all belligerent nations should voluntarily withdraw their gunboats and troops from areas in China under Japanese military control, Secretary Hull tried to bolster British and French resistance by informing London and Paris that American forces would not be removed from China. Hull also issued a veiled warning to Tokyo that the United States, if pushed, might counterattack with economic sanctions against Japan.[126] A month later, Hull instructed Ambassador Joseph C. Grew to reiterate America's commitment to the Open Door policy when he returned to his post in Tokyo. Grew hastened to carry out his task. In an address delivered on October 19, he told his Japanese audience that he was speaking "straight from the horse's mouth." Grew explained that Americans regarded the projected New Order in the Far East as an effort "to establish control, in Japan's own interest, of large areas on the continent of Asia, and to impose upon those areas a system of closed economy."[127]

In the face of mounting rumors regarding a Japanese-Russian alliance, the State Department rejected renewed British and French proposals for appeasement. London and Paris were filled with anxiety when the Japanese and Russians called a halt to their undeclared war along the Manchurian border and agreed to negotiate a commercial treaty for their mutual benefit. The British ambassador informed Sumner Welles on November 21 that his government hoped to work with the United

States in helping Japan and China reach a settlement which would involve concessions by each side. But Welles replied that there was no need to feel intimidated. He argued that a fundamental conflict of interests would keep Moscow and Tokyo from agreeing to a partition of China. He added that the Japanese were not in a position to attack British and French interests in the Orient because they could not trust the Russians. Welles concluded that the American government would not do anything to bring pressure on the Chinese to make a peace which would give the Japanese a preferential place in the China market.[128]

Adolf Berle explained in his diary in early December 1939 the basic reasons underlying the American refusal to appease Japan at the expense of China. He pointed out that the conversations between Ambassador Grew and the Japanese foreign minister were "disposing only of chicken-feed." Even if the Japanese agreed to protect American economic interests in return for the recognition of their military conquests in China, Berle maintained, the gain for the United States would be only temporary. "When the war is over," he asserted, "Japan will be a not very important power surrounded by enemies; the effect of sacrificing China would be to make permanent enemies of that whole population, which was there before the Japanese came and will be there after they go." In line with their desire to maintain American access to Asiatic markets in the future, Berle and his associates wanted to pressure Japan rather than China. "Fundamentally," he concluded, "we would like to have the Japanese get out of China and they are not going to get out until they are driven out. Diplomatic interchanges do not have much effect."[129]

The Roosevelt administration decided in December 1939 to play a guessing game with the Japanese. On the one hand, Cordell Hull recommended that the United States should neither renew nor replace the commercial treaty with Japan when it expired in the next month. On the other hand, he advised that the United States should not impose discriminatory duties on Japanese ships and cargoes permitted by American law. Roosevelt approved this strategy designed to exert psychological pressure on Tokyo. Trade with Japan would be allowed to continue on a regular basis for the present, but the United States would be free to terminate at any time in the future the shipment of raw materials that were vital to Japan. The American policy resembled a game of stud poker in which Uncle Sam showed that the card still turned down was an ace. In other words, American leaders hoped to intimidate the Japanese by keeping them uncertain about what the United States might do to their commerce.[130]

Many Americans believed that with the commercial treaty out of the way, the Japanese should and could be forced to abandon their imperial program in China. Their views were vigorously advanced in January 1940 by Henry L. Stimson in a letter published by the *New York Times*. The former secretary of state argued that the Japanese war machine depended upon American fuel oil and scrap iron, and he claimed that economic sanctions would not provoke Japan to fight the United States. Stimson therefore concluded that the time had come to cut off the supply of strategic materials to Japan.[131] But President Roosevelt and Cordell Hull disagreed. They feared that an embargo might spur the Japanese either to declare war on the United States or to invade the East Indies to obtain the natural resources that they needed. "Perhaps it was just as well for us to ship these supplies to Japan," Roosevelt told his Cabinet, "because otherwise Japan might raid the Dutch East Indies."[132] Administration spokesmen in Congress, acting on the president's instructions in January 1940, quashed several bills and resolutions calling for restrictions on American exports to Japan. As an alternative to imposing economic sanctions against Japan, Roosevelt and Hull decided that the United States should give financial aid to China, and on March 7 the Export-Import Bank made arrangements for a twenty million dollar loan to China.[133]

But the Japanese relentlessly pushed forward with their quest for empire in the Far East. After months of hesitation, Japan installed a puppet Chinese government in Nanking under Wang Ching-wei. Hull responded on March 30 with a public statement that the United States would continue to recognize the Kuomintang headed by Chiang Kai-shek in Chungking as the legal government of China. "The setting up of a new regime at Nanking," Hull declared, "has the appearance of a further step in a program of one country by armed force to impose its will upon a neighboring country and to block off a large area of the world from normal political and economic relationships with the rest of the world."[134] An article printed by *Foreign Affairs* in April 1940 likewise warned that the Japanese intended to close the door against American commerce in China. "If Chinese resistance collapses, or if there is an undeclared peace, or if China accepts a compromise that leaves the Japanese a foothold on the mainland," the article concluded, "Japan will carry through her plans for the economic development of China. And we may be certain that those plans call for the development of China in the exclusive interest of Japan."[135]

The Roosevelt administration feared that the intensification of hostilities in Europe would provide Japan with a tempting opportunity to snatch the Dutch East Indies. A week after Germany invaded Norway in April 1940, therefore, Secretary Hull issued a public warning that many countries including the United States had economic interests in the Netherlands East Indies and that any alteration in their status quo would threaten the peace of the entire Pacific region. President Roosevelt, in a related effort to deter Japan from attacking the rich South Seas colonies, moved the American fleet from San Diego to Pearl Harbor, in Hawaii.[136] The German invasion of Holland on May 10 heightened American anxiety, and a day later the British and French made matters worse by landing forces on the Dutch islands of Curaçao and Aruba in the Caribbean. American leaders were worried that the Allied occupation of the Dutch West Indies would furnish the Japanese with an excuse to dispatch troops to the Dutch East Indies. Thus, Roosevelt swiftly induced the British to give assurances that they would not intervene in the Netherlands East Indies and that the Allied forces would be removed from the Dutch possessions in the Caribbean at the earliest possible moment.[137]

The American response to the Japanese menace in Asia remained cautious as the German army made rapid advances in Europe. American military authorities did not believe that the United States was prepared to fight a two-ocean war, and they regarded Germany as a much more dangerous potential

enemy than Japan.[138] Consequently, American statesmen hesitated to take any action that might precipitate a conflict in
the Pacific. President Roosevelt did not even respond when, in
a personal message on May 15, the new British prime minister,
Winston Churchill, requested that the United States send naval
forces to Singapore to help Great Britain restrain Japan.[139] A
few American diplomats did favor a militant Asian policy. In
an important State Department meeting held on May 31, Stanley K. Hornbeck suggested that the American navy should attack the Japanese fleet if it moved against the Dutch East
Indies. But his colleagues disagreed. Sumner Welles explained
that under the circumstances the United States fleet should
not engage in hostilities in the Far East. "We would need it for
defensive purpose in the event of a German victory," he declared. "We should not risk the loss of a considerable portion
of it in such a remote adventure."[140]

Global strategic considerations continued to influence the
shaping of American diplomacy. Officials in Washington never
stopped debating about the best way to deter Japan without at
the same time precipitating a war in the Pacific. A few continued to advocate economic sanctions and even military force
if necessary in order to check the Japanese, but the majority
preferred to employ persuasion rather than coercion in dealing with Tokyo, for although a solid consensus supported the
Open Door policy in China, American decision makers regarded Nazi Germany as the key to the world crisis. One
State Department observer put the matter bluntly just prior to
the Nazi onslaught on the western front. "If Germany does not
win this war in Europe, Japan cannot possibly hold out in the
Far East," he reasoned in March 1940. "While the issues in the
Far East are important and vital to us, the real issue will be
decided in Europe."[141] Almost everyone agreed. As the German
panzer divisions raced toward the English Channel in May
1940, therefore, Americans turned their attention across the
Atlantic toward the epic contest that would determine the fate
of Europe.

If this man makes the peace...

...what real difference will it make to the 130 million of us in America?

This is the one cold question you find behind all talk and all debate. This is a question that concerns the Tomorrow of every man, woman, and child in the United States.

There should be clear answer to it.

The automotive worker in Detroit should know what chance there is for European-made motor cars to sell in South American showrooms at $300 less than the Detroit-made product from which he earns his livelihood.

The American merchant sailor should be able to estimate his chances of "standing by" while foreign crews clear vessels from his port at less than half his U. S. wage.

The American business man should know exactly what his odds of competition are if this next Peace is written in Berlin.

We believe the American business man *does* know ... exactly. We believe he got clear, complete answers from the pages of his own magazine, Business Week.

It's only natural that Business Week should have handled this big subject as a SPECIAL REPORT TO EXECUTIVES.

It's natural, too, that "The Economic Consequences of a German Peace" should have been handled in the pages of this magazine with frankness, brevity, and thoroughness. No other magazine has quite the same privilege of talking purely Management language to a purely Management audience.

but ... you may not consider it "natural" that the Editors of Business Week handled this subject *when* they did.

For ... it didn't appear in last week's issue. It didn't appear in the issue of the week before. It appeared *more than a year ago* ... in Business Week of June 22, 1940.

Which (if you happen to know Business Week well) is the most natural part of all!

Small supply of "Economic Consequences of a German Peace" still available twenty cents each ... Editorial Rooms, 330 West 42nd St., New York City.

ONE OF THE MOST *USEFUL* MAGAZINES IN AMERICA

BUSINESS WEEK, 27 September 1941

six

The Nightmare of a
Closed World

WITH LIGHTNING speed
in the spring of 1940, the ferocious Wehrmacht smashed
through the Allied fortifications along the German frontier.
The Nazi assault, launched on May 10, was not to be turned
back. Holland surrendered within five days, Belgium capitulated on May 28, and the British hurried to evacuate their troops
entrapped at Dunkirk. Left alone on the European continent
to try to stem the unrelenting German tide, the French made
desperate pleas for American war planes. Although it was il-
legal for the United States army to sell to foreign governments
arms needed for national defense, President Roosevelt decided
to circumvent the law by trading back "surplus" military
equipment to private firms for resale to England and France.[1]
Treasury Secretary Henry Morgenthau thereupon assured the
head of the Anglo-French Purchasing Commission that American officials were bending every rule in their effort to supply
arms to the Allies. "We are doing everything we can," he asserted on June 9, "within and without the law."[2] But the die
had already been cast. Nazi soldiers marched triumphantly into
Paris on June 14, 1940, and three days later France asked Germany for an armistice.

The Nazi onslaught had a profound impact upon the internal politics and the external policies of Great Britain. On
the eve of the awesome blitzkrieg, Prime Minister Neville
Chamberlain had hoped that the Allies could defeat Germany
without relying upon an American expeditionary force.

"Heaven knows I don't want the Americans to fight for us," he confided in January 1940. "We should have to pay too dearly for that if they had a right to be in on the peace terms."[3] Chamberlain had become ever more optimistic as the winter stalemate on the western front continued. "After seven months of war," he declared on April 5, "I feel ten times as confident of victory as I did at the beginning." By giving England and France time to prepare for the anticipated German offensive, Chamberlain boasted, Hitler had "missed the bus."[4] Yet only a few days later, German forces suddenly occupied Denmark and Norway. England was soon filled with cries for a change in leadership, and on May 10, First Lord of the Admiralty Winston Churchill formed a new government in London. Churchill immediately launched a vigorous crusade to convince the British people that they could hold their own against the Third Reich. But the new prime minister insisted in private that it was "vital to our safety that the United States should be involved in totalitarian warfare."[5]

Endeavoring to induce the United States to declare war on Germany, Churchill repeatedly warned that Hitler might defeat England and gain control of the British fleet. He wrote President Roosevelt on May 20 that his government was determined to fight to the bitter end, but that if the battle were lost a new regime might come to power in London and parley for peace. "You must not be blind to the fact," Churchill emphasized, "that the sole remaining bargaining counter with Germany would be the fleet."[6] The prime minister reiterated to Roosevelt on June 15 that in case of defeat, he and his associates might be overthrown and others might surrender the Royal Navy in order to obtain a favorable settlement. "Never cease to impress on the President and others," Churchill instructed the British ambassador in Washington on June 28, "that, if this country were successfully invaded and largely occupied after heavy fighting, some Quisling Government would be formed to make peace on the basis of our becoming a German Protectorate. In this case the British fleet would be the solid contribution with which this Peace Government would buy terms."[7]

Americans differed in their reaction to the plight of the Allies. Several prominent people from various parts of the country advocated an immediate declaration of war against Germany.[8] Some believed that the United States should become a belligerent in order to have a voice in formulating the peace settlement. "Without real cooperation on our part toward securing victory," Henry L. Stimson reasoned on May 3, "we would have little influence at the end."[9] Others favored American intervention to speed the process of industrial mobilization and military training. "I am afraid we won't unitedly strive for an adequate preparedness," Frank Knox of the *Chicago Daily News* wrote his wife on June 15, "until we do declare war."[10] But the president remained cautious. Although Roosevelt proceeded to appoint Knox as secretary of the navy and Stimson as secretary of war, he realized that the overwhelming majority of Americans did not want their country to become involved in the European conflict. Antiwar sentiment was particularly strong on college campuses, and the attitude of the students did not go unnoticed in Washington.[11] Roosevelt told Stimson on May 21 that he was worried about "the large number of college student groups who are not only isolationists but complete pacifists."[12]

The State Department, following the lead of the White House, hesitated to push for any action beyond the popular program of providing all aid to the Allies short of war. Even if the American people were willing to fight, Assistant Secretary Adolf A. Berle did not believe that an American task force could get to Europe fast enough to do any good. "The outcome of the battle which will decide the fate of Europe," he reasoned on May 15, "obviously will be decided before anything can get across the Atlantic."[13] Under Secretary Sumner Welles was not so sure. "Our influence would probably be a decisive factor," he argued on May 31, "if we could send our fleet and air force to Europe." But Welles admitted that American military participation was out of the question in an election year and in the face of an unfavorable public opinion. "When the American people might be ready to act," he fretted, "it might be too late to save the Allies." Nevertheless, Welles and his colleagues agreed that the United States should create a powerful military establishment which could be used "for other purposes, if advisable, than the strict defense of the hemisphere."[14]

President Roosevelt had already decided to sponsor a gigantic rearmament program. In a special message to Congress on May 16, Roosevelt said that he would like to see the nation geared to the production of 50,000 war planes a year. Then he asked for almost 1.2 billion dollars to provide new weapons for all branches of the armed forces. Two weeks later, he requested an additional 1.3 billion dollars to equip an enlarged army and to begin the construction of a two-ocean navy. Congress quickly passed bills appropriating even more money than the president had requested. When Roosevelt asked for another huge military appropriation on July 10, he assured the country that his intentions were peaceful. "We will not use our arms in a war of aggression," he promised; "we will not send our men to take part in European Wars." Taking the president at his word, Congress once again responded generously by authorizing more than 5 billion dollars for national defense.[15]

The American people, frightened by the specter of a German invasion of the Western Hemisphere, provided solid support for the arms build-up. Public opinion polls published in early June indicated that about two-thirds of those interrogated believed that the Nazis, if victorious in Europe, would attempt to seize territory in Latin America and eventually launch a direct attack on the United States. A like number of those questioned, besides advocating all aid to the Allies short of war, favored using the army and navy to protect South America.[16] As the panic about Hitler's ambitions swept across the country, the clamor for national defense became almost hysterical. But *Business Week* warned that public support for the preparedness campaign was subject to change. "If Hitler doesn't remain in the public mind as a continuing military threat," the editors predicted on June 29, "the country will sooner or later balk at continually increasing expenditures for armament, particularly when taxes begin to pinch."[17]

At the same time, foreign policy experts were already discounting the danger of a German attack on American shores. Alexander C. Kirk, the American chargé d'affairs in Berlin, pointed out on June 17 that the Nazis had no plans for invading the Western Hemisphere.[18] Hugh R. Wilson, the former American ambassador to Germany, likewise countered the popular notion that Hitler would become a threat to the physical security of the New World. "It does not seem to me," Wilson wrote Secretary of State Cordell Hull on July 16, "that an attack on the United States or the Americas is worth the effort to him."[19] Others concerned with strategic questions concluded that Hitler could not direct a successful assault across the Atlantic Ocean even if he were rash enough to make the attempt. "A cool appraisal of our present military, naval and air establishments does not support the current panic regarding the danger of a direct invasion of the United States," observed William T. Stone of the Foreign Policy Association. "Virtually every competent authority agrees that such an enterprise is beyond the bounds of military practicability."[20]

The fact is that the Roosevelt administration regarded Nazi Germany as a formidable economic threat rather than a dangerous military menace. As news of the German advances in Belgium came across the ticker tape during a Cabinet meeting on May 17, therefore, the president interposed to ask Secretary of Agriculture Henry A. Wallace to investigate what could be done for American farmers "if England and France were completely wiped out and we lost the entire European market."[21] Wallace went over to the State Department on the next day to discuss the problem, but he found that Cordell Hull "steadfastly refused to do anything but paint a very bad situation."[22] Secretary of the Treasury Henry Morgenthau was equally pessimistic. "The Germans will form a sort of overall trading corporation," he worried, "and what are we going to do about our cotton and wheat."[23] Assistant Secretary of State Breckinridge Long put the matter bluntly. "If Germany wins this war and subordinates Europe," he warned on May 28, "every commercial order will be routed to Berlin and filled under its orders somewhere in Europe rather than in the United States."[24]

Private leaders and public officials feared not only that Hitler would close the doors of Europe to American exports but also that he would launch an economic blitzkrieg against the United States in the markets of the world. "Germany's long experience in the organization of domestic and international cartels will undoubtedly be applied to the organization of world trade," the National Policy Committee declared on June 8.

"The requirements of all Europe will be lumped together for bargaining purposes and expressed through bilateral treaties accompanied by exchange controls."[25] American diplomats stationed in Germany likewise warned that Hitler would employ totalitarian trade tactics in a concerted drive to capture overseas markets. "He will confront the United States within a brief measure of time," Alexander Kirk reported on June 17, "with the impossible task of adjusting its system to an economy in which it will be excluded from access to all foreign markets."[26] Two months later, Joel C. Hudson wrote from his consular post in Berlin that if the German export plans came into effect, the position of the United States would be much like that of "an old-fashioned general store in a region of hard-boiled chain stores."[27]

Many spokesmen for the corporate community agreed that individual American entrepreneurs would be unable to compete successfully in world markets if the entire European continent came under Nazi rule. "Germany does not have to conquer us in a military sense," Bernard M. Baruch explained on May 31. "By enslaving her own labor and that of the conquered countries, she can place in the markets of the world products at a price with which we could not compete. This will destroy our standards of living and shake to its depths our moral and physical fiber, already strained to the breaking point."[28] W. Averell Harriman also noted that the real danger to the United States would come not from a military invasion but rather from a commercial rivalry with a regimented Europa Germania. "The idea that American free enterprise," he lectured on June 1, "can compete in the foreign markets against such competition is ludicrous."[29] A few days later, Lewis W. Douglas similarly warned that if Germany defeated England and France, Hitler would initiate a trade war that would profoundly affect "our traditional social, political and economic structure."[30]

The nightmare of a closed world horrified businessmen who subscribed to the leading commercial and financial journals published along the eastern seaboard. "If the German military machine is triumphant," *Bankers' Magazine* asked rhetorically, "won't our products be frozen out of world markets?"[31] Many other influential business periodicals were filled with similar forebodings that the United States would be forced into an economic vacuum as the result of a complete Allied defeat. "Our foreign trade prospect," the *Magazine of Wall Street* lamented on June 15, "would be indeed dismal."[32] In a special article on the economic consequences of a German victory, *Business Week* warned on June 22 that Hitler would set wage scales and price levels with the sole aim of capturing foreign markets for goods manufactured under his control. "The United States," the article concluded, "would tend to become a lone island in a world dominated by a philosophy of industrial coordination."[33]

The State Department was particularly frightened by visions of Dr. Schacht's Frankenstein goose-stepping with renewed vigor across the South American landscape. In the past, when Schacht had served as the purchasing agent for less than 60 million Germans, the United States had maintained a comfortable lead over the Third Reich in competition for Latin American markets. But if in the future Hitler acquired the power to purchase for more than 300 million Europeans, the Nazi bargaining position would be greatly enhanced. Adolf Berle warned on May 25 that should Hitler win the war in Europe, he would immediately attempt to induce South American countries to exchange their raw materials for aski marks which could be used only to buy industrial goods made in Germany.[34] Sumner Welles was equally alarmed about the economic implications of a Nazi victory. "If there were a German customs and monetary union throughout Europe and the Argentine were notified that it could only export its goods to Europe under the terms dictated by Germany," Welles asserted on May 31, "the Argentine would be obliged to acquiesce."[35]

If Hitler conquered the entire European continent, many business editors and corporate executives believed that the United States might be compelled to fight fire with fire in order to avoid economic isolation. The president of International Westinghouse, for example, concluded on June 7 that Americans might have "to adopt similar methods to the German barter system to maintain any foreign trade."[36] *Business Week* agreed that the United States should be prepared for a bitter trade war with Nazi Germany after the close of the military conflict in Europe. "We may be forced to adopt some of the totalitarian ways of doing things," the editors observed on June 22. "We may have to sacrifice some of the notions we have held about the rights of private property owners to dispense of their property as they see fit."[37] Will Clayton also thought that in the event of a German victory, American businessmen might have to accept some form of government control over all their commercial transactions beyond the water's edge. "If the rest of the world adopts totalitarian methods of trade," Clayton reasoned on June 27, "we will be compelled to conform if we wish to sell our surpluses."[38]

George N. Peek, the perennial champion of economic nationalism, delighted in the prospect that the United States might have to abandon the reciprocal trade agreements program, which had just been extended for three more years. "The rest of the world has changed the rules of the game," he wrote a former associate on June 18. "We can play the game according to their rules better than almost any other country because we are more nearly self-contained."[39] Peek believed that Uncle Sam would hold a strong trump card in any commercial contest with Hitler because the American market was the largest in the world. "Under conditions such as have prevailed in recent years, it is difficult to find words to define the stupidity of the Hull program with its unconditional most-favored-nation treatment, and its generalization of concessions to all countries except Germany," he wrote Raymond Moley on July 4. "We should control imports, and negotiate trade country by country, and when necessary, commodity by commodity."[40] Thus, Peek hoped that the government would establish a Foreign Trade Board which would have plenary power over all American imports and exports.

The State Department was simultaneously developing plans for the creation of a colossal hemispheric cartel designed to counter a Nazi trade offensive in the New World. It was feared that Hitler would win the war and that the individual South American countries would be helpless in bargaining with an enormous European economic bloc directed by Germany. "The logical riposte," Adolf Berle reasoned on May 25, "is to work up an agreement by which the twenty-one governments agree that so far as commercial relations are concerned they will deal as a bloc and not individually."[41] Berle wanted to put the surplus products of the entire Western Hemisphere in a vast export pool so that a huge European consumptive unit could be met by an equally immense American productive unit. Several of his colleagues favored the cartel scheme as a last resort if Hitler gained full control of the European market. But they realized that such an arrangement could not work without production controls. The Division of American Republics therefore recommended on June 10 that the hemispheric marketing organization should be "empowered to make the necessary decisions as to how much production of individual commodities would be permitted and in what directions individual nations would be encouraged to develop."[42]

President Roosevelt, infected by the mood of desperation prevailing in Washington, reacted favorably to the cartel proposal. Just one day after Nazi troops marched into Paris on June 14, he asked for the combined opinion of the secretaries of state, treasury, agriculture, and commerce regarding inter-American economic relations.[43] The Cabinet heads immediately referred the question to the Interdepartmental Group to Consider Post-War Economic Problems and Policies. But the members of the group held conflicting attitudes toward the creation of an All-American Trading Corporation. Some advocated a cartel that would act as a clearinghouse with total control over all import as well as export transactions between the Western Hemisphere and Europe. Others proposed a more limited arrangement among the twenty-one American nations covering only the production and distribution of their main exportable commodities.[44] The Cabinet heads favored the less comprehensive alternative, and on June 20 they recommended that the president should propose the establishment of an Inter-American Trading Corporation designed to "operate as an effective agency for joint marketing of the important export staples of all the American Republics."[45]

Roosevelt wanted to advance the cartel project without delay. During a White House conference on June 27, he urged that it was "necessary to move forward at once in as much as if England blew up Germany would begin making effective trade agreements in Latin America and we would be on the scene too late."[46]

The grandiose cartel scheme, however, encountered serious criticism during the ensuing weeks. On the one hand, many pointed out practical difficulties which might prove to be insurmountable. "If the German Government sought to defeat the monopoly," an economic expert in the State Department warned on June 28, "it might be able to do so by developing alternative sources for Western Hemisphere products."[47] Others argued that even if the Latin American countries were willing to risk the wrath of Hitler, they might not be willing to commit themselves to a crop-control accord. "No matter who sets the quotas or prices," *Barron's* predicted on July 29, "disagreements would be bound to arise."[48] On the other hand, many feared that the cartel plan, should it prove workable, would endanger the free enterprise system. William S. Culbertson, a former member of the United States Tariff Commission, noted that the marketing monopoly would violate the norms of liberal trade. "The tragedy of a proposal such as the inter-American marketing organization," Culbertson declared on August 1, "is that it plays into the hands of those reformers who oppose the system of private enterprise."[49] Dismayed by such considerations, the president and his advisers quickly abandoned the desperate cartel proposal and affirmed their commitment to liberal trade principles.

The Roosevelt administration used the National Foreign Trade Convention as a forum to promote the doctrine of equal commercial opportunity. In a message read before the gathering on July 30, Roosevelt pledged his continued support for the tenets underlying the reciprocal trade program. "It is naive to imagine," the president admonished, "that we could adopt a totalitarian control of our foreign trade and at the same time escape totalitarian regimentation of our internal economy."[50] Meanwhile, the State Department did its part behind the scenes to counter those who were advocating government control of overseas commerce. "They would have us 'meet fire with fire,' " Assistant Secretary Henry F. Grady warned Edgar W. Smith of General Motors, "not realizing that in the process a large part of our free enterprise structure would be burned up."[51] Smith then promptly addressed the convention on the relationship between "Foreign Trade and the Free Enterprise System."[52] The Final Declaration of the convention, in line with the advice given by Harry C. Hawkins of the Trade Agreements Division, gave "full support to the unconditional most-favored-nation principle."[53]

Business internationalists also joined together in an effort to secure bipartisan support for the reciprocal trade program. Raymond Leslie Buel, the Fortune Round Table editor, discussed the matter with Charles F. Darlington, who had left the State Department to become the foreign exchange manager of General Motors Overseas Operations. Darlington agreed to prepare a memorandum on American commercial policy for Wendell Willkie after the Republicans nominated him as their candidate for president. "In all probability if Germany is victorious we will have to fight it commercially in various parts of the world," Darlington lectured Willkie. "The principles of our action in the event of a German victory should be to hold steadfast to the commercial policies that we believe in, to defend our domestic market, our imports and our exports against any aggressive actions that Germany might take, and finally shape our own conduct so as to leave the way always open to Germany, and to encourage it, to abandon its offensive trading methods." In a letter to Secretary of State Hull on September 25, Darlington explained that his memorandum was intended to keep Willkie committed to liberal trade policies. "Whichever party may win the election," he wrote, "it seems to me essential that these policies be continued."[54]

But many farm belt leaders, never enamored of the reciprocal trade program, were already advocating the establishment of a Fortress Americas. These agrarians were willing to acquiesce in the division of the world into four great areas of trade. They believed that if Hitler won the war, Germany would dominate the markets of Europe, Russia would continue to function as a closed economic system, and Japan would achieve commercial supremacy throughout the Far East. Then the United States would be left to cultivate the resources of the Western Hemisphere. "This means to my mind the equivalent of a two ocean navy," an associate wrote George Peek on May 16. "It means a closer regional economic relation with the nations within our effective sphere of influence."[55] Some agricultural spokesmen in the midwest admitted that their dream of a self-contained hemisphere would also mean the restriction of entrepreneurial freedom in the United States. "We will have to arrange matters so that all our people have an opportunity to earn and buy more of the things they want," the publisher of an Iowa farm journal wrote on July 27. "More planning will be necessary—more regimentation, if you want to call it that."[56]

President Roosevelt and his advisers agreed that the United States could obtain an abundant supply of raw materials within the confines of a Fortress Americas. They realized that the Western Hemisphere, with its varied climate and diversified geography, provided a vast natural resource base which could sustain a rapidly expanding military-industrial complex in the United States. They also knew that chemists were creating synthetic products to serve as substitutes for many organic materials not readily available in the New World. The Standard Oil Company, for example, had acquired exclusive patent rights from I. G. Farben of Germany to manufacture artificial rubber in the United States.[57] Hoping to quiet fears about a possible shortage of raw materials, Roosevelt assured the Business Advisory Council on May 23 that tin could be obtained in sufficient quantities from Bolivia and that synthetic rubber could be produced at home in a short space of time. The president added that newspaper columnists who were worried about the question of strategic materials did not "know a damn thing about it."[58] Henry Wallace concurred. "Within the hemisphere, if it should come to that," he declared on October 11, "we can find all the materials we must have for defense and economic life."[59]

Indeed, in a series of studies prepared for the Council on Foreign Relations, economists Arthur R. Upgren and Alvin H. Hansen pointed out that even an integrated quartersphere would provide the United States with both an adequate resource base and an ample security perimeter. Upgren presented an impressive array of statistical data showing that the tropical countries between the Rio Grande and the Amazon River had a high degree of dependence upon the United States as a market for exports and as a source of imports. Thus, he concluded on July 26, 1940, that the region between the Gulf of Mexico and the bulge of Brazil could easily be integrated with the United States into a Pan American economic union.[60] A few months later, Hansen noted that the tropical territory which produced essential minerals for the United States also afforded strategic outposts needed for the defense of the Panama Canal. "We are told on competent military authority that the protection of this country against foreign aggression does not require that we develop military bases beyond a line extending roughly from the bulge of Brazil westward to the Pacific," Hansen explained. "We may conclude, then, that the area which is complementary to the United States from the economic standpoint is, in its geographic position, exactly the area which of necessity must be included in any defense program."[61]

The studies authorized by the Council on Foreign Relations, however, demonstrated that it would be exceedingly difficult for a Fortress Americas to function successfully as a self-sufficient commercial unit. The problem was rooted in the fertile soil of the Western Hemisphere where two great agrarian regions produced competitive rather than complementary commodities. Although the tropical countries in Central America produced crops like bananas, coffee, and sugar which were demanded in the United States, the countries located in the temperate parts of South America produced commodities such as cotton, wheat, and beef that were also being produced in great abundance in the United States. In other words, the New World contained two vast agricultural areas but only one major industrial center, and the resulting imbalance meant that the Western Hemisphere as a whole produced more food and fiber than it could consume. Consequently, several South American countries depended heavily upon urban markets in Europe to absorb their surplus farm commodities. And their ability to purchase industrial goods from the United States rested upon their capacity to obtain foreign exchange through their agricultural exports to metropolitan Europe.

Business executives and government officials in the

United States feared that if Hitler won the war, the old multilateral trade patterns would be replaced by new bilateral barter arrangements. "A victorious Germany," James S. Carson of the American and Foreign Power Company warned on July 30, "could, through barter and clearing agreements, compel the countries from which Europe buys its necessary foodstuffs and raw materials to spend the proceeds for German and conquered territory manufactured goods."[62] Under Secretary of Commerce Edward J. Noble agreed that the South American nations might be forced into the German economic orbit. "Wielded by a single power," Noble declared, "the economic might of a dictator-dominated Europe might be found irresistible by any single nation standing alone."[63] Howard J. Trueblood, just prior to accepting a position with the State Department, expressed similar fears about an intensive Nazi trade drive in Latin America. "Since the United States, under normal conditions, takes no more than a third of Latin American exports, while Europe imports more than half," Trueblood explained on August 1, "Germany's bargaining position would be considerably stronger than that of this country."[64]

Alvin Hansen and Arthur Upgren responded to this problem by arguing that a trade bloc which combined the British Empire with the Western Hemisphere would afford the minimum amount of economic power needed to counter a National Socialist Europe. For if the United Kingdom joined with the United States, the new commercial union would have two major industrial centers to balance the two great agricultural regions of the New World. Then the South American countries could export their surplus foodstuffs to metropolitan England in order to obtain foreign exchange needed to purchase manufactured goods from the United States. Such a triangular trade pattern would make it easier for Latin Americans to resist Nazi demands for bilateral barter. "The Anglo-American union," Hansen asserted on June 28, "would probably be sufficiently strong both in military defense and economic self-sufficiency to hold its own against the German Empire."[65] Upgren agreed. "The addition of the United Kingdom to the trade area in which the United States and the Western Hemisphere can function," he reasoned on October 19, "does appear to solve the major portion of the problem presented by the agricultural and raw material export surpluses."[66]

The top officers in the influential National Foreign Trade Council had already come to the same conclusion. Chairman James A. Farrell, in his keynote address to the organization on July 29, advocated the formation of an Anglo-American commercial union. "Pan America and the British Empire combined," Farrell proclaimed, "would establish an economic front to the rest of the world with bargaining power adequate to secure equality of treatment and fair dealing in international commerce."[67] President Eugene P. Thomas agreed that an economic alliance between the Western Hemisphere and the British Empire would prove strong enough to uphold the principle of commercial equality even if the entire European continent came under the shadow of the swastika. "Closer economic ties between the British and Pan American democracies," Thomas declared on September 19, "will provide economic power and strategy capable of holding our own in any bargaining negotiations."[68]

These proponents of a liberal commercial front urged the Roosevelt administration to continue its program of promoting economic solidarity among the peoples of the Western Hemisphere. Their fundamental aim was to make the two American continents less competitive and more complementary. The National Foreign Trade Convention therefore recommended on July 31 that the government should extend funds to Latin American countries to facilitate the production of commodities which could be sold in the United States. The members of the organization hoped that Latin Americans would thereby be able to acquire "dollar exchange to pay for our exports."[69] A week later, Congress appropriated $500,000 to finance a survey of Latin America to determine the most suitable areas for the cultivation of rubber.[70] The president, in turn, appointed Nelson A. Rockefeller on August 16 to head a new Office for Coordination of Commercial and Cultural Relations between the American Republics, and Rockefeller immediately organized a staff to promote the economic defense of the Western Hemisphere.[71]

Prominent businessmen also urged the administration

to continue its policy of doing everything short of war to defend the British Empire. Shortly after the Nazi occupation of Norway in April 1940, Thomas W. Lamont helped organize the Committee to Defend America by Aiding the Allies.[72] Many other bankers were active in forming local chapters to generate grass-roots support for the crusade to assist the adversaries of the Third Reich.[73] Following the fall of France in June 1940, William Allen White, the influential editor of the *Emporia (Kansas) Gazette*, led the organization in an intensive propaganda campaign designed to get the man on the street to view England as the first line of American defense. Some of the more militant members of the association split away and joined with Lewis W. Douglas to establish the Century Group, which was even more aggressive in advocating aid for Great Britain. The smaller organization enlisted the support of several prominent business leaders including Will Clayton, James P. Warburg, and Whitney H. Shepardson. Then the influential Century Group banded together with the Committee to Defend America in a concerted drive to persuade the president to transfer a large number of old American destroyers to the British navy.[74]

Many in official circles, however, feared that it might already be too late to save England from the clutches of Hitler. Ambassador Joseph P. Kennedy was filled with apprehensions that Great Britain would be beaten and that the United States would be left holding the bag. Kennedy warned again and again from his post in London that the United States should not jeopardize its own defense program by sending scarce military supplies to the beleaguered British.[75] Nor did his grave misgivings about the fate of England fall on deaf ears in the United States. Thomas Lamont noted with disapprobation that "all Washington turned defeatist for several weeks following the fall of France."[76] Lord Lothian, the British ambassador in Washington, made the same observation. "There is a wave of pessimism passing over this country," he reported on June 27, "to the effect that Great Britain must now inevitably be defeated and that there is no use in the United States doing anything more to help and thereby getting entangled in Europe."[77]

American military authorities, ever sensitive about their responsibility for national security, were especially fearful that aid to Great Britain would interfere with their own preparedness program. The joint planners of the War and Navy Departments made their position clear on June 27 when they sent the president a paper calling for immediate decisions concerning national defense. "The further release of war material now in the hands of our armed forces will seriously weaken our present state of defense," the document argued. "Therefore, in general, further commitments for the sale of military equipment of the armed forces of the United States will be made only if the situation should indicate that Great Britain displayed an ability to withstand German assault." The joint planners concluded that as long as the British Isles remained in grave peril, military supplies should not be sent abroad at the expense of American rearmament requirements. A day later, the Senate passed a naval expansion bill with an amendment prohibiting the disposal of any army or navy material unless the chief of staff or the chief of naval operations should certify that the supplies were not essential to the defense of the United States.[78]

President Roosevelt was given pause. After having played a leading role in the campaign to convince the American people of the need to help the enemies of the Third Reich, Roosevelt became conspicuously silent. "Up till a few weeks ago," Thomas Lamont noted on July 10, "F.D.R. was way out in front. Now he is quiescent."[79] Roosevelt harbored deep fears that the British might not be able to hold out against the anticipated Nazi invasion. Despite his strong desire to help check the Germans, the president hesitated to authorize the release of any weapons which his military advisers might deem necessary for national defense. Roosevelt was particularly reluctant to transfer old American destroyers to the British navy while the survival of the United Kingdom remained in serious doubt. "I always have to think of the possibility," he confided to a Cabinet member on July 6, "that if these destroyers were sold to Great Britain and if, thereupon, Great Britain should be overwhelmed by Germany, they might fall into the hands of the Germans and be used against us."[80]

Colonel William J. Donovan, an American expert on military strategy, helped allay the widespread apprehension in

Washington that Great Britain might go under in the near future. Secretary of the Navy Knox, with the full approval of the president, dispatched Donovan to England on July 14 to get a firsthand view of the situation. Distressed by the pessimism of Ambassador Kennedy, the British welcomed the opportunity to give the American emissary a detailed look at their military preparations. Donovan was able to examine defense installations throughout England and to confer with everyone from Prime Minister Churchill on down. Upon his return to the United States in the first days of August, he made optimistic reports to congressmen, Cabinet members, and the president. Donovan argued that the British would probably be able to beat back a German attack and urged that more American weapons should be delivered to England at once. The British were pleased. Ambassador Lothian credited Donovan with helping his country obtain warships from the United States. "I think the trick has been done," Lothian wrote from Washington on August 6. "Donovan has helped a lot."[81]

Heartened by Donovan's mission, the Roosevelt administration promptly began searching for a politically viable and legally acceptable formula for transferring American destroyers to the British navy. During an important Cabinet meeting on August 2, it was decided that the American warships should be offered in exchange for naval and air bases in British possessions in the Western Hemisphere. It was also agreed that in return for the destroyers, the United States should ask for positive assurance that the Royal Navy would under no circumstance fall into German hands if England lost the war.[82] The president immediately tried to get Wendell Willkie to influence Republican leaders in Congress to support legislation to implement such an arrangement. When Willkie refused to cooperate, the administration began to look for a legal justification to circumvent Congress. Attorney General Robert H. Jackson, after brief consideration, rendered an opinion that it would be proper for the chief of naval operations to approve the transaction if in his judgment the exchange of American destroyers for British bases would strengthen rather than impair the total defense of the United States. Finally, on September 3, 1940, Roosevelt announced the destroyer-base deal.[83]

In the meantime, the Roosevelt administration feared that the Japanese would view the German offensive in Europe as a golden opportunity to acquire a vast empire in the South Pacific. The besieged European colonial powers were in no position to prevent their rich Oriental possessions from being drawn into a Greater East Asia Co-Prosperity Sphere. As alluring vistas opened before the Land of the Rising Sun, the United States was faced with a serious dilemma. Although American policymakers were determined to keep Japan from closing the door into the markets of the Orient, they did not want to risk a war in the Far East while Hitler was on the rampage in Europe. Roosevelt and his advisers realized that if the United States became involved in hostilities in the Pacific, the flow of American military supplies would be diverted from the European conflict. They also realized that if the Nazis emerged victorious in Europe, American naval forces would be needed in the Atlantic to assure the security of the Western Hemisphere.

The State Department, worried by the initial success of the Nazi blitzkrieg in the spring of 1940, hoped to work out an agreement with Japan to keep peace in the Pacific. Secretary Hull cabled Ambassador Joseph C. Grew on May 30 to open negotiations in Tokyo. Grew was instructed not only to urge the Japanese to cooperate with the United States in expanding the area of liberal trade but also to warn them that a German victory would result in the "flooding of world markets with low-priced goods produced under conditions of virtually forced labor."[84] In a series of conversations beginning on June 10, Grew warned Foreign Minister Hachiro Arita that "our relations cannot be expected to move into fundamentally happier channels so long as Japanese interference with American rights and interests in China continues."[85] Arita requested a temporary commercial accord to remove the threat of an American embargo against Japan, but Grew refused to make any practical concessions until the Japanese committed themselves to support liberal commercial principles. Thus the talks led nowhere. "The vicious circle is complete," Grew noted in his diary, "and how to break it is a Chinese puzzle which taxes imagination."[86]

Immediately after the fall of France, the Japanese imperialists decided that the time had come to solve the Chinese tangle in their own way. They aimed to force the Nationalist regime of Chiang Kai-shek into submission by shutting off vital supply routes to the Kuomintang headquarters in Chungking. Japan therefore pressed France on June 19 to close the Indo-China border to prevent shipments of gasoline, trucks, and munitions from getting through to Chungking. Tokyo also insisted that Japanese inspectors should be stationed along the French Indo-China railroad to make sure that trains did not carry provisions to the Kuomintang army. The vanquished French, after learning that the United States would not come to their aid, decided to yield rather than resist.

A short time later, Japan demanded that Great Britain close the Hongkong frontier and the Burma Road to keep essential supplies from reaching the Nationalist forces in China and also urged the British to withdraw their troops from Shanghai.[87] Ambassador Lothian visited the State Department on June 27 and handed Secretary Hull a long memorandum expounding the views of his government toward the whole Far Eastern situation. The British argued that acquiescence would only lead to further Japanese demands, which would ultimately imperil the interests of the United States. They also reasoned that British forces by themselves could not successfully oppose aggression in both Europe and Asia. Thus the government in London concluded that only two courses remained open. On the negative side, the United States could put increased pressure on Tokyo to maintain the status quo either by imposing a full embargo on exports to Japan or by sending naval forces to reinforce the British base at Singapore. The British acknowledged that this course might result in war. On the positive side, the United States could take part in an effort to bring about a peace settlement that would leave China independent and yet give Japan some satisfaction. The Japanese would be expected in return to remain neutral in the European war and to respect the integrity of Occidental possessions in the Orient. The British offered to cooperate in whichever of the two courses the United States might select.[88]

On the following day, after discussing the British proposals with the president, Secretary of State Hull called Lothian back into his office to elucidate the American position. Hull said that the United States would neither impose an embargo against Japan nor dispatch warships to Singapore. "We've been doing and are doing everything possible short of a serious risk of actual military hostilities," he explained, "to keep the Japanese situation stabilized." The secretary also stated that his government would not join with Great Britain in paying tribute to Tokyo. While adding that the United States would not object if the British tried to reach an accord by offering concessions to the Japanese, Hull insisted that Great Britain must not make an accommodation with Japan at the expense of China or in violation of the Open Door policy. "The principles underlying Japan's application of her 'new order in East Asia' would need negating or at least serious modifying," he explained. In short, Hull left no doubt that the United States would not participate in either a program of harassment or a policy of appeasement.[89]

The Roosevelt administration was disappointed when on July 12 Great Britain announced that it would close the Burma Road for a period of three months. Secretary Hull protested to Ambassador Lothian that the American government regretted the British decision "on account of the blow that would result to China in the general contest with Japan."[90] Several other Cabinet officers, however, while bemoaning the British willingness to back down, believed that it was time for the United States to adopt a much stronger line against Tokyo. Secretaries Morgenthau, Knox, and Stimson all advocated economic sanctions to restrain the Japanese from further expansion in the Orient. They wanted the president to take advantage of an act passed by Congress on July 2 allowing him to prohibit or curtail exports of materials required for national defense. These proponents of a tougher policy against Japan urged Roosevelt on July 19 to impose an oil embargo, which could be justified on the grounds of domestic fuel needs. "The only way to treat Japan," Stimson advised the president, "is not to retreat."[91]

During the ensuing week, the Roosevelt administration engaged in a vigorous debate over the best way to deter Japan without provoking a war in the Pacific. The Treasury Department sparked the controversy when it prepared an executive order which would place controls on the exportation of *every* kind of oil and *every* grade of scrap metal. Henry Morgenthau sent the draft to Hyde Park on July 22, and Roosevelt hastily signed the document without consulting anyone. The senior officials in the State Department, with the notable exception of Stanley K. Hornbeck, were aghast. Maxwell M. Hamilton, the chief of the Division of Far Eastern Affairs, warned that the proposed restrictions on strategic exports might incite Japan to declare war on England. Under Secretary Welles immediately telephoned Roosevelt and persuaded him to backtrack, and as soon as the president returned to Washington he called a Cabinet meeting to reconsider the whole issue. After a stormy session on July 26, the Treasury proposal was discarded in favor of a proclamation drawn up by the State Department. Roosevelt then affixed his signature to the new executive order, which established export controls over *only* those kinds of gasoline and lubricants used for aviation and over *only* the highest grades of melting iron and scrap steel.[92]

Nevertheless, the Treasury Department, smarting from defeat at the hands of the State Department, continued to press the president for a harder line against Japan. Harry Dexter White argued that American diplomats were nothing but appeasers who should not be allowed to control the decision-making process. "Our State Department is replete with budding Chamberlains," White complained on August 13. "I am convinced that the time has come when a strong, clear-cut foreign policy must be formulated and enforced for the State Department to execute."[93] Secretary Morgenthau agreed. Two days later, he urged the president to expand the embargo to cover all petroleum products. But Roosevelt hewed to the State Department position. "We must not push Japan too much at this time," he lectured Morgenthau on August 16, "as we might push her to take the Dutch East Indies."[94]

The Japanese were already attempting to gain control of Indo-China. That French colony had great economic value as a source of rice, rubber, and tin needed in Japan. It also had strategic importance as a military base for Japanese operations against the Nationalist armies in southern China. In a memorandum to the French government in Vichy on August 1, Tokyo demanded the right to transport Japanese troops through

Indo-China, permission to construct airfields in the colony, and an economic agreement which would bring Indo-China into the Japanese sphere of influence. The French did what they could to stall off the Japanese, but Tokyo threatened to take military action, and on August 29 the Vichy government signed an accord which recognized the "preponderance of Japanese interest" in Indo-China. Finally, on September 22, the French agreed to provide Japan with three airfields in Indo-China and to permit the eventual passage of 25,000 Japanese soldiers through Tonkin to Yunnan.[95]

The Roosevelt administration waited to see how the Battle of Britain developed before retaliating against Japan. Cordell Hull advised caution as Germany launched wave after wave of attack planes in an attempt to bomb England into submission. "If the British go down," he reasoned on September 12, "the Japs will probably spread out over all the Pacific just like wild men. If the British hold on, why we'll be able to restrain them and put on additional impediments to them and a loan to China."[96] As the Royal Airforce fought successfully against the German Luftwaffe in the skies over the United Kingdom, Hull advocated stronger action in the Far East. "It's a question of how far we can go," he explained on September 20, "without running too much risk of a military clash."[97] Roosevelt agreed that the time had arrived to pursue a tougher policy in the Pacific. The American government consequently announced on September 25 that the Export-Import Bank would make a new loan to the Nationalists in China. On the next day, in an effort to throttle Japanese war production, the president ordered export controls on all grades of iron and steel scrap.[98]

At that very moment, Japan and Germany were maneuvering to discourage the United States from intervening in the military conflicts then raging in Europe and Asia. The Japanese formally joined hands with Hitler and Mussolini on September 27 in an alliance designed to intimidate Roosevelt. Tokyo agreed to respect the leadership of Germany and Italy in the establishment of a New Order in Europe. In return, Berlin and Rome recognized the leadership of Japan in the creation of a New Order in Greater East Asia. Without specifically mentioning the United States, the three contracting parties also promised to assist each other with all political, economic, and military means if any one of them were attacked by a power not yet involved in the European war or the Sino-Japanese conflict.

The conclusion of the Rome-Berlin-Tokyo Axis provoked varied reactions in the United States. Stimson and Morgenthau promptly renewed their arguments for a hard line against Japan. "If it should come to a showdown, at present and so long as the British Fleet lasts," Stimson reasoned on September 27, "the Axis in Europe could not help Japan if she got into trouble with us, and Japan could not help Germany or Italy if they got into trouble with us. So in substance the new arrangement simply means making a bad face at us."[99] Stimson not only regarded the Rome-Berlin-Tokyo alliance as a bluff, but he also remained convinced that soft words or inconsistent behavior would encourage the Japanese to become more aggressive in the Orient. "Japan has historically shown that she can misinterpret a pacifistic policy of the United States for weakness," Stimson wrote on October 2. "She has also historically shown that when the United States indicates by clear language and bold actions that she intends to carry out a clear and affirmative policy in the Far East, Japan will yield to that policy even though it conflicts with her own Asiatic policy and conceived interests."[100] But when Morgenthau pleaded on the same day for a tough policy against Tokyo, Roosevelt retorted that he and Hull were "handling foreign affairs."[101]

The State Department was reconsidering the whole Far Eastern question in the light of the tripartite pact. Stanley Hornbeck and Norman Davis were bellicose in their attitude toward Japan. Hornbeck had for some time been advocating a stiff policy in the Orient, and he remained convinced that the Japanese neither could nor would strike back.[102] During a meeting called by Secretary Hull on September 29, Hornbeck argued that the time had come for the United States to checkmate Japan. But the Far Eastern Division advised caution unless the United States was prepared to go to war in the Pacific. "It was obvious to everyone," Adolf Berle recorded in his diary, "that the Germans hope to embroil us in the Far East as rapidly as they can, thereby assuring to themselves—as they think—a clearer prospect in the Atlantic."[103] A day later, Hull told the British ambassador that the United States wanted to see his country defeat Germany. "Our acts and utterances with respect to the Pacific area," he explained, "will be more or less affected as to time and extent by the question of what course will most effectively and legitimately aid Great Britain in winning the war."[104]

Yet Prime Minister Churchill, anxious about the decision of his Cabinet to reopen the Burma Road, proposed an American naval demonstration in Asian waters. "Would it not be possible for you to send an American squadron, the bigger the better, to pay a friendly visit to Singapore," Churchill cabled Roosevelt on October 4. "Anything in this direction would have a marked deterrent effect upon a Japanese declaration of war upon us over the Burma Road opening."[105] But the senior officials in the State Department persuaded Roosevelt to reject the British proposal. Hornbeck and Davis were alone in their willingness to fight to protect Singapore. While Hornbeck seemed to regard "Japan as the sun around which her satellites, Germany and Italy, were revolving," Hull, Welles, Berle, and Long all concurred that the United States should avoid any action which might provoke a military showdown in the Pacific. "We must realize," Hull argued, "that the main theatre where the war will be won or lost is in England itself and there must be no lessening of our supplies to England." Welles was equally determined to prevent the United States from being trapped by a military entanglement in the Far East. "If we went to war with Japan," he reasoned, "all our efforts would have to be directed toward supplying our ships and our troops in the field and England would correspondingly suffer."[106]

President Roosevelt and his counselors in the State Department continued to regard Nazi Germany as the root of the world crisis. Francis B. Sayre, while serving as the American high commissioner in the Philippines, repeatedly advised against any provocative action in the Pacific. "Always in the background of my mind is the fact that there is nothing which Hitler would love better than to get the United States into a war with Japan," Sayre wrote from Manila on October 19. "As I see it, the whole Far Eastern situation depends upon the outcome of the war between England and Germany. If Germany is beaten, Japan can be made to behave; but if Germany succeeds in beating England, Japan will become, I fear, the unbearable dictator of all Asia."[107] Roosevelt was well aware of the need for a global strategy. "For practical purposes," he wrote Sayre on December 31, "there is going on a world conflict, in which there are aligned on one side Japan, Germany and Italy, and on the other side China, Great Britain, and the United States. This country is not involved in the hostilities, but there is no doubt where we stand as regards to the issues."[108]

Predicating their actions on that perspective, Roosevelt and his advisers continued to search for ways to deter Japan without provoking hostilities in the Pacific. They decided on October 23 to send two squadrons of pursuit planes to the Philippine Islands, which were strategically located on the flank of a possible Japanese drive to the south. They likewise decided three weeks later to base ten additional submarines at Manila.[109] Meanwhile, the Council on Foreign Relations was advocating increased financial support for Nationalist China. "By assisting the Chinese to intensify their resistance to Japanese conquest," a council study group argued on October 11, "the United States might help so to burden Japan that its reserves of shipping, material, and manpower would not be adequate to embark on the conquest of the Netherlands East Indies and of Singapore." The group added that American economic assistance "would also permit Chiang Kai-shek to accept increased Russian aid without disturbing the internal balance of political force within China."[110] Roosevelt agreed that the United States should act fast to check Communist influence in China and to help the Kuomintang resist Japan. When Tokyo formally recognized its puppet government entrenched at Nanking on November 30, therefore, Washington announced a new 100 million dollar credit for the Nationalist regime headquartered at Chungking.[111]

The Roosevelt administration also decided to apply increased economic pressure on Japan. William Diebold of the Council on Foreign Relations pointed out in November 1940 that the Japanese archipelago was vulnerable to a combined program of economic sanctions.[112] Although the State Department still opposed an oil embargo which might impel Tokyo to attack the Dutch East Indies, Secretary Hull gave his assent in December 1940 to a widening ban on exports to Japan. Under the guise of national defense, the president issued a series of executive orders which extended the export licensing system to such important raw materials as iron ore, copper, brass, zinc, nickel, and potash. The State Department concurrently made efforts to induce South American nations to put restrictions on the shipment of strategic materials to Japan.[113] In line with this campaign to undermine the war-making capacity of Japan, the Reconstruction Finance Corporation agreed to purchase materials from Latin American countries in quantities far exceeding stockpiling requirements for national defense.[114]

An additional reason for the stockpiling program was the desire to assure the United States an adequate supply of rubber in case Japan moved against the East Indies.[115] "Our existing supply of new and 'scrap' rubber now in the United States or on the way here are sufficient to carry us for two and a half to three years under war conditions even if our source of supply were cut off at once," the deputy federal loan administrator explained in February 1941. "If we should get into war, however, we could build plants for a modified type of 'neoprene' suitable for tires, and these plants could be constructed in time to take care of us before our existing supplies of rubber were exhausted."[116] The Council of National Defense had already reported to the president that "it would be possible to erect synthetic rubber plants capable of supplying our emergency needs."[117] *Fortune* magazine likewise noted that the rapid advances made in producing ersatz rubber had removed the danger of a Japanese monopoly of natural rubber. "With the development of synthetic rubber," the editors declared in December 1940, "the fear that Japan could permanently deprive our automobiling civilization of an absolute necessity has little ground."[118]

Government officials and business spokesmen were concerned much more about Japan as a threat to Oriental markets for American commodities than as a menace to Asian sources of raw materials. The dream of the China market continued to captivate the American imagination. "With a population of more than 400 million China is the biggest single potential market in the world," *Fortune* proclaimed in May 1941. "A strong China, able and willing to defend the principle of the open market in the Far East, would be worth billions of dollars to the United States."[119] Although American exports to China remained far below American shipments to Japan, it was not simply a matter of putting potential sales to China above actual business in Japan. Informed officials in Washington realized that the Japanese would become increasingly less dependent upon American products if they succeeded in establishing their own version of a *Grossraumwirtschaft* in the Far East. In such case, a State Department memorandum warned in December 1940, the United States would be hurt not only by the loss of the Chinese market but also by the "loss of much of the Japanese market for our goods as Japan would become more and more self-sufficient."[120]

Meanwhile, many individuals throughout the United States who wanted to keep out of the European conflict were joining the America First Committee. The organization, formed in September 1940 and headquartered in Chicago, gave vent to the strong grass-roots desire to avoid war. While appealing to a wide variety of people, the America First movement drew strong support from several prominent midwestern businessmen including Henry Ford, Jay Hormel, and Robert E. Wood, the chairman of the board at Sears, Roebuck and Company. These business leaders worried that a war to liberate the European market from totalitarian controls would destroy free enterprise in the United States.[121] "At the end of the last war President Wilson gave back the vast war powers given him," Wood wrote a fellow committee member in April 1941. "Railroads went back to their owners." But Wood feared that President Roosevelt would use wartime powers to fetter the American economy with increased New Deal regulations. "It is fairly certain," he concluded, "that capitalism cannot survive American participation in the war."[122]

Those who participated in the America First movement were convinced that a Nazi victory in Europe would present no threat to the vital interests of the United States. They did not believe that the Western Hemisphere was vulnerable to military attack. Nor did they think that the United States was in danger of economic strangulation. Even those who realized the importance of foreign trade had no fears of competition with Germany in the markets of the world.[123] "After all," Wood reasoned in October 1940, "when two nations or two continents each have things the other needs trade eventually results regardless of the feelings each may have for the other. Europe needs us more than we need Europe—our materials and products are more important to her than hers to us."[124] Senator Burton K. Wheeler of Montana was equally confident that Americans could hold their own in competition with Germany for overseas commerce. "Free American industry is superior to controlled Nazi industry," Wheeler told an America First rally in May 1941. "Free American workers can produce more than Nazi slaves and I know that American businessmen can compete anywhere in the world today."[125]

The same reasoning prompted George Peek to become active in the America First campaign. Peek played a leading role in the effort to persuade Americans that they could live prosperously in the same world with a victorious Germany. "Hitler cannot impoverish America by stifling our foreign trade," he asserted in May 1941. "Other things being equal, free labor can out-produce slave labor." Peek remained convinced that Yankee exporters could beat the Nazis at their own game of bilateral barter. "If we are going to engage in trade with other countries," he continued, "we should use our strategic advantages to negotiate country by country in our own interest."[126] Peek was quick to challenge the argument advanced by Douglas Miller in his book entitled *You Can't Do Business With Hitler.* "I do not care anything about Professor Miller's theories about trade with Hitler because I demonstrated to my own satisfaction in 1934 that we could trade with advantage to ourselves," Peek proclaimed in August 1941. "I am not willing to swap my practical experience for his theories."[127]

Although most business spokesmen and government officials rejected the economic arguments advanced by America First proponents, many admitted the validity of their strategic calculations. "If Hitler can't cross the English Channel," the *Magazine of Wall Street* queried in October 1940, "how can he cross the Atlantic Ocean?"[128] Josephus Daniels, the American ambassador in Mexico City, was equally skeptical about the threat of a Nazi military assault against the Western Hemisphere. "I can hardly believe," Daniels wrote Bernard Baruch in November 1940, "that it would be possible for any man to be crazy enough to try to invade this hemisphere."[129] Nor could *Fortune* magazine envision a clear and present danger to the physical security of the United States. "The danger of a direct attack upon our shores," the editors acknowledged in April 1941, "is relatively remote."[130]

The United States was also not vulnerable to an aerial attack, Hanson W. Baldwin, the eminent military correspondent of the *New York Times*, explained in March 1941. German bombers did not have nearly enough range to fly across the Atlantic Ocean, drop their payloads on American targets, and return to their European bases, he pointed out. "The ability to dispatch fleets of planes to bomb an enemy objective, to avoid or crash through the enemy defenses, to return safely to base and repeat the operation again and yet again—these are the realistic measures of effective air power," Baldwin noted. "No air power now assembled is capable of bringing that kind of force to bear against the United States." Baldwin did not believe that Hitler would be irrational enough to send great squadrons of planes and pilots on a one-way trip to imprisonment or death. "Colonel Charles Lindberg obviously was right," he observed, "when he declared that this country could not be invaded or seriously assaulted by air, so long as no Eurasian air power possessed bases in this hemisphere."[131]

The State Department made a similar estimate of the strategic importance of air power. "The time has come to control foreign air lines in South America," Adolf Berle declared in March 1941, "and the way to do that is to control the sale of aviation gasoline."[132] Thus, he and his colleagues got the Standard Oil Company to stop selling aviation fuel to Axis-controlled airlines in Latin America.[133] They also succeeded in getting several South American governments to eliminate Axis influence from their national airlines.[134] Meanwhile, the State Department was quick to grasp the strategic significance of the sinking of the *Bismarck* in May 1941. The powerful 16,000-

ton German battleship was torpedoed by British planes launched from pursuing aircraft carriers. "The fact that the *Bismarck* was sunk (substantially) by air power," Berle wrote in his diary, "seems to make it plain that if there is anything like an adequate air force, a naval invasion of the Western Hemisphere is out of the question. Even if the Germans conquered Europe, and if they outbuilt us navally and with merchant marine, it would still be a question whether these ships could live long enough to reach the United States."[135]

However, although the Roosevelt administration discounted Germany as a military threat, it became increasingly convinced that the economic consequences of a Nazi victory in Europe would be intolerable. "Our economy cannot compete with slave labor," Secretary of Commerce Jesse Jones declared in April 1941. "Maybe we can't be invaded, but we might become isolated economically."[136] Louis Domeratzky of the Bureau of Foreign and Domestic Commerce was equally alarmed about German plans for the conquest of foreign markets in the postwar period. "Confronted by a compact political-economic combination on the continent of Europe under the domination of the National Socialist State," Domeratzky warned, "the individual American entrepreneur would hardly be strong enough to find a market for his product."[137] President Roosevelt agreed. "Tariff walls—Chinese walls of isolation—would be futile," he lectured in May 1941. "Freedom to trade is essential to our economic life. We do not eat all the food we produce; we do not burn all the oil we can pump; we do not use all the goods we can manufacture. It would not be an American wall to keep Nazi goods out; it would be a Nazi wall to keep us in."[138]

Such dire forebodings continued to cause acute anxiety in the corporate community. "Under a Hitler victory," Thomas Lamont warned in January 1941, "we should find ourselves in the midst of a country-wide depression so deep and so prolonged as to make the worst of the last ten years here look like a happy and bountiful time."[139] Lamont feared that the Nazis, if triumphant, would employ commercial policies that would "ruin our trade and destroy our standard of living, rearing want and Bolshevism in our midst."[140] W. H. Schubart of the Bank of Manhattan was similarly disturbed about the prospects of a trade

185

war between Hitler and Hull. "If Germany wins, she will most certainly extend her clearing system," Schubart declared in March 1941. "In such a barter economy we shall not fit and much of the world trade will be denied us."[141] President Eugene P. Thomas of the National Foreign Trade Council agreed. "Unless the Axis Powers are defeated in this war and rendered incapable of putting into execution their plans for a new world order," Thomas exclaimed, "we must face the prospect of continental isolation."[142]

Business journals reflected the widespread apprehension that a Nazi victory in Europe would spell doom for the American free enterprise system. "The great danger facing the Western Hemisphere in the event of a totalitarian victory," *Barron's* declared in January 1941, "is not the immediate threat of armed invasion, but rather the threat of trade aggression."[143] A few months later, the same periodical warned against resorting to totalitarian trade tactics to meet German competition in overseas markets. "The inevitable consequence of federal control of the export portion of the business," the editors cautioned, "would be that government agencies would eventually find it necessary to extend their authority to the company's whole operations, domestic and foreign."[144] Such reasoning led *Fortune* to conclude that capitalism would perish in the United States if Hitler destroyed entrepreneurial freedom in Europe. "Industry and trade, labor and agriculture would become part of a state system, which in its own self-defense, would have to take on the character of Hitler's system," the editors argued in June 1941. "Freedom cannot be national. It must be international."[145]

Agreeing that the world could not endure half slave and half free, State Department officers had become increasingly skeptical about the economic viability of a Fortress Americas proposed by the agrarians. "Some of the greatest of the South American nations depend almost entirely upon Europe for their export trade," Sumner Welles pointed out in January 1941. "Because of the fact that these other American nations produce the same commodities as we ourselves produce, there is clearly no opportunity for the United States, in the event of a German domination of Europe, to take more than a relatively small percentage of such exports in addition to those which they now consume."[146] Harley A. Notter similarly believed that "the position of the United States with respect to trade with the other American republics would be disasterously inferior to that of Germany."[147] Consequently, William Phillips, then serving as the American ambassador in Rome, explained, the United States would not be content to rest secure in the Western Hemisphere. "Our policy was to encourage trade relations with all countries," Phillips noted in January 1941. "We would never be satisfied to be bottled up in the American continent."[148]

State Department officials also questioned the economic viability of a joint Pan American-British Empire trading bloc. "A German-Japanese dominated world could and would offer inducements to countries in this hemisphere greater than would be willingly supported by the United States or remnants of the British Empire," Herbert Feis admonished in January 1941. "In short, it gets to be more and more obvious each day that a German victory would be followed by division and conflict among countries of this hemisphere."[149] Lynn R. Edminster, a special assistant to the secretary of state, likewise argued that the United States could not afford to write off the European market. "Our country should exercise leadership," he concluded in May 1941, "in an endeavor to establish and maintain the largest possible sphere in the world in which trade and other economic relations can be conducted on the basis of liberal principles."[150]

Those studying economic and financial questions for the Council on Foreign Relations gradually reached the same conclusion. Percy W. Bidwell and Arthur R. Upgren had pointed out in January 1941 that a military stalemate in Europe would allow for the establishment of a Pan American-British Empire commercial union. "The British area," they had argued, "furnishes the markets and supplies the materials which can keep the Western Hemisphere a going concern."[151] But it did not take long for them to change their minds. "Only by preserving a trade area that is even wider than that of the Western Hemisphere and Britain," Upgren warned the following summer, "can our economy face the future with assurance."[152] Reasoning in like fashion, Bidwell calculated that the commerical results of a military stalemate would be disastrous for the United States. "We ought to recognize frankly that South Americans are going to want to trade with both England and the European Continent after this war is over," he asserted in August 1941. "Defeating Hitler is the first step in the process of assuring ourselves and our Latin American neighbors of this wider trading area."[153]

seven

Roosevelt's Dilemma

A CONSENSUS had gradually emerged in business and government circles that the economic consequences of a German victory would be intolerable for the United States. Before the fall of France in June 1940, many corporate executives had worried that American intervention in the European conflict would undermine free enterprise in the United States. At the same time, President Roosevelt and his advisers in the State Department had hoped that, with the help of American armaments, the Allies would be able to contain the Third Reich. But American thinking underwent a fundamental transformation after France capitulated. It became increasingly evident that the beleaguered British could not by themselves prevent Adolf Hitler and his Axis partners from dividing the world into exclusive spheres of influence. A few prominent businessmen who participated in the America First movement believed that the United States could bask in the sunshine of prosperity within the confines of the Western Hemisphere. However, most corporate chiefs and government officials agreed that the defeat of Nazi Germany was vitally important for the survival of American capitalism.

During the autumn of 1940, the Roosevelt administration remained anxious about the outcome of the contest in Europe. The failure of the Luftwaffe to gain control of the skies over England had prompted Hitler to cancel his plans for an invasion of the British Isles. But the European continent was still under the shadow of the swastika. Under Secretary of Commerce Wayne C. Taylor, just back from the United Kingdom, reported on October 10 that he doubted that the British blockade could force the Nazis to surrender.[1] Former Assistant Secretary of War Louis Johnson made the same point a day later. Johnson thought that the British might be able to hold their own against the Third Reich, but he did not believe they could ever win the war.[2] Neither did the State Department. "It looks now," Assistant Secretary Adolf A. Berle observed on September 18, "as though there would be nothing but a long, bitter stalemate."[3] J. Pierrepont Moffat, upon returning a few weeks later from his post as the American minister to Canada, found that his colleagues in Washington were pessimistic regarding England's ability to defeat Germany without American intervention. "Summing up my impressions," Moffat noted in his diary on October 10, "I had the feeling that we were fast moving toward war."[4]

Prominent members of the eastern establishment were already debating among themselves whether or not the United States should immediately enter the war. Many who were still doves, like Thomas W. Lamont, reasoned that direct American intervention would interfere with the flow of military supplies across the Atlantic and thereby hinder the British war effort. "I think that if we were in the actual armed conflict, we might for at least a year be a drag rather than otherwise," Lamont wrote a friend in England on October 11. "I am fearful that a good many of the priorities now granted to Britain might be turned aside to our own fighting forces which we should be endeavoring to equip."[5] But many others who had become hawks, like Secretary of War Henry L. Stimson, worried that the American people would not get behind the rearmament program unless they felt the heat of battle. Stimson warned on December 13 that it would be impossible to expand military production sufficiently "until we got into the war ourselves."[6]

There was a growing feeling among those closest to the president that the United States must sooner or later enter the war as an ally of Great Britain. Although many State Department officers hated to contemplate going to war twice in their lifetime, they were under no illusion that the British could safeguard American interests around the world. "We have now learned," Assistant Secretary Berle confided in his diary on September 29, "that if we are going to get our farm work done, it is we, and not our neighbors, our friends or relatives, who are going to do it."[7] Secretary of the Navy Frank Knox concurred. "The English are not going to win this war without our help, I mean our military help," Knox insisted at a high-echelon meeting on October 29. "That is what we have got to keep in our minds," he continued. "We needn't talk it outdoors, but I think it is true."[8]

During his campaign for a third term, President Roosevelt did little to enlighten the American people about the major foreign policy issues confronting the country. Roosevelt said nothing about the risk of war involved in his program of providing extensive assistance to England. Nor did he address the fundamental question of what the United States should do if Great Britain proved unable to defeat Nazi Germany. The president simply hewed to the Democratic party platform which promised that "we will not send our army, naval, or air forces to fight in foreign lands outside of the Americas, except in case of attack." Roosevelt repeatedly pledged that he would do his utmost to keep the nation at peace. "I hate war, now more than ever," he declared on September 11, 1940. "I have one supreme determination—to do all that I can to keep war away from these shores for all time."[9]

Despite such assurances, the question of American intervention in the European war became the predominant issue during the last weeks of the presidential campaign. Wendell Willkie, the Republican candidate, hoped to catch Roosevelt in the polls by charging that the president was leading the country into the military vortex. Willkie asserted that the peaceful proclamations emanating from the White House were insincere and that Roosevelt, if he were reelected, would send American boys to fight on the battlefields of Europe.

The president was quick to counterattack. In a nationwide speech delivered on October 30, Roosevelt told the American people what he knew they wanted to hear. "And while I am talking to you mothers and fathers I give you one more assurance," he declared. "I have said this before, but I shall say it again and again and again: your boys are not going to be sent into any foreign wars." Many placed their trust in Roosevelt, and a week later he won the election by a narrow margin in popular votes.[10]

Almost immediately after the election, Roosevelt received an important memorandum from Chief of Naval Operations Harold R. Stark. The document, referred to as Plan Dog, advanced a Europe-first war strategy. After arguing that the defeat of Germany would require a massive land offensive, Admiral Stark warned that the British did not have sufficient manpower to assure a victory. "I believe," he emphasized, "that the United States, in addition to sending naval assistance, would also need to send large air and land forces to Europe or Africa, or both, and to participate strongly in this land offensive." Hence, he reasoned that if the United States became involved in a two-ocean war, "we would then be able to do little more in the Pacific than remain on a strict defensive." Stark concluded with a recommendation for staff conversations between American and British military authorities.[11] Although Roosevelt withheld formal approval of Plan Dog, he promptly authorized joint staff talks based upon the assumption of hostilities in both Europe and Asia. After three months of secret discussions in Washington, the American and British military planners endorsed a grand strategy which called for the concentration of forces on Germany while conducting a war of attrition against Japan.[12]

Yet the president still refused to take the American people into his confidence. In a fireside chat to the nation on December 29, 1940, he reiterated the popular theme of all aid to Great Britain short of actual combat. "We must," he declared, "be the great arsenal of democracy." Roosevelt insisted that the British needed more weapons of every kind from the United States, but he denied that they wanted Americans to do their fighting. "There is no demand for sending an American Expeditionary Force outside our own borders," the president assured his audience. "There is no intention by any member of your Government to send such a force. You can, therefore, nail any talk about sending armies to Europe as a deliberate untruth." Candor remained in the closet. "Our national policy is not directed toward war," Roosevelt reasserted. "Its sole purpose is to keep war away from our country and our people."[13]

But President Roosevelt did not conceal his belief that the United States should redouble its efforts to help Great Britain resist the Third Reich. Realizing that the British were running low on foreign exchange needed to buy American munitions, he openly argued that the United States should ship weapons to England without demanding payment in dollars. The president used a homely analogy to cushion the shock of his proposal. If your neighbor's house was on fire, he told reporters at a press conference on December 17, you would not charge him for the use of your garden hose. Rather you would connect the hose, and your neighbor would return it after he put the fire out. Roosevelt moved quickly to secure congressional approval for his proposal. During the first week in January 1941, he asked Treasury Secretary Henry Morgenthau to prepare legislation which would empower the Chief Executive to lend or lease war materials to foreign governments. Morgenthau and his aides promptly drafted a bill authorizing the president to have manufactured in the United States any military article for any country whose defense he deemed vital to American security.[14]

The Lend-Lease bill provoked a heated debate over American foreign policy. On the one side, business internationalists like Russell C. Leffingwell of the J. P. Morgan Company stood firmly behind Roosevelt. "I can promise you," Leffingwell wrote the president on January 9, "that we will all of us so far as we have a voice to raise be using it in aid of your program of aid to Britain."[15] On the other side, economic nationalists who marched under the America First banner charged that passage of the Lend-Lease bill would be a giant step toward war. Senator Burton K. Wheeler likened the measure to the Agricultural Adjustment Act: "it will plough under every fourth American boy."[16] Although spokesmen for the administration insisted that aid to England would obviate the need for American military intervention, those close to the president knew better. Two days before Roosevelt signed the Lend-Lease Act on March 11, 1941, Adolf Berle concluded that the country was moving into a state of semibelligerency. "What I think it means," he noted in his diary, "is a steady drift into a deep gray stage in which the precise difference between war and peace is impossible to discern."[17]

The passage of the Lend-Lease Act did, in fact, bring the United States closer to combat. Hitler regarded the measure as an American declaration of economic war against Germany, and on March 25 he retaliated with a decree which extended the North Atlantic war zone westward to the coast of Greenland. Admiral Erich Raeder, the commander of the German navy, welcomed the opportunity to unleash his submarines in the expanded combat area. He hoped that Nazi U-boats would be able to sink enough tonnage in the North Atlantic to force Great Britain to sue for peace. Thus, the Roosevelt administration, having obtained billions of dollars to provide military aid for the British, was at once confronted with the grave problem of how to assure the safe delivery of American munitions to the United Kingdom.[18]

Many in official circles in Washington believed that an American naval escort would provide the only way to protect the shipping lanes across the Atlantic. This argument had been vigorously advanced for several months by Stimson, Knox, Stark, and General George C. Marshall, the chief of staff. During a meeting in December 1940, all four concurred that before long the United States would have to enter the war against Germany. They also agreed that "the eventual big act will have to be to save the life line of Great Britain in the North Atlantic."[19] As the menace in the Atlantic grew during the spring of 1941, those around the president became increasingly convinced of the need for American warships to accompany convoys headed for the British Isles. "The situation is obviously critical in the Atlantic," Stark wrote a fleet commander on April 4. "In my opinion, it is hopeless except as we take strong measures to save it."[20]

But President Roosevelt hesitated to order the American navy to escort convoys across the Atlantic. During a private conference at the White House on April 2, he insisted that "public opinion was not yet ready for the United States to convoy ships."[21] Despite continued prodding from his top advisers for a naval escort, Roosevelt searched for an alternative way to protect convoys. "He has made up his mind that it was too dangerous to ask the Congress for the power to convoy," Stimson recorded in his diary on April 10. "His plan is that we shall patrol the high seas west of the median line." In other words, Roosevelt decided to extend the American neutrality zone to the mid-Atlantic. "We can patrol and follow the convoys and notify them of any German raiders or submarines that we may see and give them a chance to escape," Stimson explained. "Also notify the British warships so they can get at the raider."[22] The new system was put into operation on April 24, and a month later a quarter of the Pacific fleet was transferred to the North Atlantic to help cover the enlarged patrol area.[23]

A pro-war consensus was then crystallizing in Washington. Pierrepont Moffat took note of the bellicose spirit when he returned home for a short vacation from his post in Ottawa. "The emotional pitch in Washington is very strong, with the interventionists in the saddle," Moffat observed on April 9. "There is an intolerant attitude in Washington toward those who do not think like the majority."[24] A few of his colleagues in the State Department did remain cautious. Assistant Secretary Breckinridge Long continued to argue that the United States should avoid hostilities until the military was ready to fight.[25] But Assistant Secretary Dean G. Acheson believed that the United States should get into the war immediately in order to speed up the defense program.[26] Many others, such as William C. Knudson of the Office of Production Management, added their voice to the mounting interventionist chorus.[27] "If we are going to save England," Treasury Secretary Morgenthau concluded on May 14, "we would have to get into this war." On the same day, Harry L. Hopkins told Morgenthau that the president had to do something and that "most of his friends felt that the next move was to get us into the war." But Hopkins, a presidential confidant who was living in the White House, thought that Roosevelt "would rather follow public opinion than lead it."[28]

The warhawks in the Cabinet had by this time become impatient with Roosevelt. Stimson and Knox met on May 12 with Interior Secretary Harold L. Ickes and Attorney General

Robert H. Jackson to discuss the need for bold and resolute executive leadership. "All four of us were feeling very acutely the need of forthright declarations from the President," Knox recorded in his diary. "We all four thought that the country was ready for action and a movement forward but awaited the President's word."[29] Stimson was particularly disappointed by the disingenuous attitude of the president. He realized that the American navy, by reporting the position of German warships to the British fleet, was engaged in "a clearly hostile act."[30] Stimson also believed that Roosevelt hoped that the aggressive naval patrol would provoke a clash with Germany. "The President," he noted on May 23, "shows evidence of waiting for the accidental shot of some irresponsible captain on either side to be the occasion of his going into war."[31]

Stimson was correct. The president did desire an incident that would justify American military action against Germany. Roosevelt told William C. Bullitt on April 23 that Stimson wanted an immediate declaration of war but that the American people were not yet willing to fight. "The President," Bullitt noted, "felt that we must await an incident and was confident that the Germans would give us an incident."[32] Roosevelt likewise told Morgenthau that he thought something might happen at any time. "I am," the president confided on May 17, "waiting to be pushed into this situation."[33] While he waited for the Nazi naval commanders to make some kind of blunder in the Atlantic, Roosevelt tried to prepare public opinion for battle. In a fireside chat broadcast to the country on May 27, the president asserted that Hitler was embarked upon a quest for "world domination." If Great Britain fell, he claimed, Germany would "close in relentlessly on this hemisphere." Roosevelt ended his address by proclaiming the existence of "an unlimited national emergency."[34] As Adolf Berle observed, the speech "was calculated to scare the daylights out of everyone."[35]

But it was not only his sensitivity to popular sentiment which made Roosevelt reluctant to fire the first shot in the Atlantic. Secretary of State Cordell Hull explained to a subordinant on April 17 an additional reason for caution in dealing with Hitler. "If we took the initiative in war on Germany—if we brought on war with her by our act—then Japan, under the terms of her Tripartite Treaty will be obligated to war on us. But if Germany takes the offensive Japan is not obligated. So we must be very careful not to do the thing which could be construed as initiating the war."[36] Joseph C. Grew, the American ambassador in Tokyo, agreed that the United States should avoid becoming involved in hostilities with enemies in the Atlantic and Pacific at the same time. He believed that prominent influences in Japan would like to obtain a release from their obligations under Article III of their treaty with Germany and Italy. "It would appear reasonable to suppose that if a German attack on an American warship or other American vessel should bring about war," Grew cabled on May 13, "the Japanese Government would take the position that Germany had taken provocative action and had given the *casus belli*. On the other hand, the obligation of Japan under Article III might in good faith be made effective if an American warship fired the first shot."[37]

American apprehensions grew as the Japanese appeared to be preparing for an advance southward. In February 1941, Washington was flooded with reports that in the near future Japan would launch a military expedition against Singapore. Hitler had already decided to urge the Japanese to attack the British stronghold, which commanded Asian trade routes essential to the survival of England. If the United States became involved in hostilities with Japan in the Pacific, the führer deduced, the Americans would be obliged to reduce their aid to Great Britain in the Atlantic. Before accepting the role Hitler had assigned them in his grand strategy, however, the Japanese hoped to work out an accord with the Russians. Thus, Tokyo dispatched Foreign Minister Yosuke Matsuoka to Moscow, and on April 13 he secured an agreement which provided that Russia and Japan would remain neutral in case either country were attacked by another power. The Japanese hoped that the pact with the Soviet Union would secure their northern flank if they embarked upon a southern campaign.[38]

The Russians in turn hoped that the neutrality agreement would remove the threat of a Japanese attack on their Siberian frontier if they needed to defend their European border from a German invasion. After the fall of France, the Soviets acutely realized that their Nazi allies presented a grave danger to their homeland. Yet Premier Stalin continued to fulfill his commitments to ship strategic goods to Germany in order to avoid as long as possible a military confrontation with Hitler. Soviet suspicions were reinforced in March 1941 when Washington informed the Kremlin that the United States had obtained an authentic copy of German plans for an assault on Russia. Hitler believed that the British had rejected his peace overtures because they expected that the Soviet Union and the United States would eventually join them in the war against Germany. But if their hope for Russian intervention were destroyed, the führer reasoned, their hope for American involvement would also vanish because the elimination of the Red Army would enormously increase Japanese power in Asia. Thus, Hitler ordered the Wehrmacht to strike on June 22 in an effort to liquidate the Soviet Union before the winter snows blanketed the vast stretch of territory between Berlin and Moscow.[39]

Most advisers to President Roosevelt assumed that the German invasion of Russia would provide no more than a temporary breather in the Battle of the Atlantic. On the eve of the Nazi assault, Ambassador Laurance Steinhardt wrote from Moscow that the Wehrmacht would have little trouble crushing the Red Army and that the victorious Germans would be able to increase the production of wheat in the Ukraine and oil at Baku.[40] Hull and Berle agreed that Hitler would make quick work of the Soviet Union and then be in a stronger position to subdue England.[41] Stimson and Knox, along with Admiral Stark and General Marshall, likewise thought that Germany would win within a brief period ranging anywhere from two weeks to three months. All four believed that the United States should take advantage of the short respite afforded by the diversion of German military power in Russia to give increased aid to Great Britain. Hence, they urged Roosevelt to seize the opportunity at hand to push with the utmost vigor American operations in the Atlantic.[42]

While he agreed that the moment was opportune to redouble American aid to England, the president had greater confidence than the military men in the staying power of the Soviet Union. Joseph E. Davies, the former American ambassador in

Moscow, persuaded Roosevelt that the Red Army would effectively resist the Nazi onslaught. Davies believed that the Russians could maintain themselves for a considerable time behind the Ural Mountains even if their first line of defense collapsed, but he argued that they would ultimately need war supplies from the United States in order to turn back the German armies. Davies also warned that Stalin might accept peace overtures from Hitler if Germany succeeded in taking the Ukraine and White Russia. He therefore insisted that everything should be done to encourage the Soviet leaders to continue their resistance, and that nothing should be done to induce them to think that they were being used as tools to pull American chestnuts out of the fire.[43] Roosevelt agreed that word should be sent to Stalin that the United States would furnish all possible assistance to Russia in the fight against Germany, and on July 10 he informed the Soviet ambassador that American supplies would be shipped to Russia as fast as possible.[44]

Following up on this initiative two weeks later, the president authorized Harry Hopkins to fly to Moscow as his personal envoy to let Stalin know that the United States meant business. Hopkins landed in the Russian capital on July 30 and found the Soviet leader willing to give him a candid assessment of the military situation. "Stalin said that he believed it was inevitable that we should finally come to grips with Hitler on some battlefield," Hopkins reported to Roosevelt. "The might of Germany was so great that, even though Russia might defend herself, it would be very difficult for Britain and Russia combined to crush the German military machine." Hopkins also reported that Stalin "asked me to tell the President that, while he was confident that the Russian army could withstand the German army, the problem of supply by next spring would be a serious one and that he needed our help."[45] Thus, the Hopkins mission to Moscow both confirmed the analysis advanced by Davies and strengthened Roosevelt in his determination to speed the shipment of vital war materials to the Soviet Union.

But the president had to overcome strong domestic opposition, particularly from Roman Catholics, to the extension of Lend-Lease aid to Russia. The Catholic hierarchy in America continued to stand on the papal encyclical *Divini Redemptoris*, which defined communism as intrinsically wrong and forbade any collaboration with the godless philosophy. Roosevelt approached the problem in two ways. First, he had Myron C. Taylor, his personal representative to the Vatican, return to Rome where on September 9 he urged the Pope to intrepret the encyclical of Pius XI in a way that would allow American Catholics to support a program of aid for Russia in good conscience. The Holy Father promptly sent the Apostolic Delegate in Washington a statement which argued that the troublesome encyclical was not intended to condemn the Russian people. Second, Roosevelt suggested to the Soviet ambassador that Moscow should "get some publicity back to this country regarding the freedom of religion." The Kremlin complied, and on October 4 the Soviet press chief released a public statement which asserted that freedom of worship existed in Russia. A month later, Roosevelt announced that he would make Lend-Lease aid available to the Soviet Union.[46]

President Roosevelt also succeeded in overcoming domestic opposition to measures that inevitably led to an undeclared naval war in the Atlantic. Admiral Stark urged Roosevelt on June 24 to introduce a convoy escorting system which "would almost certainly involve us in war."[47] But the president still hesitated to take actions that he feared would provoke a hostile public reaction. Instead, Roosevelt decided to send a task force of marines to occupy Iceland. He told Lord Halifax, the British ambassador in Washington, confidentially that "the whole thing would now boil up very quickly and that there would soon be shooting."[48] Secretary of War Stimson then proposed that Roosevelt should tell the country the whole truth: that American troops were going to Iceland to protect the supply routes to Britain; and that the United States might have to resort to armed force to assure the defeat of Germany. In an address to Congress on July 7, however, the president portrayed the occupation of Iceland as a defensive measure which was designed primarily to protect the Western Hemisphere from an eventual Nazi invasion. The message was well received.[49] "I think," Thomas Lamont wrote a friend in England on July 9, "Mr. Roosevelt is moving just about as rapidly as he can considering the fact that he must keep a united country and a not too divided Congress."[50]

But Stimson criticized President Roosevelt for circumventing the constitutional prerogative of Congress to declare war. Stimson believed that it was imperative for Roosevelt to obtain authority from Congress before getting the country into war with Germany. "This was in my opinion," he told Hopkins on July 9, "a grave question of constitutional relations between the President and the Congress—a relation which went to the very fundamentals of free government."[51] Hopkins agreed.

Nevertheless, Roosevelt continued to pursue a devious course, and on July 25 he had Admiral Stark order the Atlantic fleet to escort American convoys proceeding to Iceland. Stark thought that the directive to destroy any naval forces which threatened American and Icelandic shipping might provoke an incident that would justify a declaration of war against Germany.[52] Stimson was distressed. He likened the situation to the period between the inauguration of Abraham Lincoln and the attack on Fort Sumter, when there had been considerable "pulling back and forth, trying to make the Confederates fire the first shot."[53]

President Roosevelt was wrestling with a difficult dilemma. The British and Russians, he feared, would not be able to prevent Hitler and his Axis associates from partitioning the planet into closed economic blocs. Convinced that capitalism could not exist in isolation, Roosevelt and his intimate advisers concluded that the United States should enter the war. But the president had to face the fact that the overwhelming majority of Americans did not want to become involved in military operations on the European continent. Rather than acting in the fashion of a bold lion and openly debating the issue, Roosevelt behaved like a sly fox and attempted to manipulate public opinion. He repeatedly promised to preserve peace for the United States while he steadily maneuvered the country in the direction of war. In so doing, Roosevelt put his determination to make the world safe for free enterprise over and above his commitment to the democratic political process.

But the maneuvers of the president did not fool everyone.

Roosevelt had authorized the War Department on June 21 to propose an amendment to the Selective Service Act extending the period of conscription beyond the current one-year limit and removing the prohibition against the use of draftees outside the Western Hemisphere. The suggestion stirred a great protest throughout the country. General Marshall tried to calm the storm by denying that the Roosevelt administration had any plans for sending an American Expeditionary Force to Europe. Still, the opposition persisted, and finally Roosevelt decided to drop the recommendation to lift the ban on using conscripts beyond the confines of the Western Hemisphere. Then, after a heated debate ending on August 12, Congress passed a bill which added eighteen months to the length of service for draftees. But the incredibly close contest in the House of Representatives, with 203 votes for and 202 votes against the measure, revealed that many legislators deeply distrusted the president.[54] "Undoubtedly," Representative Roy C. Woodruff charged, "he will continue to prod and jab the Axis powers in the hope that they will commit some overt act which will enable him to find at least what appears to be a plausible excuse for going to war."[55]

Roosevelt had already informed Prime Minister Winston Churchill that he was going to expand the naval patrol to cover British as well as American merchant ships along the route to Iceland. The prime minister was happy to report to his War Cabinet on August 19 that the American escort system would be in full operation by the end of the month. "The President had said that he would wage war but not declare it, and that he would become more and more provocative," Churchill explained. "The President's orders to these escorts were to attack any U-boat which showed itself, even if it were two hundred or three hundred miles away from the convoy." Churchill noted that Hitler would be confronted with the choice of either attacking the convoys and clashing with the American naval forces or holding off and thus losing the Battle of the Atlantic. "Everything was to be done to force 'an incident,' " Churchill emphasized, adding that Roosevelt had "made it clear that he would look for an 'incident' which would justify him in opening hostilities."[56]

But Hitler had no intention of giving Roosevelt an excuse to lead the American people into the European war. Despite repeated pleas from Admiral Raeder for permission to go all out to stop the flow of Lend-Lease supplies to England, the führer refused to allow the German navy to attack American convoys crossing the Atlantic. "Under no circumstances," Raeder noted in his diary on May 22, "does he wish to cause incidents which would result in U.S. entry into the war." After the Russian campaign began a month later, Hitler was even more determined to avoid any naval skirmishes with the United States. He hoped that Japan would attack Russia from the rear and that the quick defeat of the Soviet Union would reduce the chance of American intervention. "America will have less inclination to enter the war," Hitler reasoned, "due to the threat from Japan which would then increase." Meanwhile, he wanted his submarine commanders in the Atlantic to steer clear of any incidents which might unite the American people behind a call to arms. And on July 19, the führer issued special orders against attacking, "in the extended zone of operations, U.S. merchant ships, whether single or sailing in English or American convoys."[57]

President Roosevelt was therefore pleased to learn later in the summer that the American destroyer *Greer* had exchanged shots with a German submarine. Captain John R. Beardall, the White House naval aide, provided Roosevelt with a full account of the episode, which occurred on September 4 in the vicinity of Iceland. After having received information from a British patrol plane about the location of a submerged U-boat, the *Greer* began trailing the German submarine and broadcasting its position to the pursuing aircraft. The British plane thereupon dropped four depth charges without effect and then returned to base. But the American destroyer continued the chase, and after two hours the harassed submarine launched three torpedoes, which missed their mark. The *Greer* countered by dropping eight depth charges with no apparent effect and then lost contact with the U-boat through its sound gear. "Submarine was not seen by *Greer*," the navy report concluded, "hence there is no positive evidence that the submarine knew nationality of ship at which it was firing."[58]

Nevertheless, the president seized upon the opportunity to describe the incident as an unprovoked and deliberate assault against the United States. In a national radio address delivered on September 11, Roosevelt claimed that the attack on the *Greer* was part of a concentrated Nazi plan to secure control of the oceans as a prelude to domination of the whole world. "We have sought no shooting war with Hitler," the president insisted. "But when you see a rattlesnake poised to strike, you do not wait until he has struck before you crush him." Then Roosevelt announced that the American navy would henceforth protect all merchant ships, regardless of their flag, which were engaged in commerce in the North Atlantic. "From now on," he declared, "if German or Italian vessels of war enter the waters, the protection of which is necessary for American defense, they do so at their own peril." Two days later, the Atlantic fleet received official orders to shoot on sight any Axis warship operating in the American patrol area. "So far as the Atlantic is concerned," Admiral Stark informed the commander of the Asiatic fleet on September 22, "we are all but, if not actually, in it."[59]

President Roosevelt had already decided that it was time for the United States to prepare the general outlines of a Victory Program. Roosevelt asked the secretaries of war and navy on July 9 to explore at once "the overall production requirements required to defeat our potential enemies." The president acknowledged that it would be necessary for them to make "appropriate assumptions as to our probable friends and enemies and to the conceivable theatres of operation which will be required."[60] Stimson welcomed the directive to make a broad estimate of the manpower and materials that the United States would need to defeat Germany. "It means," he recorded in his diary on August 28, "a strategic plan for the means necessary to produce a successful termination of the war against Hitler."[61] But he warned Roosevelt on the next day that the industrial mobilization program would be delayed as long as the American people still hoped to remain at peace. Thus, Stimson argued that the United States should immediately enter the conflict "so as to get the benefit of the speed which could be obtained by a war psychosis."[62]

On September 11, the Joint Planning Committee of the Army and Navy submitted to General Marshall and Admiral Stark the strategic estimate requested by the president to provide the basis for military production. "It is the opinion of the Joint Board," the report asserted, "that Germany and her European satellites can not be defeated by the European Powers now fighting against her. Therefore, if our European enemies are to be defeated, it will be necessary for the United States to enter the war." The Joint Board believed that the complete military defeat of Germany should be the first major objective of the United States and its associates. "If Germany were defeated, her entire European system would collapse, and it is probable that Japan could be forced to give up much of her territorial gains," the report continued. "The principal strategic method employed by the United States in the immediate future should be the material support of present military operations against Germany, and their reinforcement by active participation in the war by the United States, while holding Japan in check pending future developments." The Joint Board had absolutely no faith in the British idea that Germany could be vanquished by aerial bombardment. "It should be recognized as an almost invariable rule," the report concluded, "that only land armies can finally win wars."[63]

Chief of Staff Marshall and Chief of Naval Operations Stark reinforced the Joint Board estimate with their own personal views. "Our broad strategic concept of encircling Germany and closing in on her step by step is the only practical way of wearing down her war potential by military and economic pressure," Marshall wrote Roosevelt on September 22. "In the final decisive phase we must come to grips with and annihilate the German military machine. Forces deemed necessary at this time to accomplish role of ground units in supreme effort to defeat Germany comprise five field armies of about 215 divisions."[64] In a similar memorandum sent to Cordell Hull on October 8, Stark advocated an immediate declaration of war against Germany even if such action provoked Japan to join in hostilities against the United States. "It has long been my opinion that Germany cannot be defeated unless the United States is wholeheartedly in the war and makes a strong military and naval effort wherever strategy dictates," Stark wrote. "It would be very desirable to enter the war under circumstances in which Germany were the aggressor and in which case Japan might then be able to remain neutral. However, on the whole, it is my opinion that the United States should enter the war against Germany as soon as possible, even if hostilities with Japan must be accepted." Stark added in a postscript that he did not believe Germany would declare war on America until Hitler had calculated that it would be advantageous to do so. "He has every excuse in the world to declare war on us now," Stark concluded. "When he is ready, he will strike, and not before."[65]

But President Roosevelt still did not believe that either Congress or the American people would support a forthright declaration of war against Germany. "As you know," he confided to Canadian Prime Minister Mackenzie King on September 27, "I have to watch this Congress and public opinion like a hawk and actual events on the ocean, together with my constant reiteration of freedom of the seas, are increasing our armed help all the time."[66] Roosevelt was equally candid in private conversations with Lord Halifax. "He said that if he asked for a declaration of war he wouldn't get it and opinion would swing against him," Ambassador Halifax reported to Churchill on October 10. "He therefore intended to go on doing whatever he best could to help us, and declarations of war were, he said, out of fashion." Halifax also informed Churchill that he had urged Roosevelt to tell "the country straight out what he wanted."[67] But others, like Thomas Lamont, believed that the president was proceeding as fast as he could. "Mr. Roosevelt," Lamont wrote General Jan C. Smuts of South Africa on October 10, "has brought the country along step by step in a masterly way."[68]

Business internationalists throughout the United States closed ranks behind the president. "All I want to do is see Hitler licked," Lamont wrote John Foster Dulles on October 8, "and anything in the world that I can contribute to that end in thought, word, or deed I am ready to turn in."[69] The speakers at the National Foreign Trade Convention, held in New York between October 6 and 8, gave vent to the same basic feeling. "The tremendous power of the Nazi-dominated and regimented economy in the field of foreign trade," Winthrop W. Aldrich warned those attending the meeting, "would make it necessary for our own government to regiment our own foreign commerce." W. Randolph Burgess of the National City Bank similarly noted that the United States had joined Great Britain in the battle against Hitler so that "his conception of foreign trade does not become dominant on this planet." Joseph C. Rovensky, an aide to Nelson A. Rockefeller, agreed. "We are committed to the fight for freedom of economic life and for freedom of the seas," Rovensky proclaimed, "in a word, the fight for a free world." The Final Declaration, expressing the militant mood which prevailed at the convention, gave the "fullest support to the government's policy of naval, military and economic defense."[70]

President Roosevelt, encouraged by widespread support from big business, continued to maneuver the country steadily down the road to war. On October 9, he asked Congress to repeal the provision in the Neutrality Act which prohibited the arming of American merchant ships. While the House of Representatives was debating the question, a German submarine torpedoed the American destroyer *Kearny*, which had gone to the aid of a convoy under attack about four hundred miles south of Iceland. The *Kearny* had, in fact, dropped several depth charges before being struck by a German torpedo. Yet Roosevelt, in a Navy Day address on October 27, made the most of the incident. "We have wished to avoid shooting," he declared. "But the shooting has started. And history has recorded who fired the first shot." Roosevelt also professed that he had in his possession a secret map showing how the Nazis planned to divide Latin America into five vassal states. But the document was never made public, and Roosevelt lost some credibility. News that German submarines had actually sunk the American destroyer *Reuben James* on October 31 failed to dispel charges that the president was deceiving the people. A week later, however, Roosevelt narrowly succeeded in getting Congress to repeal both the ban on arming American merchant ships and the provision in the Neutrality Act which prohibited them from entering war zones.[71]

The hawks in the Roosevelt administration applauded this escalation in the undeclared war with Germany. Now that armed American merchantmen could for the first time carry Lend-Lease supplies all the way across the ocean to ports in England, Hitler would either have to unleash Admiral Raeder or lose the Battle of the Atlantic. A formal declaration of war seemed inevitable when on November 1 Roosevelt confided to Admiral William D. Leahy that he would never "join in any effort to bring about a negotiated peace with Nazism."[72] A week later, Harry Hopkins wrote an old college classmate that he did not believe that "we can ever lick Hitler with a Lend-Lease Program."[73] Vice-President Henry A. Wallace likewise assumed that the United States would have to fix bayonets in order to assure the defeat of Nazi Germany. "We must mechanize and train to the utmost in mechanized and density of fire terms an army of two million," he insisted on November 21. "The broad outlines must be known so that Don Nelson can allot the scarce raw materials with greater certainty." Wallace therefore recommended that Roosevelt should announce the Victory Program to the country "in a most solemn way on New Year's Eve."[74]

Though he agreed to make a public pronouncement to further the objectives of the Victory Program, the president still hoped to push Hitler into the position of seeming to fire the first shot. Roosevelt continued to look for a dramatic incident in the Atlantic not only to manipulate public opinion at home but also to avert hostilities in the Pacific. "The idea that Hitler is trying to control the seas for the purpose of using them as a pathway to the Americas and that we are placed upon the defensive to prevent him from coming to the Americas and that we are acting against him in a purely defensive way has been the theory which the Secretary has evolved and in which we have concurred," a State Department official noted in his diary on October 29. "Under that theory Hitler cannot point to our policy as a directive to Japan to join him in war against the United States on the theory that Japan is bound to follow Germany if Germany is attacked by the United States."[75] In accepting this procedure, Roosevelt hoped to maneuver the United States into war with Germany through the front door in the Atlantic while keeping Japan from attacking American holdings through the back door in the Pacific.

Roosevelt realized that the German invasion of Russia on June 22 had provided Japan with a golden opportunity to establish suzerainty throughout the Orient. Officials in Tokyo thereupon engaged in fateful debate over whether, where, and when to strike. The Japanese army was bent on obtaining bases in Indo-China even if an advance toward the rich East Indies would mean war with the United States. Foreign Minister Yosuke Matsuoka wanted the warlords to launch an immediate attack against Siberia to protect their northern flank before moving southward. But Premier Fumimaro Konoye still hoped that negotiations with the United States would remove the need for risky military adventures. He wanted to make a bargain to secure American recognition of a Greater East Asia Co-Prosperity Sphere in return for a Japanese promise to remain neutral with regard to the European war. Despite these differences over timing and tactics, a basic consensus existed concerning ultimate imperial objectives. Japanese leaders hoped that a quick Nazi victory over the communist colossus would allow them to consolidate their position in the Pacific while the United States concentrated its attention in the Atlantic.[76]

Nevertheless, some American leaders remained confident that a get-tough policy would deter Japan rather than provoke hostilities in the Far East. "Japan's bark is much bigger than Japan's potential bite," Stanley K. Hornbeck wrote Thomas Lamont on June 25. "If only the United States would get Japan's 'number,' and, having done so, look Japan squarely in the eye and utter a few quiet words, there would be little need to fear that Japan would bite us or even bite our friends."[77] Lamont concurred. "In what you say in regard to Japan's real capacity in raising cain," he replied, "I am in hearty accord. I myself think they would curl up."[78] So did Interior Secretary Harold L. Ickes. He had been advocating the imposition of a complete oil embargo against Japan for more than a year, and the strategic implications of the German invasion of Russia did nothing to change his mind. As the petroleum coordinator for national defense, Ickes wanted to suspend the issuance of all licenses for the export of oil to Japan.[79]

But President Roosevelt refused to permit him to put an immediate halt on petroleum shipments to Japan. "Please let me know," Roosevelt wrote Ickes on June 23, "if this would continue to be your judgment if this were to tip the delicate scales and cause Japan to decide either to attack Russia or to attack the Dutch East Indies."[80] An aggrieved Ickes offered to resign, but the president stood his ground. "I think it will interest you to know," Roosevelt lectured Ickes on July 1, "that the Japs are having a real drag-down and knock-out fight among themselves and have been for the past week—trying to decide which way they are going to jump—attack Russia, attack the South Seas (thus throwing their lot definitely with Germany) or whether they will sit on the fence and be more friendly with us. No one knows what the decision will be but, as you know, it is terribly important for the control of the Atlantic for us to keep peace in the Pacific. I simply have not got enough Navy to go round—and every little episode in the Pacific means fewer ships in the Atlantic."[81]

Japanese rulers did not take long in making their crucial decision. The Tokyo government concluded on July 2 that it would pursue an imperial policy aimed at establishing hegemony in the Far East no matter what obstacles it might encounter. The Japanese Privy Council thereupon approved a program which advocated not only continued diplomatic negotiations with Washington but also a push southward even at the risk of war with the United States. Several months before, American cryptographers had succeeded in breaking the secret Japanese diplomatic code by means of an electronic device known as MAGIC. American officials were therefore able to read deciphered messages which regularly passed between Tokyo and its overseas embassies, including those in Washington, Rome, and Berlin. When Roosevelt learned through MAGIC intercepts that the Japanese were determined to advance into Indo-China, he began contemplating the imposition of additional economic sanctions on Tokyo. Sumner Welles informed the British ambassador on July 10 that the president had authorized him to say that if "Japan took any overt step through the exercise of pressure or force to acquire or conquer territories of other nations in the Far East, the Government of the United States would immediately impose various embargoes."[82]

Japan moved quickly to obtain military sites in French Indo-China which could be used as staging grounds for eventual attacks against both British Malaya and the Dutch East Indies. Tokyo sent a message on July 12 instructing Sotomatsu Kato, the Japanese ambassador at Vichy, to demand the right to occupy eight airfields in southern Indo-China and to use the naval bases at Saigon and Camranh Bay. Kato was to warn the French government that if consent were not given by July 20, Japanese forces would seize the bases without delay. Intercepts from MAGIC provided officials in Washington with detailed information about the Japanese demands, and the whole situation was reviewed on July 18 during a Cabinet meeting. American policymakers favored some kind of action against Japan if France acquiesced, but the Cabinet discussion produced different opinions as to just how far the United States should go.[83] President Roosevelt wanted to proceed with caution. He explained that he was against a complete American oil embargo because "it would simply drive the Japanese down to the Dutch East Indies, and it would mean war in the Pacific."[84]

News that France had submitted to the Japanese demands prompted renewed discussions about the kind of countermeasures which should be taken by the United States. During a Cabinet meeting on July 24, the president ruled in favor of freezing Japanese funds in the United States, but he left open for future determination the core question: whether the Treasury Department should be lenient or severe in issuing licenses to permit Japan to draw on the frozen dollar balances to pay for American oil. Roosevelt said that he did not think that the contemplated measure would spur Japan to move against the East Indies to secure a dependable fuel supply. The president explained that he was "inclined to go ahead with the order in the regular way and grant licenses for the shipment of petroleum as the applications are presented to the Treasury." But he added that the policy "might change any day and from there on we would refuse any and all licenses."[85] When Roosevelt signed the freezing order on July 26, he did not intend to strangle

Japan. "He thought that it might be better to slip the noose around Japan's neck," Harold Ickes observed, "and give it a jerk now and then."[86]

But the rope around Japan's neck was soon drawn tight. "I think we need to keep a stiff rein," Cordell Hull advised on July 29, "and consider making it just as stiff as possible short of actual military activity."[87] Two days later, President Roosevelt approved a licensing policy which would prevent the Japanese from purchasing any more crude oil and low grade gasoline than they had bought from the United States during what was considered a normal period in the past. But Roosevelt soon became even more hostile, and no licenses allowing Japan to obtain American petroleum products were issued. Within a week after the American freezing order, moreover, the British placed strict controls on all funds which the Japanese might use to purchase goods from anywhere within the vast imperial preference area. The Dutch likewise decided to require special permits for all exports to Japan from their East Indian possessions. Time was running out for the Japanese. If the oil embargo continued, their fuel reserves would be used up within two years. Thus, Foreign Minister Teijiro Toyoda concluded on July 31 that Japan "must take immediate steps to break assunder this ever-strengthening chain of encirclement."[88]

News that Japan was already preparing for full-scale economic warfare with the western powers created a stir in the American diplomatic community. When Tokyo announced on July 28 the freezing of American, British, and Dutch assets in Japan, Ambassador Grew feared that his efforts to maintain peace in the Pacific were doomed to fail. "The vicious circle of reprisals and counter reprisals is on," Grew lamented. "Unless radical surprises occur in the world, it is difficult to see how the momentum of this downgrade movement in our relations can be arrested, nor how far it will go. The obvious conclusion is eventual war." Secretary of State Hull was also beginning to lose faith in his ability to avert a military clash through negotiations with Ambassador Kichisaburo Nomura. But he still hoped to buy time before the ultimate showdown with the Japanese. "Nothing will stop them except force," Hull advised on August 2. "The point is how long we can maneuver the situation until the military matter in Europe is brought to a conclusion."[89]

Meanwhile, after several conferences between civilian and military authorities, the Japanese decided to pursue conversations in Washington looking toward a general settlement which would leave them free to complete their imperial program in the Far East. Ambassador Nomura called upon Hull on August 6 and presented a new set of proposals. The Japanese would promise not to station any more troops in the Southwest Pacific and to remove their soldiers from Indo-China after settling the war in China. In return, the United States was to suspend all military preparations in the Southwest Pacific, restore normal trade relations with Japan, help the Japanese obtain raw materials from the East Indies, use its good offices to get Chiang Kai-shek to make peace with Japan, and recognize that the Japanese were entitled to a special position in Indo-China even after the withdrawal of their forces. But Hull responded with little enthusiasm. When Ambassador Nomura called again on August 8 and proposed a personal conference between President Roosevelt and Premier Konoye, Hull replied that a final decision regarding a summit meeting could not be made until the president returned from the Atlantic Conference.[90]

The Far Eastern situation was high on the agenda during the Anglo-American talks held between August 9 and 12 off the Newfoundland coast. Sumner Welles explained to British officials that the American government desired to exploit the unacceptable Japanese proposals as a means of protracting conversations in Washington in order to put off a showdown with Tokyo. Welles pointed out that "in the opinion of both the War and Navy Departments of the United States the chief objective in the Pacific for the time being should be the avoidance of war with Japan inasmuch as war between the United States and Japan at this time would not only tie up the major portion of if not the entire American fleet but would likewise create a very serious strain upon our military establishment and upon our productive activities at the very moment when these should be concentrated upon the Atlantic."[91] President Roosevelt reiterated to Prime Minister Churchill that the United

States aimed to resume discussions with Japan in an effort to gain time. "If Russia bogs down the Germans, Japan won't move at all," he reasoned. "If Germany defeats Russia, then we shall have trouble in the Far East."[92] Roosevelt concluded that if negotiations were prolonged, "any further move of aggression on the part of Japan which might result in war could be held off for at least thirty days."[93]

The president returned to Washington on August 17, and on the afternoon of that day he and Hull received Ambassador Nomura at the White House. Roosevelt first warned Nomura that the United States would be compelled to safeguard its interests if Japan made further advances in Southeast Asia. He then emphasized that the United States would like to reach a general settlement if the Japanese were prepared to suspend their expansionist activities and embrace liberal trade principles. After indicating that Hull was ready to resume informal exploratory discussions with the ambassador, Roosevelt said that he would be glad to arrange a personal meeting between himself and Premier Konoye.[94] On the next day, Roosevelt gave Lord Halifax the gist of his talk with Nomura, and the British embassy promptly alerted London. But the British Foreign Office was not about to challenge American leadership. "We cannot prevent the negotiations from proceeding or the meeting from taking place," the Far Eastern Department concluded on August 25, "and we must put the best face on it that we can." Alexander Cadogan, the permanent under secretary, concurred. While Great Britain might have reservations, he observed, "in all this it is the United States that calls the tune."[95]

Tokyo instructed Nomura, in the meantime, to reiterate to officials in Washington that Konoye was eager to begin discussions with the president. When the ambassador raised the subject on August 28, Roosevelt conveyed the impression that he was looking forward to a conference with the Japanese premier. But Hull was firmly opposed to any meeting between the two heads of state prior to an agreement on fundamental issues. Hull told Nomura that the Japanese authorities would have to indicate in advance their intention to withdraw from close association with the Axis powers, to remove their troops from China, and to adhere to liberal commercial principles. Nomura replied that he "could not conceive of his people being prepared to go to war with the United States for the sake of Germany," but that the American insistence that the Japanese army evacuate from China might cause trouble. Hull then remarked that American officials would not mediate between Tokyo and Chungking unless they knew the terms to be offered Chiang Kai-shek.[96] Nomura was dismayed. "The United States Government," he cabled Tokyo on August 29, "is unwilling to seek adjustments in Japanese-American relations at the expense of existing American-Chinese relations."[97]

The United States and Imperial Japan were on a collision course. Despite his initial enthusiasm for a meeting with Konoye, Roosevelt quickly veered toward Hull's position, and on September 3 he told Nomura that an agreement on general principles must precede a conference aimed at adjusting specific issues. But time was running out for the Land of the Rising Sun. The Japanese army would not tolerate a long delay in negotiations, because military operations would be difficult after the start of the winter monsoons and because their oil reserves would decline with the passing of each day. As the clock continued ticking, Japan faced the mounting threat of economic strangulation and the increasing deployment of American naval and air forces in the Far East. There remained but two alternatives. The Japanese would either have to conclude a general settlement with the United States or prepare for a military confrontation in the Pacific.[98]

The Japanese High Command decided that it was time to force the issue with the United States. An Imperial Conference on September 6 concluded that if by early October Japanese diplomats failed to achieve their minimum demands through negotiations in Washington, the Japanese military must be ready for war. The terms outlined in Tokyo called upon the United States to cease all aid to China while the Japanese would remain free to impose their will on Chungking. But the State Department continued to play for time. The Far Eastern Division hoped that if the Russians were able to maintain their resistance against the German onslaught, the Japanese might yet be induced to back down. After stalling for several weeks, Hull informed Nomura on October 2 that Roosevelt would not meet with Konoye unless the Japanese first agreed to abandon their quest for a self-sufficient empire in the Orient. The hope for a summit conference was dead. Konoye therefore resigned from the Cabinet on October 16, and the Japanese emperor asked War Minister Hideki Tojo to head a new government.[99]

The Tojo Cabinet, prompted by the wishes of the emperor and the navy, reviewed the earlier resolution in favor of war. After a few weeks of debate, Japanese authorities decided that a final set of proposals should be submitted for American consideration. An Imperial Conference on November 5 concluded that if by November 25 no accord had been reached with the United States, the final decision to go to war would be placed before the emperor. The military forces were to be ready to fight by the beginning of December. The operational orders, issued on November 5, included Admiral Isoroku Yamamoto's plan to attack the American fleet at Pearl Harbor. MAGIC intercepts of messages from Foreign Minister Shigenori Togo to Ambassador Nomura indicated to American officials that the Japanese regarded the continuation of parleys in Washington as their final effort to reach an agreement with the United States. "Both in name and in spirit," Togo cabled Nomura, "this counterproposal of ours is, indeed, the last."[100]

The Roosevelt administration, however, hoped to gain more time in order to strengthen American air power in the Philippines. The success of American Flying Fortresses used by the British in bombing raids against Germany gave rise to the idea that the United States might soon be in a position to compel the Japanese to abandon their imperial program.[101] Consequently, Secretary of War Stimson urged Hull on October 6 to string out his talks with Nomura because the army needed three months to reinforce Manila with B-17 bombers capable of blockading the South China Sea.[102] "A strategic opportunity of the utmost importance has suddenly arisen in the southwestern Pacific," Stimson wrote Roosevelt on October 21. "We are rushing planes and other preparations to the Philippines." This action, he continued, "bids fair to stop Japan's march to the south."[103] A week later, Stimson told Hull that the rapid deployment of heavy bombers in Manila might strengthen "his diplomatic arm in forcing the Japanese to keep away from Singapore and perhaps, if we are in good luck, to shake the Japanese out of the Axis."[104]

The Joint Board of the Army and Navy, in a memorandum presented to President Roosevelt on November 5, endorsed the strategy of delayed showdown. "The United States Army Air Forces in the Philippines will have reached their projected strength by February or March 1942," the military planners calculated. "The potency of this threat will have then increased to a point where it might well be a deciding factor in deterring Japan in operations in the area south and west of the Philippines." The Joint Board therefore argued that "war between the United States and Japan should be avoided while building up defense forces in the Far East." But the war planners did recommend that military operations should be undertaken if the Japanese either directly attacked American, British, or Dutch possessions or moved their forces beyond a certain line in Thailand.[105] Two days later, the Cabinet approved the policy of continuing the talks with Japan while completing military preparations in Manila. The Cabinet also decided that government officials should try to prepare the American people for a declaration of war in the event that Japan attacked British Malaya or the Netherlands East Indies.[106]

On that very evening, Nomura presented Hull with proposals concerning the deployment of Japanese troops and the principle of nondiscriminatory trade. Hull was cordial but noncommittal. Then Roosevelt received Nomura at the White House on November 10 and told the ambassador that the Japanese should prove that their intentions were peaceful by withdrawing their military forces from Indo-China. A few days later, Hull informed Nomura that Japanese formulas regarding both their adherence to liberal commercial principles and their commitment to their Axis partners were inadequate. Nomura immediately reported home his belief that the United States would rather fight than abandon China for the sake of Japan. But Tokyo ordered the ambassador to make one final effort to avoid a military confrontation with the United States. Acting on his instructions, Nomura called upon Hull on

November 20 and proposed a temporary truce which would leave Japan free to impose terms on the Nationalist government in China.[107]

Though Roosevelt and Hull agreed that the Japanese offer was unacceptable, they decided to advance a counterproposal for a three-month *modus vivendi* designed to postpone a violent explosion without abandoning American interests in China. Encouraged by the Russian resistance against Germany, they hoped to gain more time to send Flying Fortresses to the Philippines and to work out a permanent accord with Japan.[108] But their enthusiasm was dampened by a telegram from Tokyo, deciphered by MAGIC on November 22, indicating that Nomura had just one more week to resolve the crisis with the United States in a peaceful manner. "After that," the cable explained, "things are automatically going to happen." Although pessimism pervaded the White House, Roosevelt decided to move fast before the Japanese deadline arrived. The president informed Churchill on November 24 that the United States intended to offer Japan a monthly quota of oil for civilian needs and a limited amount of a few other supplies in return for a Japanese promise not to advance either northward or southward. "I am not very hopeful," he concluded, "and we must be prepared for real trouble, possibly soon."[109]

President Roosevelt met with his top advisers at noon on the next day to discuss relations with Japan. Roosevelt observed that the Japanese were notorious for making surprise attacks and that they might strike without warning in the near future. He then asked what the United States should do. "The question was how we should maneuver them into the position of firing the first shot without allowing too much danger to ourselves," Stimson recorded in his dairy. "It was a difficult proposition."[110] The problem seemed difficult because American leaders believed that the Japanese would be much more likely to attack Thailand, Malaysia, or the Dutch Indies than the Philippines or Hawaii. Hull was therefore assigned the task of drafting a message designed to justify American military intervention if the Japanese confined their anticipated operations to non-American territory. Admiral Stark was left with the job of warning the commanders of the Pacific fleet to be on guard for a surprise attack. Though the chances of reaching an agreement with Japan seemed slight, American officials still hoped to arrange a temporary truce in the Far East.[111]

The British and the Chinese, however, reacted negatively to the American *modus vivendi* proposal. Chiang Kai-shek feared that the United States was inclined to appease Japan at the expense of China and that Tokyo was poised for an attack on Chungking. The generalissimo warned Washington on November 25 that the Chinese resistance would collapse if the United States relaxed the economic embargo against the Japanese while their armies remained in China. On the same day, the British ambassador handed Hull a message from Foreign Secretary Anthony Eden. Although he expressed willingness to leave the decision to Washington, Eden suggested that the United States should pitch its demands high and its price low. Prime Minister Churchill followed this message up with a direct telegram to the White House. "Of course, it is for you to handle this business and we certainly do not want an additional war," he cabled Roosevelt. "There is only one point that disquiets us. What about Chiang Kai-shek? Is he not having a very thin diet? Our anxiety is about China. If they collapse, our joint dangers would enormously increase."[112]

Roosevelt and Hull thereupon decided to scrap the *modus vivendi* project and instead advanced a comprehensive proposal for a general settlement with Japan. Hull summoned Nomura on November 26 and presented him with a ten-point program which called upon the Japanese to abandon their plans for a New Order in East Asia. The proffered terms, which provided for the withdrawal of the Japanese forces from China and Indo-China, were submitted for the record. Assuming that Tokyo would reject the uncompromising proposal and break off relations with the United States, Hull told Stimson on November 27 that he had washed his hands of the whole matter and that the Far Eastern problem was now in the hands of the army and navy. Admiral Stark immediately alerted the commanders of the Asiatic and Pacific fleets. "Negotiations with Japan looking toward stabilization of conditions in the Pacific have ceased," he warned, "and aggressive move by Japan is expected within the next few days." General Marshall issued a similar warning to General Douglas MacArthur in the Philippines. "If hostilities cannot, repeat cannot, be avoided," Marshall cabled, "the United States desires that Japan commit the first overt act."[113]

Intelligence reports that a large Japanese task force was steaming southward along the China coast heightened American anxiety about the probability of a sudden attack against Thailand. Roosevelt and his principal advisers met on November 28 and decided that the Japanese expeditionary force must not be allowed to get around the southern point of Indo-China and land in the Gulf of Siam. "It was agreed that if the Japanese got into the Isthmus of Kia the British would fight," Stimson recorded in his diary. "It was also agreed that if the British fought, we would have to fight." During a conversation with Ambassador Halifax three days later, Roosevelt remarked that in case of a direct Japanese attack on British or Dutch possessions "we should obviously be all together." Halifax inquired on December 4 to find out what the president had in mind when he said that the British could count on American support in the event of a Japanese attack. Roosevelt replied that he meant "armed" support and that the United States would help Great Britain resist a Japanese invasion of Thailand.[114]

Information that Japanese troop convoys were rounding Cape Cambodia and entering the Gulf of Siam stirred President Roosevelt into action. On Saturday evening, December 6, he sent a direct message to the emperor of Japan warning that he was sitting on a keg of dynamite and urging that he do something to prevent an explosion. Roosevelt decided that he would address Congress if the emperor did not reply within two days. He hoped to convince Congress and the American people that a Japanese attack against Thailand, Malaysia, or the Indies would require military counteraction by the United States. His aides were drafting the proposed speech on Sunday morning, December 7, when they learned through MAGIC intercepts that the Japanese were about to break diplomatic relations. Hull told Stimson and Knox that the Japanese were undoubtedly "planning some deviltry," and all three were "wondering where the blow will strike."[115]

That afternoon, word came that Japan had struck at Pearl Harbor. "My God, this can't be true," Knox exclaimed. "They must mean the Philippines!" Stimson asked Roosevelt if he meant Southeast Asia when he reported the attack. "Southeast Asia, hell," the President shot back. "Pearl Harbor!"[116]

Roosevelt and his aides, though surprised, were relieved by the air raid on Pearl Harbor. Eleanor Roosevelt recalled that on the day of the Japanese attack "Franklin was in a way more serene than he had appeared in a long time."[117] Members of his inner circle were equally calm. "When the news first came that Japan had attacked us," Stimson recorded in his diary on December 7, "my first feeling was of relief that the indecision was over and that a crisis had come in a way which would unite all our people. This continued to be my dominant feeling in spite of the news of the catastrophies which quickly developed."[118] On that afternoon, Roosevelt summoned Hull, Stimson, Knox, Stark, and Marshall to the White House. "The conference met in not too tense an atmosphere," Harry Hopkins recorded after he went upstairs to bed, "because I think that all of us believed that in the last analysis the enemy was Hitler and that he could never be defeated without force of arms; that sooner or later we were bound to be in the war and that Japan had given us an opportunity."[119]

President Roosevelt and his advisers, however, debated whether or not the United States should declare war on Germany and Japan at the same time. After a Cabinet meeting on Sunday evening, December 7, Stimson urged the president to ask Congress for "a declaration of war against Germany before the indignation of the people was over." Roosevelt replied that he intended to address that issue two days later. Meanwhile, on Monday afternoon, December 8, the president asked Congress to declare war on Japan, and both houses immediately complied with only one dissenting vote. A message from Berlin to Tokyo, intercepted by MAGIC on the same day, indicated that Germany and Italy would fall in line with Japan. Roosevelt therefore decided that from the standpoint of public opinion in the United States, he should wait for Hitler and Mussolini to take the initiative. They were not slow to oblige. On Thursday, December 11, Germany and Italy declared war on the United States, and on the same day the United States reciprocated.[120]

Roosevelt Confronts Hitler

The devastating attack against Pearl Harbor produced a dramatic change in public opinion in the United States. Dissent immediately dissipated, and Americans united in support of the Victory Program. Industrial establishments all across the country converted their machinery to produce an awesome array of military equipment, while young men and boys rushed to induction centers to enlist in the armed services. The president had finally escaped from the horns of his dilemma. Unencumbered by the problem of having to counter a widespread antiwar movement, Roosevelt was now free to confront Hitler and his Axis associates with the full weight of American military power.

eight

The Dream of a Pax Americana

LONG BEFORE the United States formally entered the Second World War, American leaders had begun thinking about the kind of international order they hoped would emerge after hostilities ceased. Government officials and corporate executives looked forward to the establishment of a liberal capitalist world system based upon the institution of private property and the principle of equal commercial opportunity. During the hiatus in European military operations following the defeat of Poland in September 1939, President Roosevelt and his State Department advisers had attempted to sponsor a peace settlement that would be favorable to American economic interests and ideological persuasions. But after the fall of France in June 1940, American policymakers gradually concluded that the United States would have to intervene in the conflict in order to determine the nature of the postwar world.

President Roosevelt and his associates in the business community hoped that the principles underlying the reciprocal trade agreements program would provide the cornerstone for a peaceful and prosperous world in the postwar era. In his annual message to Congress in January 1940, two years before the United States officially entered the war, Roosevelt had insisted that the reciprocal trade statute must not be allowed to expire in the spring. "The Trade Agreements Act should be extended as an indispensable part of the foundation of any stable and durable peace," he declared. "And when the time comes, the

United States must use its influence to open up the trade channels of the world in order that no nation need feel compelled in later days to seek by force of arms what it can well gain by peaceful conference."[1] Corporate chiefs such as Thomas J. Watson of International Business Machines likewise hoped that Congress would renew the reciprocal trade measure and thereby provide the economic basis for world peace. "We believe," Watson proclaimed in March 1940, "that the proper amount of goods and services going both ways across the borders of countries will do away with the necessity for soldiers marching across those same borders."[2]

Business internationalists and government authorities also believed that the salvation of capitalism in the United States depended upon the retention of the reciprocal trade legislation. They were determined to open foreign markets for surplus American commodities in order to avoid the need for federal intervention in the economy to keep domestic production in line with home consumption. "The alternative to the present trade agreements program," the Business Advisory Council warned in January 1940, would involve "a greater dependency on self-containment" which would in turn lead to "a degree of regulatory control destructive of free enterprise."[3] Secretary of State Cordell Hull concurred. During his testimony before the Senate Finance Committee in February 1940, Hull argued that the United States should engage in reciprocal trade with other countries rather than embark upon an isolationist policy which would require national economic planning. "The question of the survival or disappearance of free enterprise," he exclaimed, "is bound up with the continuation or abandonment of the trade agreements program."[4]

Spokesmen for American agricultural interests, however, presented a major obstacle to the continuation of the reciprocal trade program. During the public hearings conducted by the Committee on Reciprocity Information in the autumn of 1939, senators and representatives from the cattle-raising states had registered strong opposition to any reduction in the duties on beef imported from Argentina.[5] Protectionist sentiment remained especially strong in the farm belt, and many agrarian leaders wanted to prevent the extension of the Trade Agreements Act in the spring of 1940. They charged that the State Department aimed to lower duties on agricultural imports in order to gain concessions for industrial exports. They also pointed out that the flames of war had engulfed Europe despite American efforts to negotiate reciprocal trade agreements. George N. Peek, for example, never tired of ridiculing Cordell Hull for asserting that his reciprocal trade program would provide a remedy for international conflict. "I expect to hear next that it is a sure cure for leprosy," Peek quipped in November 1939. "One claim is about as valid as the other."[6]

Secretary of Agriculture Henry A. Wallace led the Roosevelt administration's fight to obtain agrarian support for the extension of the Trade Agreements Act. During his testimony before the House Ways and Means Committee in January 1940, he called attention to the fact that farmers in the United States were producing more food than the American people could eat, and he argued that reciprocal trade agreements would open foreign markets for surplus crops while affording American farmers adequate protection in the domestic market. He concluded that Hull's commercial program could be "an extremely important factor in the economic reconstruction of the post-war world."[7] Wallace reiterated this point in a published work. "When peace comes and men are no longer needed in the Army and Navy and in the production of airplanes and munitions," he warned, "we shall face the same old problem of finding markets at home and abroad for our non-military farm and city goods."[8] Though many agrarians remained skeptical of his assurance that the State Department would safeguard their interests, the powerful American Farm Bureau Federation backed the drive to maintain the reciprocal trade program.[9]

President Roosevelt and Secretary Hull were delighted when Congress voted in April 1940 to extend the Trade Agreements Act for another three years. The senior officers in the State Department immediately congratulated their chief for winning "one of the most brilliant and hard-fought victories of his long career."[10] While expressing his gratitude for the renewal of the reciprocal trade program, Hull gave vent to his deep conviction that a revival in international commerce in the postwar period would enhance the prospects for domestic prosperity as well as world peace.[11] The president shared this belief. "Our nation cannot enjoy sustained and satisfactory prosperity," Roosevelt declared in May 1940, "unless adequate foreign markets exist for our exportable surpluses." Nor could future wars be averted, he argued, if the patterns of world trade were to remain artificially diverted. Thus, Roosevelt promised that the advancement of liberal commercial practices would "continue to be a vital part and a dominant purpose of the foreign policy of the United States."[12]

Business internationalists believed that the United States should go further and underwrite the postwar economic reconstruction of Europe. John Abbink, the president of Business Publishers International, argued in March 1940 that Americans would have to extend loans and credits to revive foreign commerce after hostilities ended.[13] Russell C. Leffingwell of the J. P. Morgan Company expressed the same opinion. He thought that the rapid accumulation of gold at Fort Knox would provide the United States with the opportunity to rebuild the international financial structure when peace returned. "We must use the gold," he insisted in April 1940, "to help Europe in particular and the world at large to reestablish a gold exchange standard based upon the dollar."[14] Leffingwell remained convinced that Americans should assume responsibility for postwar economic rehabilitation. "We are going to have to lend money and provide currency and buy goods and services and invest in foreign plants and develop them," he warned in September 1940. "Or, on the other hand, we are going to be subjected after the war to, what seems more terrible than anything that has ever been known, a period of plague, pestilence, unemployment and revolution in Europe, and depression, unemployment and misery here."[15]

President Roosevelt and his State Department advisers were likewise worried about the possibility of a devastating postwar depression. They realized that the New Deal had failed to solve the twin problems of overproduction and unemployment. Although massive military spending was stimulating industrial activity and creating jobs for many who had been without work, it was feared that the country would slip back into a deflationary spiral during the period of demobilization following the war.[16] Under Secretary of State Sumner Welles wrote Roosevelt in March 1940 that the United States, like the European belligerents, would need overseas markets when the time came to convert from military to civilian production. He therefore suggested that colonial areas should be placed under international control in order to give all countries "equality of economic opportunities in non-self-governing territories."[17] The president was also thinking about how the United States could avoid a postwar business slump. During a meeting at the White House in December 1940, Roosevelt explained that he was "determined that there shall be no depression of prices after the war."[18]

Business periodicals clearly defined the two basic paths that the United States could take in attempting to prevent a postwar depression. "Should we try to make a world market for our manufacturing industry through general tariff reductions?" *Business Week* asked in February 1941. "Could we, if necessary, so rearrange the social and economic scheme at home that domestic consumption will absorb the output of our industry?"[19] Remaining true to their commitment to entrepreneurial freedom, business publications throughout the country advocated commercial expansion abroad rather than economic regimentation at home. The editors of *Fortune*, after pointing out that the New Deal had failed to achieve an internal balance between supply and demand, concluded in May 1941 that foreign markets were needed to absorb surplus American products. "The only way mass purchasing power can be effectively increased," the editors insisted, "is by increasing international trade."[20] A writer in *Bankers' Magazine* agreed. "I don't see how America in the forties should go forward better than it did in the last decade," he reasoned in September 1941, "unless you open new unlimited frontiers."[21]

As indicated by these pronouncements, spokesmen for the corporate community favored the restoration of a liberal capitalist international order after the war ended. George N. Peek stood almost alone among business leaders in his lack of enthusiasm for the principles of free trade. "With modern methods of manufacture and given reasonable demand for the product," he wrote Bernard M. Baruch in October 1941, "one

227

country can manufacture its own raw materials about as well as another and so the world is destined to divide itself up into economic areas." Peek did not believe that the United States could do in the future what Great Britain had done in the past. He warned Baruch that one great industrial nation could no longer exercise "its sphere of influence throughout the world, bringing in its raw materials and selling and financing the sale of its products."[22] But the great majority of business spokesmen disagreed. William Diebold of the Council on Foreign Relations articulated the prevailing viewpoint when he argued in June 1941 that the economic interests of the United States demanded "an interchange of goods among all parts of the world according to the comparative advantage of each part in producing certain goods."[23]

But American leaders feared that during the chaotic period following the war a wave of social revolutions might sweep across Europe and shatter their vision of an international capitalist utopia. "Let us assume that the socialist and communist elements in England, France and Germany succeed, as a result of the colossal disaster which the war had brought upon all of Europe, in developing a genuine program for the economic reconstruction of European society under the banner of a socialist commonwealth," Alvin H. Hansen of the Council on Foreign Relations wrote in June 1940. "It may be expected that a European socialist commonwealth would, equally with the Nazi system, develop a highly self-sufficient and virtually closed economy. Trade with other areas would be probably limited largely to the same products which Nazi Germany would find it necessary and useful to import. Moreover it may be expected that foreign trade purchases would be centralized in a single commonwealth controlled corporation and distributed throughout Europe from a common center." Hansen concluded that "the difference between the two systems might be relatively small so far as the United States trade is concerned."[24]

State Department officials, reasoning in the same way, hoped to keep the European continent in the capitalist orbit. Leo Pasvolsky warned in January 1940 that if the United States failed to satisfy the financial needs of the European belligerents after hostilities ceased, disastrous social upheavals might threaten "stability over wide areas and constitute a seriously disturbing element in the process of post-war reconstruction."[25] Sumner Welles was particularly concerned about the possibility that a punitive peace settlement would create the material conditions for a radical uprising in Germany. He advocated a cooperative peace arrangement which would enable the German people to enjoy prosperity in the postwar period by engaging in trade with the rest of the world. "For the last six years German industries have been progressively oriented for war," Welles explained in March 1940, "but with the return of peace German equipment, German skill and German industriousness will require large external markets if the most serious unemployment is to be avoided. Such unemployment, apart from the suffering it would involve, would provide a veritable forcing bed for communism."[26]

American leaders had for some time been grappling with the question of how to reintegrate Germany into a liberal capitalist world system. Many believed that the erection of high tariff walls in the early 1930s had set the stage for the rise of national socialism in Germany. "Hitlerism would not have come to power," Fortune Round Table editor Raymond Leslie Buel declared in November 1939, "except for the economic and political nationalism of the West."[27] John Foster Dulles, who had represented American bondholders during the first year of the Nazi regime, agreed. "I was in frequent conference with men like Schacht, Schmitt and other members of the German cabinet, and I could see the development there of nationalistic policies occurring in direct relation to the development of nationalistic economic policies in the rest of the world," Dulles asserted in November 1941. "The failure of the London Economic Conference had, to my personal knowledge, a very real bearing upon the course which Nazism adopted."[28] Americans like Buel and Dulles hoped that the removal of tariff barriers in the postwar years would enable Germany to obtain raw materials and commodity markets by engaging in overseas trade rather than by embarking upon yet another campaign to achieve continental hegemony.

But other American leaders feared that the German people would not remain content with their assigned place in a peaceful and prosperous international community even after their Nazi rulers were removed from their seat of power in Berlin. "I cannot seem to differentiate between Hitler and the German people," Thomas W. Lamont complained in February 1940. "They are all imbued with the same idea of domination. I think it is born and bred in the flesh. It dates back at least from the time of Frederick the Great. How to change that attitude, how to cure that idea fixe is beyond me."[29] Henry A. Wallace likewise believed that the German people had a deeply rooted desire to dominate others. "Those who think that getting rid of Hitler will clear up the situation," he wrote Roosevelt in March 1940, "simply don't know what they are talking about."[30] Yet even such pessimists as Lamont and Wallace continued to hope that Uncle Sam could pacify the German people by giving them reasonable commercial opportunities.[31] As Vera Michels Dean of the Foreign Policy Association pointed out in May 1941, American leaders were still thinking "in terms of throwing the resources of the whole world open to all peoples on a basis of equality, and distributing these resources in such a way as to benefit international society as a whole."[32]

Business internationalists who were thinking along these lines insisted that the United States should be prepared to run the economic affairs of the postwar world. "If we are to establish our kind of 'new world order' in the realm of economics," John Abbink declared in March 1941, "it must be launched while our growing might can accent its various provisions."[33] President Eugene P. Thomas of the National Foreign Trade Council held the same view. "It is necessary, looking ahead to what will be required of us at the close of the war," he proclaimed, "that our Government and business leaders take prompt steps to formulate plans for a postwar economic world order which will insure the resumption of normal, orthodox, international trade and investments."[34] Thomas Lamont likewise concluded in June 1941 that the United States would have to play a leading role in the advancement of a postwar economic program which would remove "trade barriers, quotas, and all the pernicious devices that intensified nationalism in so many countries, large and small."[35]

A month later, but almost a half-year before Japan attacked

Pearl Harbor, the State Department set up a special committee to draft blueprints for the eventual peace conference.[36] This action was prompted by fears that the New Deal reformers would assume control of postwar economic planning. "If they really get in the saddle," Secretary Hull warned in September 1941, "they will adopt a closed economy."[37] Hull and his subordinates continued to worry that the New Dealers would subvert their quest for New Frontiers. They remained convinced that the American free enterprise system could be preserved only through a policy of overseas expansion and not through a program of domestic reorganization. As John D. Hickerson explained in October 1941, he and his colleagues in the State Department were looking forward to the establishment of "a world-wide open economy."[38] Assistant Secretary Adolf A. Berle therefore turned his mind to the problem of working out "financial arrangements which will make possible something like open trade."[39]

The State Department planners based their dreams for the creation of a Pax Americana upon the assumption of a military victory over Nazi Germany. They realized that the United States was not yet prepared to send a huge expeditionary force to reconquer the European continent. It would take considerable time to produce enough weapons and train enough soldiers to fulfill the requirements of the Victory Program. But the postwar planners in the State Department did not remain idle while the men and materials were being transformed into an invincible military machine. Rather, they went forward with their work in the quiet confidence that American entrance into the war would ultimately turn the tide of battle against the Third Reich. "The most sweeping assumption which must of course be made in our work," Harley A. Notter of the Division of Special Research acknowledged in Setember 1941, "is that Germany will be defeated and that England with participation on the part of the United States will win the war by a clear and uncompromising victory enabling us to disarm the enemy."[40]

Disarmament of the Germans and their Axis partners was essential to the Roosevelt administration's postwar plan, both economically and strategically. Secretary of the Treasury Henry Morgenthau even suggested in June 1941 that the United States should put its gold to work after the war "by buying up all the munition plants in the world, and then destroying them, and insisting that the gold be used in each country for reconstruction purposes." He hoped that as a result "we would remove the fear of the people for another war, and would also give these countries money with which to start international commerce again."[41] A week later, President Roosevelt reminded Adolf Berle to make disarmament a central feature in his outline for a peace settlement. "Don't forget that the elimination of costly armaments is still the keystone—for the security of all little nations and for economic solvency," he lectured. "Don't forget what I discovered—that over ninety percent of all national deficits from 1921 to 1939 were caused by payments for past, present, and future wars."[42] In short, Roosevelt and his advisers hoped that disarmament would not only provide physical security for small countries but also promote economic reconstruction throughout the world.

The Roosevelt administration intended to use food as well as gold in an effort to make European reconstruction compatible with American interests. A State Department official recommended in June 1941 that surplus American farm products should be distributed to needy European countries after the war in order to induce them to abandon their nationalistic agricultural policies. "These countries might never be called upon to pay for these commodities," he explained. "One quid pro quo for such a gift, however, might be an agreement not to produce these same surplus commodities under highly uneconomic conditions with the support of high tariffs, quotas, prohibitions, government subsidies, etc."[43] The idea appealed to Agricultural Department officials, who wanted to make the European continent a large market for American crops. "The provision of food to the half-starved European population at the end of the war," they reasoned in August 1941, "will prove to be a lever by means of which influence can be brought to bear upon the political and economic reconstruction of Europe."[44]

But State Department officials feared that the British would attempt to structure the European relief and rehabilitation program to serve their own economic interests. When the English suggested the establishment of a central bureau in

London to handle all the foodstuffs and other materials that would be shipped to the European continent in the postwar years, Adolf Berle was particularly worried. He promptly warned Roosevelt in July 1941 that the British proposal for reprovisioning Europe was designed "to channelize the trade and economics of this area through London when the war is over." Berle added that "a plan to regionalize the world (leaving us the Western Hemisphere) has already been turned down by our people."[45] His colleagues shared his apprehensions about British aims. "The danger is that various British interests will certainly attempt to retain the benefits they have obtained through war-time measures that are probably necessary under present conditions," a member of the Trade Agreements Division warned in May 1941. "This means strong postwar pressure for accentuated Empire self-sufficiency, coupled with clearing arrangements of the Nazi type."[46]

The State Department had feared for some time that Great Britain would present a serious obstacle to the restoration of liberal trading practices after the war. Due to a shortage in dollar exchange, the British were restricting their purchases from the United States and increasing their imports from their Dominions, where they could pay in pounds sterling. Cordell Hull articulated the growing concern in January 1940 that these commercial discriminations would "extend into peacetime, perhaps permanently, to the detriment of American interests."[47] Two days later, Norman H. Davis noted that "whereas the British were now bent on fighting a military war, there were too many evidences that they were at the same time laying the groundwork for fighting an economic war against us."[48] J. Pierrepont Moffat likewise observed in February 1940 "the increasing evidence that Britain was planning a huge trading orbit within the pound-franc area designed to exclude us."[49] Leo Pasvolsky was equally alarmed about indications that the Allies were determined to create a European commercial union based upon preferential trade arrangements. "Such a course of developments," he lamented in March 1940, "would place before us some very serious problems."[50]

Prominent members of the corporate community were also worried about the possibility of a closed world in the postwar period even if the Nazis were defeated. Winthrop W. Aldrich explained to the shareholders of the Chase National Bank in January 1940 that "a situation must be created in which goods may move freely and in volume over international boundaries."[51] The participants in the Fortune Round Table discussions agreed. "What interests us primarily," they explained in January 1940, "is the longer-range question of whether or not the American capitalist system could continue to function if most of Europe and Asia should abolish free enterprise in favor of totalitarian economics as a result of this war."[52] Thus, the Fortune group thought that the United States should be prepared to use its financial power to induce the British and French as well as the Germans to abandon their stringent government controls over foreign trade after the war.[53]

The State Department wanted to employ the Lend-Lease Act as a lever to pry open the British imperial preference system. Pierrepont Moffat made a special pilgrimage from his post in Canada in March 1941 "to preach the gospel that unless we availed ourselves of the present situation to obtain a commitment from the members of the British Empire to modify the Ottawa Agreements after the war, we would ultimately be virtually shut out of our Dominion markets through a tendency on the part of them all to close the Empire further and further by means of increased Imperial preferences."[54] When Moffat arrived in Washington, he was delighted to find that Welles and Berle completely agreed with him. They were intent on securing economic cooperation rather than monetary compensation for Lend-Lease materials shipped to the United Kingdom. "Repayment in commodities, if pushed far enough to compensate for a large amount of destroyed military items, would deprive the British in the post-war period of foreign exchange with which to buy from us and others necessary imports," a State Department memorandum warned in June 1941. "Such a situation might provide the cause or excuse for a British control over their foreign trade and foreign payments equalling or exceeding the pre-war restraints of continental countries."[55]

Assistant Secretary Dean G. Acheson called upon a group of Treasury officials in June 1941 and explained how the State Department viewed the Lend-Lease question. If Americans wished to avoid becoming entangled once again in a serious war debt problem, Acheson argued, the United States should not make impossible demands for repayment for weapons sent to Great Britain. "The whole idea of Lend-Lease," he insisted, "was not to get in the fix that you and I unhappily were in in 1933." He pointed out that the State Department intended to exploit the British need for American military supplies by demanding a *quid pro quo* in the form of postwar commercial concessions. Acheson explained that he and his colleagues had drafted a preliminary Lend-Lease accord "in the hope that if we sat down right away before we got too deeply committed in this war with the British they would be willing to go quite a way toward either cracking now or laying the foundations for cracking the Ottawa agreements."[56]

Many in Great Britain, however, were determined to keep the imperial preference system intact when the war came to a close. Conservative leaders like Leopold S. Amery, Lord Beaverbrook, and Robert S. Hudson vigorously defended the discriminating trade agreements which had been made in 1932 at Ottawa.[57] John Maynard Keynes, the eminent liberal economist, also wanted to maintain a tariff wall around the British Empire in the postwar period. As a representative of the British Treasury, Keynes traveled to Washington in June 1941 to work out the details of a Lend-Lease agreement with the United States. The State Department immediately presented him with a draft of a temporary Lend-Lease accord which called upon Great Britain to embrace liberal commercial principles after the war. But Keynes had no intention of allowing the United States to dismantle the Ottawa system. He insisted that his country would have to maintain a bilateral policy in order to obtain preferential commercial treatment in countries with which the United Kingdom had an unfavorable balance of payments.[58]

The State Department reacted angrily to Keynes. "Despite the war the Hitlerian commercial policy will probably be adopted by Great Britain," Moffat lamented on July 14. "If and when we do become involved we shall give all and get nothing, other than a good screwing to our trade by Great Britain."[59] Berle also feared that the British would close the doors of their empire against American products. "If this is worked out," he grumbled on July 17, "the only economic effect of the war will be that we have moved a closed-economy center from Berlin to London."[60] Acheson promptly informed Keynes that the United States was going to attach strings to Lend-Lease aid and that the British must "not regard themselves as free to take any measure they chose directed against the trade of that country."[61] But Keynes refused to backtrack, and on July 29 he gave Acheson a memorandum which characterized the most-favored-nation principle as "the clutch of the dead, or at least the moribund, hand."[62] Harry C. Hawkins of the Trade Agreements Division was outraged. "Our own and the British interests will be best served if we can dissuade them from adopting the kind of policies advocated by Mr. Keynes," Hawkins advised on August 4. "The appropriate instrument for crystallizing and, if possible, settling the issue presented is the lend-lease agreement now under discussion with the British."[63]

The Anglo-American battle over postwar commercial affairs dampened the Atlantic Conference held in secret between August 9 and 12, 1941, off the Newfoundland coast. At the first opportunity, Sumner Welles proposed that Great Britain and the United States should issue a joint declaration that "they will endeavor to further the enjoyment by all peoples of access, without discrimination and on equal terms, to the markets and to the raw materials of the world." But Prime Minister Winston Churchill replied that it would take at least a week before he could get permission from the Dominion governments to do anything that would prejudice the future of the Ottawa agreements for imperial preference. Harry Hopkins then suggested that the British should rephrase the proposal so that they would not have to wait for approval from the Dominions, and the publication of the declaration could coincide with the public announcement of the meeting. Welles retorted that a vital principle was involved and not a mere question of phraseology. "If the British and United States Governments could not agree to do everything within their power to further, after the termination of the present war, a restoration of free and liberal trade policies," he asserted, "they might as well throw in the sponge and realize that one of the greatest factors in creating the present tragic situation in the world was going to be permitted to continue unchecked in the post-war world."[64]

But President Roosevelt overruled Welles and asked Churchill to try his hand at drafting some phraseology that the United Kingdom could support without first obtaining approval from the Dominion governments. Churchill thereupon submitted a redraft which inserted the qualifying clause "with due respect for their existing obligations" before the joint pledge to promote equal access to world markets.[65] This modification was designed to exempt the Ottawa agreements from the British commitment to sponsor liberal commercial practices. Welles again protested, but the president told Churchill that he "could accept temporary closed arrangements if Britain made it clear that on broad lines and as an objective it stood for non-discriminatory, free-for-all trade."[66] Roosevelt then confided to Welles that the British redraft "was better than he had thought Mr. Churchill would be willing to concede." Welles finally acquiesced, and the British revision of his original proposal became the fourth point in the highly publicized Atlantic Charter.[67]

Yet the question had not been resolved. Greatly agitated by reports that British newspapers seemed to regard point four as a loophole for preserving the imperial preference system, Cordell Hull convinced Roosevelt that the matter should be clarified at once. Hull then requested on August 23 that Churchill issue a public statement to the effect that the fourth article in the Atlantic Charter was "a forthright declaration of intention by the British and American Governments to do everything in their power" to restore a liberal world order through "the reduction or elimination of preferences and discriminations."[68] But Churchill refused. The American embassy in London reported that the prime minister was not only doubtful of Dominion approval but also keenly aware that many members of his own party were deeply attached to the Ottawa agreements.[69] Although Hull decided to drop the issue for the moment, his aides in the State Department continued to exert pressure on the British ambassador in Washington. "We had made it quite clear to Lord Halifax," Moffat informed a Canadian diplomat on September 25, "that if Keynes' philosophy prevailed and Britain entered into a system of competitive bilaterialism, using her imports to force exports, we would undoubtedly have to do the same."[70]

The State Department also used the National Foreign Trade Convention held in New York between October 6 and 8 to keep the British informed about American desires concerning the postwar world. "The creation of an economic order in the postwar world which will give free play to individual enterprise," Sumner Welles told the assembled businessmen, "is almost as essential to the preservation of free institutions as is the actual winning of this war." Welles added that "the Atlantic Declaration means that every nation has a right to expect that its legitimate trade will not be diverted and throttled by towering tariffs, preferences, discriminations or narrow bilateral practices." His speech was well received. The Final Declaration of the convention, which had been drafted by the State Department, strongly recommended that the American government "endeavor to obtain definite commitments for the progressive removal of trade discriminations against the United States throughout the British Commonwealth and elsewhere, to the extent that such discriminations are the result of British policy."[71]

The State Department, acting in line with that resolution, continued its efforts to extract commercial commitments from Great Britain. When Ambassador Halifax presented Acheson with a redraft for a master Lend-Lease agreement on October 17, Acheson and his colleagues thought that "the British proposal was too vague and did not furnish a sufficient commitment."[72] The State Department promptly prepared a counterproposal which offered to reduce American tariffs on British Empire products in return for substantial modifications in the imperial preference system.[73] After Hull secured approval from the White House, Acheson handed Halifax the American redraft on December 2, 1941, and urged that the British should accept its provisions for liberal commercial practices without delay.[74] But only after several months of procrastination did Great Britain finally capitulate to American economic demands for the postwar world. The formal Lend-Lease agreement, signed in February 1942, provided for joint Anglo-

American action directed "to the elimination of all forms of discriminatory treatment in international commerce and to the reduction of tariffs and other trade barriers."[75]

At the same time as American diplomats had been seeking to dismantle the Ottawa imperial preference system, they had also been working to keep the British from recognizing Eastern Europe as a Russian sphere of influence. Their apprehensions about Eastern Europe had begun when Stalin responded to the fall of France in June 1940 by imposing complete Soviet control over Latvia, Lithuania, and Estonia. Although President Roosevelt and his State Department advisers viewed the Russian move as an attempt to establish a security perimeter in anticipation of a future German attack against the Soviet Union, they immediately protested the annihilation of independence in the Baltic countries.[76] "Our failure to recognize Soviet conquests just now," Loy Henderson wrote Adolf Berle on July 15, "may possibly place another card in our hands when, if ever, a conference regarding the future of Europe takes place."[77] Berle agreed. He informed the Turkish ambassador in Washington on October 9 that the United States would not support Soviet attempts to build a Balkan bloc in opposition to Hitler until the Russians stopped asserting "the right to take and seize territory by violence."[78] But the British were willing to bargain away Eastern Europe in an effort to induce Stalin to switch his allegiance from Germany to England. Thus, the British ambassador in Moscow offered on October 22, 1940, "to give *de facto* recognition to the Soviet acquisition of the three Baltic States, Eastern Poland, Bessarabia and Bukowina."[79]

Though Stalin steadfastly refused to do anything which might arouse the wrath of Hitler, the British decided in early June 1941 to make another overture to the Kremlin. Prime Minister Churchill told Ambassador Ivan Maisky that if Germany invaded Russia, Great Britain would be willing to provide economic and military aid to the Soviet Union. Maisky replied that such help would be more welcome if preceded by British recognition of Soviet absorption of the Baltic States.[80] Sumner Welles promptly cautioned Ambassador Halifax that Great Britain should not attempt to achieve a rapprochement with Russia at the expense of the Baltic countries. But his admonishment had little effect. "Lord Halifax said he felt he was rather cynical with regard to the Baltic States," Welles recorded on June 15. "He said he did not think the Baltic peoples were peoples who demanded very much respect or consideration and that in the situation in which Great Britain now found herself, concentrating as her sole objective upon the defeat of Hitler, he could conceive of a situation developing in which the British Government, in order to form close relations with the Soviet Union, might desire to take some steps with regard to recognizing the Soviet claims with regard to the Baltic States."[81] A week later, Hitler ordered his troops to attack Russia, and Churchill seized the opportunity to dispatch a military mission to Moscow.[82]

The German assault on Russia immediately raised the question of the future status of Poland, divided by Hitler and Stalin in September 1939 following the Nazi-Soviet nonaggression pact. The Polish government-in-exile, which had been biding time in London, eagerly opened negotiations with Ambassador Maisky on July 5 in hopes of restoring the prewar borders of Poland. But Maisky indicated that the Kremlin would insist on the maintenance of boundaries closely corresponding to the Curzon Line, which the British had advocated in 1919 as the ethnographic frontier of Poland.[83] The State Department feared that Great Britain would try to squeeze the Poles in order to buy friendship from Soviet Russia. "It is now evident that preliminary commitments for the postwar settlement of Europe are being made, chiefly in London," Berle warned Roosevelt on July 8. "You will recall that at Versailles President Wilson was seriously handicapped by commitments made to which he was not a party and of which he was not always informed. I have suggested to Sumner that we enter a general caveat, indicating that we could not be bound by any commitments to which we had not definitely assented."[84]

The president quickly acted along the lines that Berle had recommended. Roosevelt instructed Harry Hopkins on July 11 that he was to inform Churchill during their forthcoming meetings that there must be no economic or territorial deals made between Great Britain and the Soviet Union.[85] In a direct message sent to Churchill three days later, Roosevelt suggested that the prime minister should issue a public statement "making clear that no postwar peace commitments as to territories, populations or economics have been given."[86] But Churchill refused to make a forthright declaration in accordance with American wishes. Rather, he acted in a devious manner to promote a temporary accommodation between Poland and Russia. On the one hand, he encouraged the Soviets to believe that England would support the creation of a postwar federation in Eastern Europe under the hegemony of Russia.[87] At the same time, he put pressure on the Poles to drop for the moment their territorial demands in hopes that a satisfactory settlement with the Soviets could be reached after the war. The Poles acquiesced, and on July 30, 1941, they signed a pact with the Russians which left the basic territorial issue open for future determination.[88]

The Polish-Soviet accord heightened American apprehensions that Britain would secretly consent to Russian domination of Eastern Europe. At a meeting held in Berle's office on August 1, it was decided that the United States should block any British maneuvers which might undermine the future independence of countries like Finland, Poland, Czechoslovakia, Yugoslavia, and the Baltic states.[89] "At our suggestion," Berle reported to Hull on August 4, "the President sent a message to Winston Churchill indicating that we could not recognize any postwar commitments except as a part of a general final settlement in which, presumably, we should take part."[90] A few days later, during the Atlantic Conference, Welles personally raised the question with Alexander Cadogan, the permanent under secretary of state for British foreign affairs, noting that Churchill had not yet replied to the request made by Roosevelt a month earlier for a public disclaimer regarding postwar commitments. Cadogan then gave Welles "the most specific and positive assurance that the British had entered into no agreements and had made no commitments which had to do with frontiers or territorial readjustments."[91]

British Foreign Secretary Anthony Eden also complied with American desires when he met with Stalin between December 16 and 28 to discuss war aims. The State Department had been worried that Eden might make territorial concessions to Russia in order to quiet persistent Soviet demands for Britain to open a second front on the European continent. After getting an okay from the president, Hull instructed the American embassy in London on December 5 to remind Eden that he should not "enter into commitments regarding specific terms of the postwar settlement."[92] When Eden arrived in Moscow, Stalin pressed for British recognition of Soviet claims to the area in Eastern Europe occupied by Russia in June 1941 prior to the German attack eastward. Eden replied that the resolution of all frontier questions should be deferred until the peace conference following the war and that Great Britain would not make any deals with the Soviet Union "without prior agreement with the United States." The talks ended on an ominous note when Stalin remarked that he had thought that the Atlantic Charter was directed against the Axis powers but that it was beginning to look as if it were directed against Russia.[93]

Such was the nature of the Grand Alliance linking the United States with Great Britain and the Soviet Union. American leaders had decided to postpone a showdown with Russia regarding the ultimate destiny of Eastern Europe. President Roosevelt and his advisers did not want to alienate Stalin while Soviet troops were fighting against the common enemy. Nor did they wish to confront the Kremlin until peace returned and the United States could negotiate from a much stronger position. "In looking into the future, it is clear that it is America's policy which will give the first answer to what kind of world is to come out of the war," a Council on Foreign Relations memorandum asserted in September 1941. "The United States is growing enormously in strength and power; the other nations are rapidly exhausting themselves; the disproportion between their resources and America's is constantly widening."[94] The inner circle in Washington hoped that the postwar strength of the United States would be tremendously enhanced by an Anglo-American monopoly of atomic energy. In a letter to Churchill on October 11, therefore, Roosevelt suggested that secret American and British efforts to build an atom bomb should be "coordinated or even jointly conducted."[95]

President Roosevelt had already concluded that the United States would have to join with Great Britain in the deployment of military force in order to establish a liberal capitalist world system in the postwar era. During his private conversations with Churchill off the coast of Newfoundland in August 1941, Roosevelt explained that he "would not be in favor of the creation of a new Assembly of the League of Nations, at least until after a period of time had passed and during which an international police force composed of the United States and Great Britain had an opportunity of functioning." The prime minister thought that Roosevelt was being remarkably realistic. "The President," Churchill immediately cabled his War Cabinet, "undoubtedly contemplates the disarmament of the guilty nations, coupled with the maintenance of strong united British and American armaments both by sea and air for a long indefinite period." Although Roosevelt agreed on the need for the eventual "establishment of a wider and permanent system of general security," he refused to consider sharing the role of policing the world with a group of smaller nations.[96]

Prominent members of the eastern establishment agreed that the United States would need to assume the role of world policeman if it wanted to maintain global hegemony, but they realized that it would only work if the American people were willing to shoulder the military burden. Harvard University president James B. Conant thought that Great Britain should be the junior partner in an Anglo-American alliance which would hold sway in the postwar era. "The United States should be the majority stockholder in this new enterprise," Conant wrote Lewis W. Douglas in October 1940. "I believe that the only satisfactory solution for this country is for a majority of the thinking people to became convinced that we must be a world power, and the price of being a world power is willingness and capacity to fight when necessary."[97] Douglas concurred. "I agree with you that the United States must become the dominant power," he replied. "This of course raises the fundamental question as to whether or not the American people will support a public policy resting upon the assumption of our world responsibilities." Douglas feared that the American people might not think that the game was worth the candle. "If they won't, then I think the jig is up," he continued. "The hope of the future as I see it is a very close working arrangement, political, economic, and military between the United States and the British Empire."[98]

Not all American diplomats agreed that the United States should become the policeman of the world, however. "In my mind," Hugh R. Wilson wrote in his diary in March 1940, "entry into battle either in Asia or in Europe is only justified if we are willing to assume the position in the world hitherto maintained by the British Empire of a continuous forceful maintenance of peace." Wilson did not believe that the American people were prepared to pay the price in terms of permanently stationing troops overseas and constantly interfering with the internal affairs of foreign nations. "The penalties," he reasoned, "are too high."[99] Wilson not only questioned whether the American people would be willing to support an international police force, but he also doubted the ability of the United States to exercise control over the entire planet. "We are not confronting a period of the nineteenth century," he warned his State Department colleagues in May 1940, "but are living in a century where industry and war-like power are growing in various portions of the world, thus making infinitely more difficult the maintenance of a far-flung empire."[100]

Most of Wilson's associates in the State Department, however, were eager to establish American authority on a worldwide basis. "I have been saying to myself and other people," Adolf Berle recorded in his diary in September 1940, "that the only possible effect of this war would be that the United States would emerge with an imperial power greater than the world had ever seen."[101] Berle believed that the historic moment had arrived for the United States to reverse roles with the United Kingdom. "In the World War we came so into the English camp that we became virtually an adjunct to the British war machine," he observed in October 1940. "They kept that position after the war was over, and the result of that was that we got not one single thing that we really desired in the ensuing peace. This time it seems to me that the thing should be the other way around." Berle concluded that the United States would be "the inevitable economic center of the regime which will emerge."[102] Norman Davis agreed that the British would not be strong enough to hold their vast empire together in the postwar period. "We shall in effect be the heirs of the Empire," Davis gloated in October 1940, "and it is up to us to preserve its vital parts."[103]

Confident that the United States would emerge from the war with a preponderance of economic and military power, American policymakers aimed to grasp the opportunity to create a new international order devoted to the doctrine of equal commercial opportunity. They realized that, although Great Britain had buttressed a liberal capitalist world system in the past, after the war she would no longer be able to rule the entire globe in the interests of free enterprise. Because the sun was about to set on the British Empire, American leaders believed that the United States should be prepared to fill the power vacuum. They hoped that, just as the last century belonged to England, an Allied victory over the Axis countries would mark the dawn of an American century. In short, they envisioned the establishment of a Pax Americana that would replace the Pax Britannica and thereby sustain the capitalist epoch.

It was not, however, to be an easy task. Although the United States succeeded in keeping Japan and the countries of Western Europe committed to free enterprise, it failed to prevent China from opting out of the capitalist orbit. In addition, despite their overwhelming economic and military power, American policymakers were unable to stop the Soviet Union from erecting an iron curtain that effectively closed the doors of Eastern Europe against western trade and investment. Nor were they able to deter the Russians from encouraging the rising tide of revolutions that threatened to undermine American economic interests in the Third World. As the United States assumed the role of international policeman, the dream of a Pax Americana quickly turned into the nightmare of a Cold War that would ultimately extend into the new frontier of outer space.

Notes

1. The Crisis of Capitalism

1. For a good description of Hoover's philosophy see Joan Hoff Wilson, *Herbert Hoover: Forgotten Progressive* (Boston: Little, Brown and Co., 1975). See also Melvyn P. Leffler, *The Elusive Quest: America's Pursuit of European Stability and French Security, 1919–1933* (Chapel Hill: University of North Carolina Press, 1979); Michael J. Hogan, *Informal Entente: The Private Structure of Cooperation in Anglo-American Economic Diplomacy, 1918–1928* (Columbia: University of Missouri Press, 1977); William A. Williams, *The Contours of American History* (New York: World Publishing Co., 1961); and Ellis W. Hawley, "Herbert Hoover, the Commerce Secretariat, and the Vision of an 'Associative State,' 1921–1928," *Journal of American History*, vol. 61 (June 1974), pp. 116–140.

2. Wilson, *Herbert Hoover*, p. 127.

3. Arthur M. Schlesinger, Jr., *The Crisis of the Old Order, 1919–1933* (Boston: Houghton Mifflin Co., 1957), p. 155.

4. George Soule, *Prosperity Decade: From War to Depression, 1917–1929* (New York: Harper and Row, 1947).

5. Gilbert Fite, *George N. Peek and the Fight for Farm Parity* (Norman: University of Oklahoma Press, 1954).

6. Irving Bernstein, *The Lean Years: A History of the American Worker, 1920–1933* (Boston: Houghton Mifflin Co., 1960).

7. Joan Hoff Wilson, *American Business and Foreign Policy, 1920–1933* (Boston: Beacon Press, 1971).

8. Herbert Feis, *The Diplomacy of the Dollar, 1919–1932* (New York: W. W. Norton and Co., 1950).

9. Hogan, *Informal Entente*.

10. Wilson, *American Business and Foreign Policy*.

11. Feis, *Diplomacy of the Dollar*.

12. Leffler, *The Elusive Quest*, p. 229.

13. For an excellent analysis of Hoover's domestic recovery program, see Albert U. Romasco, *The Poverty of Abundance* (New York: Oxford University Press, 1965).

14. *Ibid.*, pp. 184–187.

15. Leffler, *The Elusive Quest*, p. 270.

16. Wilson, *Herbert Hoover*, p. 166.

17. Fredrick J. Dobney, *Selected Papers of Will Clayton* (Baltimore: Johns Hopkins Press, 1971), p. 21–32.

18. Thomas W. Lamont Memorandum, April 7, 1932; Lamont to J. P. Morgan, Russell C. Leffingwell, and S. Parker Gilbert, April 19, 1932, Lamont Papers, Box 181, Baker Library, Harvard Business School.

19. Thomas W. Lamont Memorandum on Reparations and War Debts, April 5, 1932, Lamont Papers, Box 209.

20. Norman H. Davis to Thomas W. Lamont, April 29, 1932; Lamont to J. Ridgely Carter, May 4, 1932, Lamont Papers, Box 181.

21. Thomas W. Lamont to Henry L. Stimson, May 23, 1932, Lamont Papers, Box 209.

22. Henry L. Stimson Diary, July 11, 1932, Sterling Library, Yale University.

23. *Ibid.*, November 23, 1932.

24. *Ibid.*, December 4, 1932.

25. Edwin O. Reischauer, *The United States and Japan* (New York: Viking Press, 1965).

26. Thomas J. McCormick, *China Market: America's Quest for Informal Empire, 1893–1901* (Chicago: Quadrangle Books, 1967).

27. Akira Iriye, *After Imperialism: The Search for a New Order in the Far East, 1921–1931* (New York: Atheneum, 1965).

28. William L. Neumann, *America Encounters Japan: From Perry to MacArthur* (New York: Harper and Row, 1965).

29. Arnold A. Offner, *The Origins of the Second World War: American Foreign Policy and World Politics, 1917–1941* (New York: Praeger Publishers, 1975).

30. Lloyd C. Gardner, *Economic Aspects of New Deal Diplomacy* (Madison: University of Wisconsin Press, 1964), p. 21.

31. *Ibid.*, p. 71.

32. Henry L. Stimson Diary, January 9, 1933.

33. Frank Freidel, *Franklin D. Roosevelt: Launching the New Deal* (Boston: Little, Brown and Company, 1973).

34. Henry L. Stimson Diary, October 8, 1934.

2. Hull's Vision of Utopia

1. Arthur M. Schlesinger, Jr., *The Coming of the New Deal* (Boston: Houghton Mifflin Co., 1958), p. 27.

2. Irving Bernstein, *The Turbulent Years* (Boston: Houghton Mifflin Co., 1969), p. 15.

3. *Ibid.*

4. Beatrice B. Berle and Travis B. Jacobs, eds., *Navigating the Rapids: 1918–1971, From the Papers of Adolf A. Berle* New York: Harcourt Brace Jovanovich, Inc., 1973), p. 45.

5. William E. Leuchtenburg, *Franklin D. Roosevelt and the New Deal* (New York: Harper and Row, 1963), p. 19.

6. Rexford G. Tugwell, *The Brains Trust* (New York: Viking Press, 1968), pp. 295–296.

7. *The Memoirs of Cordell Hull*, vol. 1 (New York: Macmillan Co., 1948), pp. 354–355; and Dick Steward, *Trade and Hemisphere: The Good Neighbor Policy and Reciprocal Trade* (Columbia: University of Missouri Press, 1975), pp. 1–2, 77.

8. Raymond Moley, *The First New Deal* (New York: Harcourt, Brace, and World, Inc., 1966), p. 46.

9. Breckinridge Long to Edward M. House, December 13, 1932, House Papers, Series I, Box 71, Sterling Library, Yale University. See also House to Long, December 15, 1932.

10. Moley, *The First New Deal*, p. 55.

11. Frank Freidel, *Launching the New Deal* (Boston: Little, Brown and Co., 1973), p. 131.

12. Raymond Moley, *After Seven Years* (Lincoln: University of Nebraska Press, 1939), pp. 67–79; and Rexford G. Tugwell, *The Democratic Roosevelt* (Garden City, N.Y.: Doubleday and Co., 1957), pp. 255–260.

13. James M. Hall, "Franklin D. Roosevelt and the Passage of the Johnson Act of 1934," (M.A. thesis, University of South Dakota, 1978), pp. 71–78.

14. Elliot Roosevelt, ed., *F.D.R.: His Personal Letters*, vol. I (New York: Duel, Sloan, and Pearce, 1950), pp. 347–348.

15. Lewis W. Douglas to James S. Douglas, May 7, 1933, Douglas Papers, Box 31, University of Arizona Library.

16. Lewis W. Douglas to Franklin D. Roosevelt, January 19, 1933, Douglas Papers, Box 174.

17. Henry L. Stimson Diary, March 28, 1933, Sterling Library, Yale University.

18. John Foster Dulles to Westmore Willcox, Jr., March 14, 1933, Dulles Papers, Box 11, Firestone Library, Princeton University.

19. Tugwell, *The Brains Trust*, pp. 96–130; Moley, *After Seven Years*, pp. 184–190; Schlesinger, *The Coming of the New Deal*, pp. 179–184; and Leuchtenburg, *Franklin D. Roosevelt and the New Deal*, pp. 34–35.

20. J. Pierrepont Moffat Diary, January 25, 1933, Houghton Library, Harvard University.

21. Melvyn P. Leffler, *The Elusive Quest* (Chapel Hill: University of North Carolina Press, 1979), p. 304.

22. Moley, *The First New Deal*, p. 61.

23. Edgar B. Nixon, ed., *Franklin D. Roosevelt and Foreign Affairs*, vol. II (Cambridge: Harvard University Press, 1969), p. 114.

24. Tugwell, *The Brains Trust*, pp. 206–209; Freidel, *Launching the New Deal*, pp. 309–311; and Grant McConnell, *The Decline of Agrarian Democracy* (Berkeley: University of California Press, 1953).

25. Moley, *The First New Deal*, p. 205.

26. Edward L. and Frederick H. Schapsmeier, *Henry A. Wallace of Iowa: The Agrarian Years, 1910–1940* (Ames: Iowa State University Press, 1968), pp. 174, 234–240; and J. Samuel Walker, *Henry A. Wallace and American Foreign Policy* (Westport, Conn.: Greenwood Press, 1976), pp. 30–31.

27. *Report of the Secretary of Agriculture* (Washington: Government Printing Office, 1933), pp. 5–7.

28. Tugwell, *The Democratic Roosevelt*, pp. 310–312.

29. Schlesinger, *The Coming of the New Deal*, p. 122.

30. Moley, *The First New Deal*, pp. 338–340.

31. *The Memoirs of Cordell Hull*, vol. I, p. 159.

32. Freidel, *Launching the New Deal*, pp. 359–365.

33. National Archives, Record Group 59, 611.0031/428.

34. *The Memoirs of Cordell Hull*, vol. I, pp. 248–249.

35. N.A., R.G. 59, 611.0031/2870.

36. James R. Moore, "Sources of New Deal Economic Policy: The International Dimension," *Journal of American History*, vol. 61, no. 3 (December 1974), pp. 728–744; and Freidel, *Launching the New Deal*, pp. 384–389.

37. Tugwell, *The Democratic Roosevelt*, p. 291; and *The Memoirs of Cordell Hull*, vol. I, pp. 246–249.

38. Freidel, *Launching the New Deal*, p. 460.

39. Herbert Feis, Notes Before Departure for the Economic Conference, May 28, 1933, Lewis W. Douglas Papers, Box 249.

40. Franklin D. Roosevelt to Cordell Hull, June 7, 1933, N.A., R.G. 59, 611.0031/500; Roosevelt to Hull, June 11, 1933, Hull Papers, Library of Congress; and Robert W. Bingham to Edward M. House, July 31, 1933, House Papers, Series I, Box 15.

41. Robert W. Bingham Diary, June 12, 1933, Library of Congress.

42. *Foreign Policy Reports*, vol. 9, no. 18, November 8, 1933.

43. Moley, *After Seven Years*, pp. 259–260.

44. Robert W. Bingham Diary, July 21, 1933.

45. Edward M. House to Robert W. Bingham, September 10, 1933, Bingham Papers, Box 13, Library of Congress.

46. Freidel *Launching the New Deal*, pp. 493–495.

47. Josephus Daniels to Cordell Hull, September 25, 1933, Daniels Papers, Box 82, Library of Congress.

48. Herbert Feis, Memorandum, November 20, 1933, John C. Wiley Papers, Box 1, Franklin D. Roosevelt Library.

49. *Report of the Secretary of Agriculture*, 1933, p. 5.

50. James Warburg to Dean Acheson, October 12, 1933, George L. Harrison Papers, Box 3, Butler Library, Columbia University.

51. Steward, *Trade and Hemisphere*, p. 19.

52. William Phillips Diary, December 28, 1933, Houghton Library, Harvard University.

53. The *Memoirs of Cordell Hull*, vol. I, pp. 353–363.

54. William Phillips Diary, February 28, 1934; March 1, 1934; and March 29, 1934.

55. Nixon, ed., *Franklin D. Roosevelt and Foreign Affairs*, vol. II, p. 1.

56. *The Memoirs of Cordell Hull*, vol. I, p. 357.

57. Memorandum of a Conversation Between Francis B. Sayre and Stanley M. Bruce, June 6, 1934, N.A., R.G. 59, 611.473/93.

58. Steward, *Trade and Hemisphere*, p. 240.

59. The *Memoirs of Cordell Hull*, vol. I, p. 362.

60. Herbert Feis to James T. Murphy, Jr., October 10, 1934, N.A., R.G. 59, 611.0011/12. See also William Phillips to Francis B. Sayre, November 22, 1934, 611.0011/14; and Wilbur J. Carr to Murphy, November 28, 1934, 611.0011/15.

61. See, for example, *The Protectionist*, January 1934 and April 1934.

62. Lewis Murphy to Cordell Hull, April 20, 1936, N.A., R.G. 59, 611.0031/2151.

63. Henry F. Grady to Cordell Hull, April 22, 1936, N.A., R.G. 59, 611.0031/2156.

64. Henry A. Wallace to Francis P. Miller, June 29, 1938, National Policy Committee Papers, Library of Congress.

65. Henry A. Wallace Diary, November 21, 1939, University of Iowa Library.

66. William Phillips Diary, December 4, 1933.

67. *Ibid.*, December 11, 1933.

68. *Ibid.*, December 12, 1933.

69. William Phillips to Cordell Hull, January 5, 1934, N.A., R.G. 59, 611.0031 Executive Committee/80.

70. William Phillips Diary, January 6, 1934.

71. Ibid., February 27, 1934.

72. *The Memoirs of Cordell Hull*, vol. I, p. 370.

73. George N. Peek to Congressman Coffee, February 20, 1935, Peek Papers, Box 60, University of Missouri Library.

74. George N. Peek to Ellison D. Smith, January 23, 1936, Peek Papers, Box 21.

75. *Vital Speeches*, April 8, 1935, p. 443.

76. Frederick C. Adams, *The Export-Import Bank and American Foreign Policy, 1934–1939* (Columbia: University of Missouri Press, 1976), p. 85.

77. George N. Peek to Chester C. Davis, September 15, 1934, Peek Papers, Box 60.

78. George N. Peek to Douglas Osterheld, March 25, 1936, Peek Papers, Box 22.

79. George N. Peek to F. R. Eldridge, March 22, 1934, Peek Papers, Box 14.

80. Henry A. Wallace Diary, January 25, 1935.

81. George N. Peek to Congressman Coffee, June 5, 1935, Peek Papers, Box 61.

82. George N. Peek to Franklin D. Roosevelt, November 12, 1934, Peek Papers, Box 16.

83. George N. Peek to Cordell Hull, September 12, 1934, Peek Papers, Box 15.

84. George N. Peek to Sumner Welles, December 8, 1934, N.A., R.G. 59, 611/0031 Executive Committee/340.

85. George N. Peek to Cordell Hull, August 27, 1934, N.A., R.G. 59, 611.0031/1079; and Memorandum of Conversation in Office of Special Adviser to President on Foreign Trade, August 1, 1934, N.A., R.G. 59, 611.0031/1015.

86. George N. Peek to Chester C. Davis, August 30, 1934, Peek Papers, Box 15.

87. Francis B. Sayre to George N. Peek, April 8, 1935, Peek Papers, Box 17.

88. Herbert Feis to William Phillips, June 1, 1934, N.A., R.G. 59, 611.00/522.

89. Paul T. Culbertson to Franklin S. Keller, July 23, 1936, N.A., R.G. 59, 862.5151/1722.

90. Lloyd C. Gardner, *Economic Aspects of New Deal Diplomacy* (Madison: University of Wisconsin Press, 1964), p. 43.

91. *Vital Speeches*, November 19, 1934, p. 109.

92. Herbert Feis to William Phillips, June 1, 1934, N.A., R.G. 59, 611.00/522.

93. Steward, *Trade and Hemisphere*, p. 52.

94. Henry Morgenthau, Jr., to George N. Peek, June 5, 1934, Peek Papers, Box 15.

95. Henry A. Wallace Diary, January 25, 1935.

96. Thomas E. Wilson to George N. Peek, March 10, 1934; and Peek to Wilson, March 14, 1934, Peek Papers, Box 13.

97. George N. Peek to James D. Mooney, April 9, 1934; Mooney to Peek, April 13, 1934; Peek to Mooney, April 25, 1934; and Mooney to Peek, April 27, 1934, Peek Papers, Box 14.

98. Thomas E. Wilson to George N. Peek, February 28, 1934, Peek Papers, Box 13.

99. George N. Peek to Thomas E. Wilson, March 23, 1934, Peek Papers, Box 14.

100. J. Pierrepont Moffat Diary, June 1, 1934.

101. Nixon, ed., *Franklin D. Roosevelt and Foreign Affairs*, vol. II, p. 141.

102. J. Pierrepont Moffat Diary, June 6, 1934.

103. James D. Mooney to George N. Peek, April 9, 1934; Mooney to Peek, April 13, 1934; and Mooney to Peek, May 7, 1934, Peek Papers, Box 14.

104. *The Memoirs of Cordell Hull*, vol. I., p. 371.

105. Memorandum from Interdepartmental Trade Agreements Committee, December 5, 1934, N.A., R.G. 59, 662.1115/108A. See also Memorandum of Conversation Between Henry F. Grady and Carlos Joao Muniz, December 11, 1933, N.A., R.G. 59, 611.6231/477.

106. William Phillips Diary, December 13, 1934.

107. Cordell Hull to Franklin D. Roosevelt, December 14, 1934, Roosevelt Papers, P.S.F., Box 44, Roosevelt Library.

108. J. Pierrepont Moffat to John C. White, December 20, 1934, Moffat Papers, Houghton Library, Harvard University.

109. J. Pierrepont Moffat to George S. Messersmith, December 27, 1934, Messersmith Papers, University of Delaware Library.

110. Steward, *Trade and Hemisphere*, p. 54.

111. *The Secret Diary of Harold L. Ickes: The First Thousand Days, 1933–1936* (New York: Simon and Schuster, 1953), p. 360. See also J. Pierrepont Moffat Diary, December 14, 1934; and William Phillips to Francis B. Sayre, June 18, 1935, N.A., R.G. 59, 611.0031 Executive Committee/390.

112. Roosevelt, ed., *F.D.R.: His Personal Letters*, vol. I, p. 493.

113. Joseph C. Green to J. Pierrepont Moffat, January 9, 1936, Moffat Papers.

114. *Vital Speeches*, October 1, 1936, p. 796.

115. Cordell Hull to J. M. Gardenhire, August 21, 1935, Hull Papers.

116. Cordell Hull to J. E. Early, February 20, 1936, Hull Papers.

117. *Vital Speeches*, May 20, 1935, p. 545.

118. *Annals of the American Academy of Political and Social Science*, July 1936, p. 191.

119. *Ibid.*, p. 130.

120. Nixon, ed., *Franklin D. Roosevelt and Foreign Affairs*, vol. II, p. 24.

121. *Official Report of the National Foreign Trade Convention,* 1935, p. 501.

122. Thomas W. Lamont to Cordell Hull, May 3, 1935, Lamont Papers, Box 209, Baker Library, Harvard Business School.

123. *Think*, September 1935, p. 23.

124. R. Walton Moore to Claude G. Bowers, March 2, 1934, Moore Papers, Box 3, Franklin D. Roosevelt Library.

125. Cordell Hull to W. J. Fitts, December 12, 1935, Hull Papers.

126. *Annals of the American Academy of Political and Social Science*, July 1936, p. 133.

127. Steward, *Trade and Hemisphere*, p. 11.

128. *Annals of the American Academy of Political and Social Science*, July 1938, pp. 35–42.

129. *Vital Speeches*, November 19, 1934, p. 110.

130. *Ibid.*, May 15, 1938, p. 468.

131. *Annals of the American Academy of Political and Social Science*, July 1936, p. 134.

132. *Vital Speeches*, January 1, 1937, p. 173.

133. John Foster Dulles to Roswell P. Barnes, October 7, 1937, Dulles Papers, Box 16. See also Francis B. Sayre to Dulles, March 21, 1936, Box 15.

134. *Think*, February 1936, p. 8.
135. Ibid., June 1936, p. 5.
136. Thomas W. Lamont to Cordell Hull, May 3, 1935, Lamont Papers, Box 209.
137. *Report of the Secretary of Agriculture*, 1935, pp. 14–21. See also Henry A. Wallace Diary, January 25, 1935.
138. *Think*, November 1935, p. 21.
139. *Ibid.*, September 1935, p. 7.
140. *Vital Speeches*, July 1, 1936, p. 619.
141. Frederick J. Dabney *Selected Papers of Will Clayton* (Baltimore: Johns Hopkins University Press, 1971), p. 6. See also James P. Warburg to Cordell Hull, October 13, 1936, Hull Papers; and Lewis W. Douglas to Cordell Hull, October 13, 1936, Douglas Papers, Box 251.
142. George F. Bauer to George H. Lorimer, June 2, 1936, Peek Papers, Box 24. See also Edgar W. Smith to Peek, August 4, 1936, Peek Papers, Box 15.
143. George N. Peek to Rosemond Duncan, July 22, 1938, Peek Papers, Box 34.
144. *The Memoirs of Cordell Hull*, vol. I, p. 365.

3. Dr. Schacht's Frankenstein

1. Raymond J. Sontag, *A Broken World, 1919–1939* (New York: Harper & Row, 1971), pp. 53–55; Allan Bullock, *Hitler: A Study in Tyranny* (New York: Harper & Row, 1971), pp. 72–78; A. J. P. Taylor, *The Origins of the Second World War* (Greenwich, Conn.: Fawcett Publications, 1961), p. 46–50; and Arnold A. Offner, *The Origins of the Second World War* (New York: Praeger Publishers, 1975), pp. 25–26.
2. Klaus Hildebrand, *The Foreign Policy of the Third Reich* (Berkeley:. University of California Press, 1970), p. 27; and Bullock, *Hitler*, pp. 173–198.
3. Joan Hoff Wilson, *American Business and Foreign Policy, 1920–1933* (Boston: Beacon Press, 1971); Melvyn P. Leffler, *The Elusive Quest: America's Pursuit of European Stability and French Security, 1919–1933* (Chapel Hill: University of North Carolina Press, 1979).
4. Norman H. Davis to Nicholas Murray Butler, February 9, 1932, Butler Papers, Butler Library, Columbia University.
5. George S. Messersmith to Cordell Hull, April 28, 1933, National Archives, Record Group 59, 862.20/610. See also Messersmith

to Hull, May 9, 1933, N.A., R.G. 59, 862.51/3605; and Messersmith to William Phillips, June-26, 1933, N.A., R.G. 59, 862.00/3415.

6. J. Pierrepont Moffat Diary, May 2, 1933, Houghton Library, Harvard University.

7. Memorandum of Conversation Between J. Pierrepont Moffat and the Italian Ambassador, May 11, 1933, N.A., R.G., 500.A15A4/1860; and Memorandum of Conversation Between William Phillips and the German Ambassador, May 11, 1933, N.A., R.G. 59, 500.A15A4/1952.

8. Franklin D. Roosevelt to Cordell Hull, May 6, 1933, N.A., R.G. 59, 500.A15A4/1848.

9. Henry L. Stimson Diary, March 28, 1933, Sterling Library, Yale University.

10. Memorandum of Conversation Between Norman H. Davis and Adolf Hitler, April 8, 1933, N.A., R.G. 59, 55O. S1 Wash./359.

11. Hugh R. Wilson to J. Pierrepont Moffat, March 29, 1933, Moffat Papers, Houghton Library, Harvard University; J. Pierrepont Moffat to William Phillips, April 19, 1933, Moffat Papers; and Cordell Hull to Norman H. Davis, April 25, 1933, N.A., R.G. 59, 500.S1 Wash./387.

12. Robert A. Divine, *The Illusion of Neutrality* (Chicago: Quadrangle Books, 1962), pp. 41–56; Arnold A. Offner, *American Appeasement: United States Foreign Policy and Germany, 1933–1938* (New York: W. W. Norton & Co., 1969), pp. 25–37; and Robert Dallek, *Franklin D. Roosevelt and American Foreign Policy, 1932–1945* (New York: Oxford University Press, 1979), pp. 47–48.

13. J. Pierrepont Moffat to James G. Rogers, June 6, 1933, Moffat Papers.

14. Franklin D. Roosevelt to Norman H. Davis, August 30, 1933, N.A., R.G. 59, 500.A15A4/2196A. See also N.A., R.G. 59, 500.A15A4/2084; and 500.A15A4/2156.

15. Memorandum by Allen W. Dulles, October 27, 1933, Moffat Papers.

16. Telephone Conversation Between Franklin D. Roosevelt and Norman H. Davis, October 16, 1933, N.A., R.G. 59, 500.A1514/2241.

17. J. Pierrepont Moffat to Ferdinand L. Mayer, November 6, 1933, Moffat Papers. See also Moffat to Mayer, March 21. 1934.

18. Hugh R. Wilson to Cordell Hull, March 21, 1934, Wilson Papers, Box 3, Herbert C. Hoover Library. See also Edgar Mowrer to Frank Knox, November 9, 1933, Knox Papers, Box 4, Library of Congress; and George S. Messersmith to William Phillips, November 23, 1933, N.A., R.G. 59, 862.00/3417.

19. Norman H. Davis to J. Pierrepont Moffat, December 20, 1933, Moffat Papers.

20. Douglas Miller to Willard L. Thorp, Spring 1934, Moffat Papers.

21. J. Pierrepont Moffat Diary, March 28, 1934.

22. J. Pierrepont Moffat to John C. White, March 31, 1934, Moffat Papers. See also Raymond H. Geist to J. Pierrepont Moffat, June 9, 1934, N.A., R.G. 59, 662.1115/70.

23. John Foster Dulles to Cordell Hull, June 6, 1933, Dulles Papers, Box 12, Firestone Library, Princeton University.

24. Cordell Hull to William Phillips, June 11, 1933, N.A., R.G. 59, 862.51/3618; and William Phillips to American Embassy in Berlin, June 13, 1933, N.A., R.G. 59, 862.51/3616.

25. Memorandum of Conversation Between Dr. Schacht and Herbert Feis, June 13, 1933, N.A., R.G. 59, 462.00R296/5762.

26. Johh Foster Dulles to Cordell Hull, October 13, 1933, N.A., R.G. 59, 862.51/3735; Hull to William Dodd, November 1, 1933, 862.51/3725; and John C. White to Hull, November 16, 1933, 862.51/3756.

27. William Phillips Diary, January 18, 1934, Houghton Library, Harvard University; and State Department Aid Memoire to the German Ambassador, January 19, 1934, N.A., R.G. 59, 862.51/3830.

28. William Phillips to William E. Dodd, January 15, 1934, N.A., R.G. 59, 862.51/3789.

29. Hjalmar Schacht to Thomas W. Lamont, April 20, 1934, Lamont Papers, Box 182, Baker Library, Harvard Business School; and George S. Messersmith to William Phillips, April 27, 1934, Messersmith Papers, University of Delaware Library.

30. Ramsay MacDonald to J.P. Morgan & Co., June 28, 1934, Lamont Papers, Box 182.

31. Offner, *American Appeasement*, p. 79.

32. Thomas W. Lamont to E.C. Grenfell, May 22, 1935, Lamont Papers, Box 182.

33. William Dodd to R. Walton Moore, August 17, 1936, Dodd Papers, Library of Congress.

34. J. Pierrepont Moffat Diary, March 27, 1934, and July 5, 1934.

35. William Phillips Diary, July 10, 1934. See also Thomas W. Lamont to E.C. Grenfell, May 23, 1935 Lamont Papers, Box 182.

36. J. Pierrepont Moffat Diary, July 11, 1934. See also William Phillips Diary, July 11, 1934.

37. Cordell Hull to William E. Dodd, July 12, 1934, N.A., R.G. 59, 462.00R296/5820.

38. William Phillips Diary, July 5, 1934.

39. *Ibid.*, July 16, 1934.

40. *Ibid.*, October 13, 1934.

41. Cordell Hull to William E. Dodd, September 28, 1933, N.A., R.G. 59, 662.116/160. See also Hull to Dodd, October 9, 1933, 662.116/163.

42. Dick Steward, *Trade and Hemisphere: The Good Neighbor Policy and Reciprocal Trade* (Columbia: University of Missouri Press, 1975), p. 250.

43. Offner, *American Appeasement*, p. 98. See also William E. Dodd to Cordell Hull, July 3, 1934, N.A., R.G. 59, 662.1111/19.

44. Cordell Hull to William E. Dodd, October 2, 1933, N.A., R.G. 59, 862.51/3697A.

45. Herbert Feis to Cordell Hull, March 28, 1934, N.A., R.G. 59, 611.6231/320.

46. Memorandum of Conversation Between Hans Luther and Francis B. Sayre, April 12, 1934, N.A., R.G. 59, 611.6231/332. See also Memorandum of Conversation Between Luther and Cordell Hull, June 6, 1934, N.A., R.G. 59, 611.6231/357.

47. Memorandum of Conversation Between Francis B. Sayre and George N. Peek, April 26, 1934, N.A., R.G. 59, 611.6231/348. See also Memorandum of Conversation between William Phillips, James D. Mooney, and George N. Peek, June 1, 1934, N.A., R.G. 59, 611.6231/347.

48. J. Pierrepont Moffat Diary, June 1, 1934.

49. George S. Messersmith to William Phillips September 7, 1934, N.A., R.G. 59, 863.00/1084. See also Messersmith to Phillips, November 8, 1934, N.A., R.G. 59, 863.00/1135.

50. George S. Messersmith to Cordell Hull, March 22, 1934, N.A., R.G. 59, 611.6231/330.

51. George S. Messersmith to Cordell Hull, March 28, 1934, N.A., R.G. 59, 611.6231/333; and Messersmith to J. Pierrepont Moffat, April 14, 1934, Messersmith Papers.

52. George S. Messersmith to William Phillips, April 27, 1934, N.A., R.G. 59, 862.00/3422.

53. George S. Messersmith to William Phillips, March 29, 1934, Messersmith Papers.

54. George S. Messersmith to William E. Dodd, April 13, 1934, Messersmith Papers.

55. See, for example, reports by Douglas Miller to the Bureau of Foreign and Domestic Commerce for the months of April, August, and September 1934, N.A., R.G. 151.

56. Memorandum Submitted by Douglas Miller to the American Embassy in Berlin, April 17, 1934, N.A., R.G. 59, 862.00/3421.

57. George S. Messersmith to William Phillips, April 13, 1934, N.A., R.G. 59, 862.00/3420. See also Messersmith to Cordell Hull, June 4, 1934, N.A., R.G. 59, 862.50/806, and Report by John H. Morgan, August 26, 1933, N.A., R.G. 59, 862.504/351.

58. George S. Messersmith to William Phillips, March 24, 1934, Messersmith Papers.

59. George S. Messersmith to William Phillips, August 17, 1934, Messersmith Papers.

60. George S. Messersmith to William Phillips, October 28, 1933, Messersmith Papers; Messersmith to Phillips, November 8, 1934, N.A., R.G. 59, 863.00/1135; and Messersmith to Phillips, December 6, 1934, 863.00/1164.

61. George S. Messersmith to William Phillips, September 7, 1934, N.A., R.G. 59, 863.00/1084.

62. George S. Messersmith to William Phillips, July 5, 1934, N.A., R.G. 59, 862.00/3424.

63. George S. Messersmith to William Phillips, April 27, 1934, Messersmith Papers.

64. George S. Messersmith to William Phillips, December 6, 1934, N.A., R.G. 59, 863.00/1164.

65. J. Pierrepont Moffat to George S. Messersmith, May 4, 1934, Moffat Papers.

66. J. Pierrepont Moffat Diary, June 6, 1934.

67. *Ibid.*, July 19, 1934.

68. Memorandum by Herbert Feis, June 23, 1934, N.A., R.G. 59, 611.6231/379.

69. J. Pierrepont Moffat Diary, June 15, 1934. See also Moffat Diary, June 4 and June 5, 1934; and William Phillips Diary August 14, 1934.

70. William Phillips Diary, July 5, 1934.

71. Hamilton Fish Armstrong to Cordell Hull, July 24, 1934, N.A., R.G. 59, 862.50/819.

72. Cordell Hull to Hamilton Fish Armstrong, July 27, 1934, N.A., R.G. 59, 862.50/819.

73. J. Pierrepont Moffat to George S. Messersmith, August 22, 1934, Moffat Papers. See also Moffat to Messersmith, September 15, 1934, Messersmith Papers.

74. Raymond H. Geist to J. Pierrepont Moffat, September 15, 1934, Moffat Papers; William Phillips Diary, September 21, 1934; Memorandum of Conversation Between Alvin H. Hanson and L. V.

Steere, November 1, 1934, N.A., R.G. 59, 611.6231/442; and Douglas Jenkins to Moffat, December 21, 1934, Moffat Papers.

75. Memorandum on the Proposed American Policy Toward Germany, October 12, 1934, N.A., R.G. 59, 611.6231/483. See also J. Pierrpont Moffat Diary, October 9 and 12, 1934.

76. Memorandum of Conversation Between William Phillips and Hans Luther, October 13, 1934, N.A., R.G. 59, 611.6231/430.

77. J. Pierrepont Moffat to Douglas Jenkins, November 21, 1934, Moffat Papers. See also J. Pierrepont Moffat Diary, November 5, 1934.

78. Memorandum of Conversation Between Francis B. Sayre and Hans Luther, April 4, 1935, N.A., R.G. 59, 611.6231/587.

79. Cordell Hull to the American Embassy in Berlin, April 30, 1935, N.A., R.G. 59, 611.6231/597. See also William Phillips Diary, April 30, 1935.

80. J. Pierrepont Moffat Diary, September 14, 1934.

81. Thomas W. Lamont to Cordell Hull, April 19, 1935, Lamont Papers, Box 182. See also Lamont to E. C. Grenfell, May 22 and May 23, 1935, Lamont Papers, Box 182.

82. J.P. Morgan Co. to Thomas W. Lamont, July 11, 1935, Lamont Papers.

83. Thomas W. Lamont to Hjalmar Schacht, December 26, 1935, Lamont Papers.

84. Herbert Feis to Pierre de LaBoal, March 4, 1935, Feis Papers, Box 11, Library of Congress.

85. William Phillips Diary, March 8, 1935.

86. Memorandum of a State Department Meeting, September 30, 1935, N.A., R.G. 59, 611.6231/727. See also Cordell Hull to Hans Luther, June 28, 1935, N.A., R.G. 59, 611.6231/621.

87. Francis B. Sayre to Chester C. Davis, March 24, 1936, N.A., R.G. 59, 611.6231/748A.

88. *Foreign Affairs*, January 1939, p. 388.

89. Steward, *Trade and Hemisphere*, p. 133.

90. *Ibid.*, p. 249.

91. Herbert Feis to Cordell Hull, October 1, 1934, N.A., R.G.59, 662.006/137.

92. Memorandum of Conversation Between Cordell Hull and Rudolf Leitner, May 4, 1936, N.A., R.G. 59, 611.0031/2198.

93. William E. Dodd to Franklin D. Roosevelt, November 12, 1936, Dodd Papers. See also Dodd to Cordell Hull, July 3, 1937, Hull Papers, Library of Congress.

94. *National Foreign Trade Convention, Official Report*, 1936, pp. 556–61.

95. George S. Messersmith to Cordell Hull, June 24, 1936, N.A., R.G.59, 662.6331/337.

96. *Foreign Policy Reports*, November 15, 1936, pp. 214–15.

97. Douglas Miller, Monthly Economic Review from Berlin, June 1936, N.A., R.G.151.

98. Herbert Feis to John MacMurray, April 7, 1936, Feis Papers, Box 21.

99. George S. Messersmith to Cordell Hull, July 12, 1936, Hull Papers.

100. Steward, *Trade and Hemisphere*, p. 249.

101. Douglas Miller, Report on Trade Promotion Activities of the German Government, October 26, 1935, N.A., R.G. 151.

102. Herbert Feis to George S. Messersmith, July 6, 1936, Feis Papers, Box 21.

103. *National Foreign Trade Convention, Official Report*, 1936, pp. 11–12.

104. F. S. Fales to Cordell Hull, April 4, 1933, N.A., R.G. 59, 893.6363 Manchuria/l.

105. *The Memoirs of Cordell Hull*, vol. I (New York: Macmillan Co., 1948), p. 275.

106. *Foreign Relations of the United States*, 1934, vol. III, p. 56.

107. J. Pierrepont Moffat to Norman H. Davis November 3, 1934, Moffat Papers.

108. J. Pierrepont Moffat Diary, October 29, 1934.

109. Lloyd C. Gardner, *Economic Aspects of New Deal Diplomacy* (Madison: University of Wisconsin Press, 1964), p. 77.

110. Henry L. Stimson Diary, March 20, 1935.

111. W. Cameron Forbes to Henry Ford, January 7, 1936, Forbes Papers, Confidential Letterbook, Houghton Library, Harvard University.

112. *National Foreign Trade Convention, Official Report*, 1935, pp. 104–112.

113. *The Memoirs of Cordell Hull*, Vol. I, pp. 286–87.

114. Dallek, *Franklin D. Roosevelt and American Foreign Policy*, p. 75.

115. William Phillips Diary, May 24, 1934.

116. J. Pierrepont Moffat Diary, November 13, 1934.

117. William L. Neumann, *America Encounters Japan: From Perry to MacArthur* (New York: Harper and Row, 1965), pp. 229–30; Gardner, *Economic Aspects of New Deal Diplomacy*, p. 38.

118. Robert W. Bingham Diary, February 20, 1934, Bingham Papers, Box 1, Library of Congress.

119. *Ibid.*, June 22 and July 16, 1934; Offner, *The Origins of the Second World War*, p. 143.

120. Memorandum of a Conversation in the White House, October 3, 1934, Moffat Papers.

121. Edgar B. Nixon, ed., *Franklin D. Roosevelt and Foreign Affairs*, vol. II (Cambridge: Harvard University Press, 1969), p. 263.

122. Norman H. Davis to Franklin D. Roosevelt, December 14, 1934, Davis Papers, Library of Congress.

123. Nixon, ed., *Franklin D. Roosevelt and Foreign Affairs*, vol. III, p. 179.

124. *The Memoirs of Cordell Hull*, vol. I, pp. 446–50.

125. Gardner, *Economic Aspects of New Deal Diplomacy*, p. 75.

126. Neumann, *America Encounters Japan*, pp. 232–33.

127. George S. Messersmith to William Phillips, February 28, 1936, Messersmith Papers. See also Messersmith to Phillips, August 6, 1935, N.A., R.G. 59, 863.00/1229; and Messersmith to Cordell Hull, April 3, 1936, 863.00/1265.

128. William Phillips Diary, April 10, 1935. See also Raymond H. Geist to J. Pierrepont Moffat January 26, 1935, Moffat Papers.

129. Douglas Jenkins to Cordell Hull, November 4, 1935, N.A., R.G. 59, 862.00/3552. See also Raymond H. Geist to James C. Dunn, February 15, 1936, Messersmith Papers.

130. Robert W. Bingham Diary, February 20, 1934, Library of Congress.

131. Offner, *American Appeasement*, p. 105.

132. Memorandum of Conversation Between Franklin D. Roosevelt and Emile Francqui, May 16, 1934, N.A., R.G. 59, 500.A15A4/2537.

133. William Phillips to J. Pierrepont Moffat, October 22, 1934, N.A., R.G. 59, 500.A15A4/2600 1/3.

134. J. Pierrepont Moffat to William Phillips, October 23, 1934, N.A., R.G. 59, 500.A15A4/2600 2/3.

135. Robert W. Bingham Diary, March 12, 1935.

136. *Ibid.*, April 24, 1935.

137. Franklin D. Roosevelt to Edward M. House, April 10, 1935, House Papers, Series I, Box 95, Sterling Library, Yale University.

138. Franklin D. Roosevelt to Cordell Hull, March 9, 1935, Roosevelt Papers, P.S.F., Box 144, Franklin D. Roosevelt Library.

139. John C. Wiley to Robert F. Kelley, March 16, 1935, Wiley Papers, Box 1.

140. Offner, *American Appeasement*, p. 117.

141. George S. Messersmith to William Phillips, July 8, 1935, N.A., R.G. 59, 863.00/1209.

142. Henry L. Stimson Diary, May 5, 1935.

143. J. Pierrepont Moffat to Hugh R. Wilson, May 28, 1935, Moffat Papers.

144. J. Pierrepont Moffat to Ferdinand L. Mayer, April 18, 1935, Moffat Papers.

145. Thomas W. Lamont Diary, June 9, 1935, Lamont Papers, Box 173.

146. Thomas W. Lamont to Russell C. Leffingwell, July 9, 1935, Lamont Papers, Box 173.

147. Thomas W. Lamont Memorandum, July 1935, Lamont Papers, Box 173.

148. Divine, *The Illusion of Neutrality*, pp. 57–60.

149. *The Memoirs of Cordell Hull*, vol. I, pp. 397–410.

150. William Phillips Diary, July 22, 1935. See also Robert W. Bingham Diary, September 10, 1935.

151. Divine, *The Illusion of Neutrality*, pp. 122–125.

152. Hugh R. Wilson to Cordell Hull, November 13, 1935, N.A., R.G. 59, 740.00/40 1/2. See also Wilson to Hull, January 27, 1936, N.A., R.G. 59, 740.00/41 1/2.

153. Norman H. Davis to Hugh R. Wilson, November 7, 1935, Wilson Papers. See also James C. Dunn to George S. Messersmith, September 30, 1935, Messersmith Papers.

154. R. Walton Moore to William C. Bullitt, October 1, 1935, Moore Papers, Box 3, Franklin D. Roosevelt Library. See, for a contrary view, J. Pierrepont Moffat to William R. Castle, February 28, 1936, Moffat Papers.

155. Divine, *The Illusion of Neutrality*, pp. 134–152.

156. Franklin D. Roosevelt to William E. Dodd, December 2, 1935, N.A., R.G. 59, 862.00/3558.

157. Divine, *The Illusion of Neutrality*, pp. 152–161.

158. Offner, *American Appeasement*, pp. 139–146.

159. Norman H. Davis, Meeting of the Board of Trustees of the Carnegie Endowment for International Peace, May 7, 1936, Carnegie Endowment for International Peace Papers, Box 22, Butler Library, Columbia University.

160. George S. Messersmith to Cordell Hull, July 2, 1936, Hull Papers. See also Messersmith to Hull, July 10, 1936, Hull Papers.

161. George S. Messersmith to Cordell Hull, August 28, 1936, Hull Papers. See also Messersmith to Hull, September 18, 1936, Hull Papers.

162. George S. Messersmith to R. Walton Moore, December 5, 1936, Messersmith Papers.

163. Edgar B. Nixon, ed., *Franklin D. Roosevelt and Foreign Affairs*, vol. III (Cambridge: Harvard University Press, 1969), p. 267.

164. William E. Dodd to Franklin D. Roosevelt, October 19, 1936, Roosevelt Papers, P.S.F., Box 45.

165. William E. Dodd to Franklin D. Roosevelt, December 7, 1936, N.A., R.G. 59, 862.00/3634 1/2.

166. *Foreign Policy Reports*, November 15, 1936, pp. 214–15; and March 15, 1937, pp. 9–16.

167. William E. Dodd to Cordell Hull, November 12, 1936, N.A., R.G. 59, 862.00/3627; and Dodd to Hull, January 21, 1937, 862.50 Four Year Plan/30.

168. Memorandum of Conversation Between Cordell Hull and Hans Luther, August 15, 1935, N.A., R.G. 59, 611.6231/675. See also Memorandum of Conversation Between Hull and Luther, March 28, 1935, N.A., R.G. 59, 662.0031/89; and Memorandum of Conversation Between Hjalmar Schacht and Samuel R. Fuller, September 23, 1935, 862.00/3558.

169. George S. Messersmith to William Phillips, November 8, 1934, N.A., R.G. 59, 863.00/1135. See also Messersmith to Phillips, June 19, 1934, 863.00/1075; Douglas Jenkins to Cordell Hull, January 11, 1935, 862.50/861; and William E. Dodd to Hull, October 15, 1936, 862.50/957.

170. H. Merle Cochran to Cordell Hull, June 13, 1936, N.A., R.G. 59, 611.6231/796.

171. Thomas W. Lamont to Hjalmar Schacht, August 13, 1936, Lamont Papers, Box 182.

172. Hugh R. Wilson to Cordell Hull, June 17, 1935, N.A., R.G. 59, 862.20/1059. See also Wilson to Hull, November 13, 1935, 740.00/40 1/2; and Wilson to Hull, January 26, 1936, 740.00/41 1/2.

173. *Foreign Policy Reports*, June 19, 1935, p. 104.

174. Robert W. Bingham to Daniel C. Roper, March 28, 1935, Bingham Papers, Box 22, Library of Congress.

175. *Annals of the American Academy of Political and Social Science*, July 1936, p. 16.

176. *Vital Speeches*, September 1, 1936, p. 731.

177. *Think*, January 1936, p. 12.

178. Daniel C. Roper to Franklin D. Roosevelt, November 4, 1935, Roosevelt Papers, P.P.F., Box 2975.

179. Francis B. Sayre to John Foster Dulles, March 21, 1936, Dulles Papers, Box 15.

180. Herbert Feis to George S. Messersmith, November 5, 1936, Feis Papers, Box 21.

181. *Vital Speeches*, December 15, 1936, p. 134.

182. J. Pierrepont Moffat to Norman H. Davis, June 19, 1936, Moffat Papers.

183. J. Pierrepont Moffat to Hugh R. Wilson, August 21, 1936, Wilson Papers, Box 3. See also Moffat to Joseph C. Green, June 13, 1936, Moffat Papers.

184. J. Pierrepont Moffat to Norman H. Davis, June 19, 1936, Davis Papers, Library of Congress. See also Moffat to William Phillips, May 28, 1936, N.A., R.G. 59, 611.4731/162 1/2.

185. J. Pierrepont Moffat to George S. Messersmith, October 15, 1936, Moffat Papers.

186. Leo Pasvolsky, Memorandum on the Possibilities of Concerted Action with the British Government in the Sphere of Commercial Policy, February 27, 1936, N.A., R.G. 59, 641.0031/69.

187. Norman H. Davis to J. Pierrepont Moffat, July 29, 1936, Moffat Papers.

188. J. Pierrepont Moffat to Norman H. Davis, October 7, 1936, Moffat Papers.

189. Memorandum of Conversation Between Cordell Hull and Ronald Lindsay, February 5, 1936, N.A., R.G. 59, 611.4131/141.

190. Memorandum of Conversation Between Cordell Hull and Ronald Lindsay, October 22, 1936, N.A., R.G. 59, 611.4131/195.

4. The Quest for Economic Appeasement

1. Sumner Welles to William E. Dodd, May 25, 1937, N.A., R.G. 59, 600.0031 World Program/123. See also Bernard M. Baruch to Henry A. Wallace, October 18, 1937, Baruch Papers, Mudd Library, Princeton University.

2. Division of Trade Agreements Memorandum on What Might Be Said to M. van Zeeland, June 24, 1937, National Archives, Record Group 59, 640.0031/136.

3. John Cudahy to Franklin D. Roosevelt, December 26, 1936, Roosevelt Papers, P.S.F., Box 65, Franklin D. Roosevelt Library. See also Cudahy to R. Walton Moore, March 20, 1937, Moore Papers, Box 4, Franklin D. Roosevelt Library.

4. Leo Pasvolsky to Cordell Hull, January 18, 1937, Pasvolsky Papers, Box 7, Library of Congress.

5. Memorandum of a Conversation in the State Department, December 10, 1937, N.A., R.G. 59, 611.0031/3087/1/2.

6. Breckinridge Long to Franklin D. Roosevelt, April 5, 1935, Edgar B. Nixon, ed., *Franklin D. Roosevelt and Foreign Affairs*, vol. II (Cambridge: Harvard University Press, 1969), p. 457. See also John C. Wiley to Robert F. Kelley, April 4, 1935, Wiley Papers, Box 1, Franklin D. Roosevelt Library.
7. William E. Dodd to Cordell Hull, February 8, 1936, N.A., R.G. 59, 862.20/1107.
8. William C. Bullitt, December 20, 1936, Roosevelt Papers, P.S.F., Box 43. See also Bullitt to Cordell Hull, July 19, 1937, Hull Papers, Library of Congress.
9. *Vital Speeches*, May 1, 1937, p. 447.
10. Cordell Hull to Mackenzie King, April 2, 1937, N.A., R.G. 59, 600.0031 World Program/63. See also Hull to Premier Colijn, March 19, 1937, N.A., R.G. 59, 640.0031/97.
11. Memorandum of a Conversation Between Cordell Hull and H. O. Chalkley, August 9, 1937, N.A., R.G. 59, 611.4131/355.
12. Memorandum of a Conversation Between Cordell Hull and Frederick Phillips, September 22, 1937, N.A., R.G. 59, 611.4131/383. See also Henry L. Stimson Diary, April 4, 1938, Sterling Library, Yale University.
13. Cordell Hull to Thomas W. Lamont, November 30, 1937, Lamont Papers, Box 209, Baker Library, Harvard Business School.
14. Herbert Feis to John MacMurray, February 17, 1937, Feis Papers, Box 21, Library of Congress. See also Feis to Edwin C. Wilson, October 2, 1937, Feis Papers, Box 28.
15. Herbert Feis to Felix Frankfurter, October 6, 1937, Feis Papers, Box 16. See also J. Pierrepont Moffat Diary. June 20, 1937 Houghton Library, Harvard University.
16. Norman Davis to Cordell Hull, April 10, 1937, N.A., R.G. 59, 740.00/143. See also Memorandum of a Conversation Between Francis B. Sayre and H. O. Chalkley, March 2, 1937, N.A., R.G. 59, 611.4131/274.
17. Division of Trade Agreements Memorandum on What Might Be Said to M. van Zeeland, June 24, 1937, N.A., R.G. 59, 640.0031/136. See also Memorandum of a Conversation Between Sumner Welles and van Zeeland, June 25, 1937, 600.0031 World Program/142 1/2.
18. Herbert Feis to John C. Wiley, July 2, 1937, Wiley Papers, Box 7.
19. Memorandum of a Conversation Between Sumner Welles and Ronald Lindsay, July 31, 1937, N.A., R.G. 59, 611.4131/359 1/2.
20. Thomas W. Lamont to William North Duane, July 18, 1937, Lamont Papers, Box 92.

21. Thomas W. Lamont to Cordell Hull, May 27, 1937, Lamont Papers, Box 173. See also Lamont to Lord Lothian, March 22, 1937, Lamont Papers, Box 105; and Lamont to Lady Astor, June 4, 1937, Lamont Papers, Box 82.

22. Thomas W. Lamont to Sir James Arthur Salter, June 11, 1937, Lamont Papers, Box 129. See also Lamont to General Jan C. Smuts, June 29, 1937, Lamont Papers, Box 131.

23. Leo Pasvolsky to James C. Dunn, April 29, 1937, N.A., R.G. 59, 600.0031 World Program/93. See also Joseph E. Davies to Cordell Hull, June 8, 1937, Hull Papers.

24. J. Pierrepont Moffat to Earl C. Squire, August 14, 1937, Moffat Papers, Houghton Library, Harvard University.

25. Francis B. Sayre to William Phillips, April 12, 1937, Sayre Papers, Library of Congress. See also Memorandum of a Conversation Between Sayre and Kenneth Banta, October 6, 1937, N.A., R.G. 59, 611.4131/398.

26. J. Pierrepont Moffat to Earl C. Squire, August 14, 1937, Moffat Papers. See also Wayne C. Taylor to Henry Morgenthau, August 28, 1937, Morgenthau Papers, Correspondence, Box 282, Roosevelt Library.

27. Memorandum of a Conversation Between Harry C. Hawkins, John D. Hickerson, and O. D. Skelton, September 1, 1937, N.A., R.G. 59, Hickerson Files, Box 4.

28. John D. Hickerson to J. Pierrepont Moffat, November 2, 1937, Moffat Papers.

29. Memorandum of a Conversation in the State Department, December 10, 1937, N.A., R.G. 59, 611.0031/3087 1/2. See also Henry L. Stimson Diary, March 24, 1938.

30. *Business Week*, July 23, 1938, p. 36. See also November 19, 1938, p. 13; and November 26, 1938, pp. 14–16.

31. Samuel R. Fuller, Jr., to Franklin D. Roosevelt, October 11, 1935, Cordell Hull Papers; Fuller to Roosevelt, October 10, 1936, Morgenthau Papers, Correspondence, Franklin D. Roosevelt Library, Box 1.

32. Douglas Miller, Hitler's Second Four-Year-Plan, October 5, 1936, N.A., R.G. 151.

33. *Foreign Affairs*, January 1937, pp. 229–230. See also William C. Bullitt to Cordell Hull, April 29, 1937, N.A., R.G. 59, 740.00/153.

34. William E. Dodd to Cordell Hull, August 18, 1936, N.A., R.G. 59, 711.62/116; William E. Dodd, Jr. and Martha Dodd, eds., *Ambassador Dodd's Diary* (New York: Harcourt, Brace, and Co., 1941), pp. 380, 388–89; Memorandum of a Conversation Between Dr. Schacht

and Lord Lothian, May 5, 1937, Franklin D. Roosevelt Papers, P.S.F., Box 44.

35. *Ambassador Dodd's Diary*, pp. 376–77.

36. Joseph E. Davies to Franklin D. Roosevelt and Cordell Hull, January 20, 1937, N.A., R.G. 59, 740.00/100.

37. William C. Bullitt to R. Walton Moore, December 17, 1936, N.A., R.G. 59, 751.62/381; Bullitt to Franklin D. Roosevelt, December 20, 1936, Roosevelt Papers, P.S.F., Box 43.

38. William C. Bullitt to R. Walton Moore, January 12, 1937, N.A., R.G. 59, 751.62/386; Bullitt to Cordell Hull, February 20, 1937, Franklin D. Roosevelt Papers, P.S.F., Box 24.

39. William C. Bullitt to Franklin D. Roosevelt, December 7, 1936, Roosevelt Papers, Box 43. See also Bullitt to Roosevelt, November 24, 1936, Roosevelt Papers, P.S.F., Box 41; Bullitt to R. Walton Moore, January 13, 1937, Roosevelt Papers, P.S.F., Box 24; and Memorandum of a Conversation Between M. Bonnet and Edwin C. Wilson, February 4, 1937, N.A., R.G. 59, 862.00 Four Year Plan/28.

40. William C. Bullitt to R. Walton Moore, January 13, 1937, N.A., R.G. 59, 751.62/387. See also Bullitt to Franklin D. Roosevelt, January 10, 1937, Roosevelt Papers, P.S.F., Box 43.

41. George S. Messersmith to Cordell Hull, March 2, 1937, Hull Papers. See also Messersmith to John Hickerson, January 27, 1937, Messersmith Papers, University of Delaware; and Messersmith to Herbert Feis, March 4, 1937, Messersmith Papers.

42. *Ambassador Dodd's Diary*, pp. 388–389. See also Dodd to Francis B. Sayre, January 22, 1937, N.A., R.G. 59, 611.6231/920.

43. Memorandum for the Honorable Norman H. Davis: Contribution to a Peace Settlement, February 16, 1937, Davis Papers, Library of Congress.

44. R. Ralton Moore to John Cudahy, February 24, 1937, Moore Papers, Box 4.

45. Hugh R. Wilson to Cordell Hull, January 25, 1937, N.A., R.G. 59, 740.00/104; Memorandum of a Conversation Between Ray Atherton and Sir Robert Vansittart, April 20, 1937, 740./160; and William C. Bullitt to Cordell Hull, May 20, 1937, 740.00/178.

46. Norman H. Davis to Franklin D. Roosevelt and Cordell Hull, April 29, 1937, Roosevelt Papers, P.S.F., Box 28; William C. Bullitt to Hull, May 1, 1937, Roosevelt Papers, P.S.F., Box 24.

47. Robert W. Bingham Diary, March 20, 1937, Bingham Papers, Box 1, Library of Congress; Memorandum of a Conversation Between Bingham and Anthony Eden, May 3, 1937, N.A., R.G. 59, 740.00/170.

48. *The Memoirs of Cordell Hull*, vol. I (New York: Macmillan

Co., 1948), pp. 527–28; Wayne C. Taylor to Henry Morgenthau, February 19, 1937, Morgenthau Papers, Correspondence, Box 282.

49. Norman H. Davis to Franklin D. Roosevelt, April 13, 1937, Roosevelt Papers, P.S.F., Box 88.

50. William C. Bullitt to Cordell Hull, April 30, 1937, N.A., R.G. 59, 740.00/156; Bullitt to Hull, May 6, 1937, 740.00/164.

51. Franklin D. Roosevelt to William Phillips, May 17, 1937, in Elliot Roosevelt, ed., *F.D.R.: His Personal Letters, 1928–1945*, vol. I (New York: Duell, Sloan, and Pearce, 1950), pp. 680–81. See also Herbert Feis to John C. Wiley, May 20, 1937, Wiley Papers, Box 7.

52. William Phillips Diary, January 29, 1936, Houghton Library, Harvard University. See also James C. Dunn to J. Pierrepont Moffat, December 19, 1936, Moffat Papers.

53. Joseph E. Davies, *Mission to Moscow* (New York: Simon and Schuster, 1941), pp. 139–144.

54. J. Pierrepont Moffat Diary, September 16, 1937, Houghton Library, Harvard University. See also Moffat to Raymond H. Geist, April 20, 1938, Moffat Papers.

55. Arnold A. Offner, *American Appeasement: United States Foreign Policy and Germany, 1933–1938* (New York: W. W. Norton, 1969), pp. 204–210; Robert Dallek, *Democrat and Diplomat: The Life of William E. Dodd* (New York: Oxford University Press, 1968), p. 321.

56. William L. Langer and S. Everett Gleason, *The Challenge to Isolation*, vol. I (New York: Harper and Row, 1952), pp. 19–23. See also Beatrice B. Berle and Travis B. Jacobs, ed., *Navigating the Rapids, 1918–1971: From the Papers of Adolf A. Berle* (New York: Harcourt Brace Jovanovich, 1973), pp. 143–44.

57. Langer and Gleason, *Challenge to Isolation*, vol. I, pp. 24–25. See also Adolf A. Berle Diary, December 2, 1937, Berle Papers, Box 210, Franklin D. Roosevelt Library.

58. Neville Chamberlain to Franklin D. Roosevelt, January 14, 1938, N.A., R.G. 59, 740.00/264 A.

59. Franklin D. Roosevelt to Neville Chamberlain, January 17, 1938, N.A., R.G. 59, 740.00/264 B.

60. Langer and Gleason, *Challenge to Isolation*, vol. I, pp. 26–27; Offner, *American Appeasement*, pp. 219–222.

61. Offner, *American Appeasement*, pp. 224–29.

62. Hugh R. Wilson to Cordell Hull, March 24, 1938, Hull Papers.

63. Douglas Miller, Annual Economic Review: Germany 1937, Pt. II, March 29, 1938, N.A., R.G. 151.

64. Anthony Biddle to Cordell Hull, June 19, 1938, N.A., R.G. 59, 740.00/441.

65. *Business Week*, May 7, 1938, p. 33. See also February 26, 1938, p. 13.

66. Adolf A. Berle Diary, March 19, 1938.

67. *Ibid.*, February 16, 1938.

68. *Ibid.*, February 21, 1938. See also Hugh R. Wilson to Cordell Hull, March 24, 1938, Hull Papers; and R. Walton Moore to John Cudahy, May 16, 1938, Moore Papers, Box 4.

69. Adolf A. Berle to Cordell Hull and Sumner Welles, March 16, 1938, Berle Papers, Box 210. See also Bernard N. Baruch to Joseph P. Kennedy, March 30, 1938, Baruch Papers.

70. Henry L. Stimson Diary, March 24, 1938. See also Hugh R. Wilson to Cordell Hull, March 24, 1938, Hull Papers; George S. Messersmith to Hugh R. Wilson, March 4, 1938, Wilson Papers, Box 3, Herbert C. Hoover Library; and J. Pierrepont Moffat to Wilson, April 30, 1938, Moffat Papers.

71. J. Pierrepont Moffat Diary, January 18, 1938. See also September 29, 1937.

72. *Ibid.*, March 11, 1938.

73. George S. Messersmith to Cordell Hull, July 31, Hull Papers.

74. William E. Dodd to Franklin D. Roosevelt, April 1, 1936, Dodd Papers, Library of Congress.

75. *The Memoirs of Cordell Hull*, vol. I, p. 544.

76. William L. Neumann, *America Encounters Japan: From Perry to MacArthur* (New York: Harper and Row, 1965), pp. 240–42.

77. Moffat Diary, October 10, 1937. See also entry for October 8, 1937.

78. Hugh R. Wilson to Joseph C. Grew, October 18, 1937, Wilson Papers, Box 2.

79. Herbert Feis, *The Road to Pearl Harbor* (Princeton: Princeton University Press, 1950), p. 13; and Berle and Jacobs, eds., *Navigating the Rapids*, p. 140.

80. *The Memoirs of Cordell Hull*, vol. I, pp. 550–53.

81. Norman H. Davis to Cordell Hull, November 2, 1937, N.A., R.G. 59, 793. 94 Conference/176. See also Memorandum of a Conversation Between Sumner Welles and Robert Lindsay, November 13, 1937, 793.94 Conference/251.

82. Norman H. Davis to Franklin D. Roosevelt, November 10, 1937, N.A., R.G. 59, 793.94 Conference/219; and Davis to Cordell Hull, November 19, 1937, 793.94 Conference/274.

83. Neumann, *America Encounters Japan*, pp. 234–36.

84. Lloyd C. Gardner, *Economic Aspects of New Deal Diplomacy* (Madison: University of Wisconsin Press, 1964), p. 138.

85. Neumann, *America Encounters Japan*, p. 248

86. Stimson Diary, April 27, 1938.

87. *Ibid.*

88. Arnold A. Offner, *The Origins of the Second World War: American Foreign Policy and World Politics, 1917–1941* (New York: Praeger Publishers, 1975), p. 154.

89. *The Memoirs of Cordell Hull*, vol. I, p. 569.

90. Langer and Gleason, *The Challenge to Isolation*, pp. 42–43.

91. *Ibid.*, pp. 44–45.

92. Neumann, *America Encounters Japan*, p. 246.

93. Moffat Diary, November 5, 1938.

94. Offner, *The Origins of the Second World War*, p. 157.

95. Hugh R. Wilson to Cordell Hull, May 18, 1938, Franklin D. Roosevelt Papers, P.S.F., Box 26; Wilson to Hull, September 15, 1938, Roosevelt Papers, P.S.F., Box 27; William C. Bullitt to Hull, September 15, 1938, Roosevelt Papers, P.S.F., Box 24.

96. William C. Bullitt to Franklin D. Roosevelt, May 20, 1938, Roosevelt Papers, P.S.F., Box 43.

97. Adolf A. Berle to Franklin D. Roosevelt, September 1, 1938, Roosevelt Papers, P.S.F., Box 94. See also Berle Diary, August 29, 1938.

98. Adolf A. Berle Diary, September 1, 1938. See also Hugh R. Wilson to Cordell Hull, September 15, 1938, Franklin D. Roosevelt Papers, P.S.F., Box 27.

99. J. Pierrepont Moffat Diary, September 26, 1938. See also Joseph P. Kennedy to Cordell Hull, September 21, 1938, Franklin D. Roosevelt Papers, P.S.F., Box 28.

100. Offner, *American Appeasement*, p. 261. See also Robert Dallek, *Franklin D. Roosevelt and American Foreign Policy, 1932–1945* (New York: Oxford University Press, 1979), pp. 164–65; and Joseph P. Lash, *Roosevelt and Churchill, 1939–1941* (New York: W. W. Norton, 1976), pp. 25–27.

101. Berle and Jacobs, eds., *Navigating the Rapids*, pp. 186–87.

102. Langer and Gleason, *Challenge to Isolation*, vol. I, p. 33.

103. J. Pierrepont Moffat Diary, September 27, 1938.

104. Berle and Jacobs, eds., *Navigating the Rapids*, pp. 187–89.

105. Langer and Gleason, *Challenge to Isolation*, vol. I, pp. 33–34; and Offner, *American Appeasement*, pp. 264–66.

106. Berle and Jacobs, eds., *Navigating the Rapids*, p. 188.

107. Offner, *American Appeasement*, p. 269.

108. J. Pierrepont Moffat to Joseph P. Kennedy, September 20, 1938, Moffat Papers.

109. Thomas W. Lamont to Cordell Hull, October 4, 1938, Lamont Papers, Box 209. See also Bernard M. Baruch to Hugh R. Wilson, September 30, 1938, Wilson Papers, Box 1.

110. Franklin D. Roosevelt to William Phillips, October 17, 1938, in Elliot Roosevelt, ed., *F.D.R.: His Personal Letters*, vol. II, p. 819.

111. Franklin D. Roosevelt to Mackenzie King, October 11, 1938, Roosevelt Papers, P.S.F., Box 35.

112. *Foreign Affairs*, January 1939, p. 280.

113. *Business Week*, October 8, 1938, p. 47.

114. Anthony Biddle to Franklin D. Roosevelt, October 15, 1938, Roosevelt Papers, P.S.F., Box 65. See also Ray Atherton to Cordell Hull, October 18, 1938, Roosevelt Papers, P.S.F., Box 23.

115. *Foreign Affairs*, January 1939, p. 301.

116. Douglas Miller, Implications of the Annexation of the Sudeten Land, October 3, 1938, N.A., R.G. 151.

117. J. Pierrepont Moffat Diary, November 3, 1938. See also Memorandum on Germany's Future in Southeastern Europe by Mr. Straight, January 30, 1939, N.A., R.G. 59, 600.6217/43.

118. *Business Week*, September 24, 1938, p. 43.

119. *Official Report of the National Foreign Trade Convention*, 1938, pp, 36–37.

120. Dick Steward, *Trade and Hemisphere: The Good Neighbor Policy and Reciprocal Trade* (Columbia: University of Missouri Press, 1975), p. 256.

121. Lawrence Duggan to Hugh R. Wilson, May 31, 1938, Wilson Papers, Box 1.

122. J. Pierrepont Moffat Diary, July 24, 1939.

123. *Fortune*, December 1937, p. 178. See also May 1939, p. 97.

124. Berle and Jacobs, eds., *Navigating the Rapids*, pp. 177, 212.

125. Bernard M. Baruch to Franklin D. Roosevelt, April 29, 1938, Roosevelt Papers, P.S.F., Box 14.

126. *Business Week*, June 25, 1938, p. 38.

127. Josephus Daniels to Cordell Hull, June 30, 1938, Daniels Papers, Box 83, Library of Congress.

128. Josephus Daniels to Cordell Hull, July 8, 1938, Hull Papers. See also Daniels to William E. Dodd, February 20, 1939, Daniels Papers, Box 75.

129. Thomas W. Lamont to Adolf A. Berle, June 22, 1938, Lamont Papers, Box 209.

130. Herbert Feis to Norman Armour, September 20, 1938, Feis Papers, Box 11; and R. Walton Moore to Frederick A. Delano, September 24, 1938, Moore Papers, Box 4.

131. George S. Messersmith to D. N. Heineman, November 7, 1938, Messersmith Papers. See also Henry A. Wallace to Cordell Hull, December 16, 1940, Wallace Papers, University of Iowa.

132. Franklin D. Roosevelt to Henry A. Wallace, January 10, 1941, Wallace Papers, University of Iowa.

133. Steward, *Trade and Hemisphere*, pp. 148, 264. See also *Business Week*, July 30, 1938, p. 38; October 29, 1938, p. 15; and March 11, 1939, p. 51.

134. *Fortune*, June 1939, p. 41.

135. David S. Wyman, *Paper Walls: America and the Refugee Crisis, 1938–1941* (Amherst: University of Massachusetts Press, 1968), pp. 28–37.

136. John M. Blum, *From the Morgenthau Diaries: Years of Crisis, 1928–1938*, vol. I (Boston: Houghton Mifflin, 1959), pp. 380–427. See also George L. Harrison to Marriner S. Eccles, March 4 and May 20, 1938, Harrison Papers, Box 4, Butler Library, Columbia University.

137. Marriner S. Eccles, *Beckoning Frontiers* (New York: Alfred A. Knopf, 1951), p. 303–311; Rexford G. Tugwell, *The Democratic Roosevelt* (Garden City, N.Y.: Doubleday, 1957), pp. 444–45; and Berle and Jacobs, eds., *Navigating the Rapids*, pp. 152, 153, 172.

138. Morgenthau Papers, Presidential Diary, January 16, 1938, Book 1. See also Berle and Jacobs eds., *Navigating the Rapids*, pp. 148, 152, 154; and Walter Lippmann to Lewis W. Douglas February 7, 1938, Douglas Papers, Box 253, University of Arizona.

139. Berle and Jacobs, eds., *Navigating the Rapids*, p. 176.

140. John M. Blum, *From the Morgenthau Diaries: Years of Urgency, 1938–1941*, vol. II (Boston: Houghton Mifflin, 1964), pp. 24–25.

141. Wyman, *Paper Walls*, pp. 3–5, 67–115, 168–183.

142. *Ibid.*, p. 43; and Henry L. Feingold, *The Politics of Rescue: The Roosevelt Administration and the Holocaust, 1938–1945* (New Brunswick, N.J.: Rutgers University Press, 1970), p. 23.

143. Confidential Statement by George S. Messersmith before the First Meeting of the President's Advisory Committee on Political Refugees, May 16, 1938, Myron C. Taylor Papers, Box 8, Franklin D. Roosevelt Library.

144. Wyman, *Paper Walls*, p. 57; and Feingold, *The Politics of Rescue*, p. 32.

145. Robert T. Pell to Myron C. Taylor, December 22, 1939, Taylor Papers, Box 5.

146. J. Pierrepont Moffat Diary, August 26, 1938. See also Moffat to Hugh R. Wilson, August 29, 1938, Moffat Papers; and Myron C. Taylor to Cordell Hull and Sumner Welles, August 5, 1938, Taylor Papers, Box 5.

147. George Rublee to Myron C. Taylor, September 19, 1938, Taylor Papers, Box 5.

148. J. Pierrepont Moffat Diary, October 24, 1938. See also Moffat Diary, October 28, 1938.

149. *Ibid.*, November 3, 1938. See also George S. Messersmith to Raymond H. Geist, November 7, 1938, Messersmith Papers.

150. Robert T. Pell to J. Pierrepont Moffat, October 19, 1938, Moffat Papers. See also Franklin D. Roosevelt to Myron C. Taylor, November 23, 1938, Taylor Papers, Box 5.

151. Minutes of the Fourteenth Meeting of the President's Advisory Committee on Political Refugees, December 23, 1938, Myron C. Taylor Papers, Box 8.

152. Myron C. Taylor, Confidential Memorandum Regarding Refugees, 1938–1947, Taylor Papers, Box 8; and Memorandum by George L. Warren, April 10, 1938, Taylor Papers, Box 8.

153. J. Pierrepont Moffat Diary, May 4, 1939. See also Moffat Diary, March 23 and April 25, 1939.

154. Robert T. Pell to J. Pierrepont Moffat, May 1, 1939, Myron C. Taylor Papers, Box 5. See also Moffat to Sumner Welles, May 11, 1939, Moffat Papers; Pell to Moffat, May 12, 1939, Taylor Papers, Box 5; and Pell to Taylor, May 15, 1939, Taylor Papers, Box 5.

155. Minutes of the Twenty-second Meeting of the President's Advisory Committee on Political Refugees, March 24, 1939, Myron C. Taylor Papers, Box 8.

156. George L. Warren, Memorandum on the Proposed Private International Corporation, April 10, 1939, Myron C. Taylor Papers, Box 8.

157. J. Pierrepont Moffat Diary, May 4, 1939.

158. George L. Warren to Myron C. Taylor, June 8, 1939, Taylor Papers, Box 8; Robert T. Pell to Cordell Hull, June 9, 1939, Taylor Papers, Box 5; and Warren to Taylor, June 14, 1939, Taylor Papers, Box 8.

159. Sumner Welles to Myron C. Taylor, June 22, 1939, Taylor Papers, Box 5. See also Taylor to Welles, June 25, 1939. Taylor Papers, Box 6.

160. *Business Week*, September 24, 1938, p. 48.

161. Josephus Daniels to Franklin D. Roosevelt, October 3, 1938, Roosevelt Papers, P.S.F., Box 61.

162. J. P. Morgan to Thomas W. Lamont, October 5, 1938, Lamont Papers, Box 108.

163. Edgar W. Smith to Henry A. McBride, October 28, 1938, Cordell Hull Papers.

164. *Think*, October 1938, p. 27.

165. *Official Report of the National Foreign Trade Convention,* 1938, p. 50.

166. Thomas W. Lamont to Cordell Hull, October 4, 1938, Lamont Papers, Box 209.

167. Berle and Jacobs, eds., *Navigating the Rapids*, p. 189.

168. *Ibid.*

169. Offner, *American Appeasement*, p. 269.

170. Franklin D. Roosevelt to Mackenzie King, October 11, 1938, Roosevelt Papers, P.S.F., Box 35.

171. Hugh R. Wilson to Cordell Hull, October 11, 1938, Wilson, *A Career Diplomat The Third Chapter: The Third Reich* (Westport, Conn.: Greenwood, 1960), pp. 55–57.

172. William E. Dodd to Cordell Hull, April 2, 1937, N.A., R.G. 59, 862.50/983; and Joseph P. Kennedy to Hull, February 27, 1939, 862.50/1040.

173. Memorandum by Mr. Sussdorff, April 17, 1937, N.A., R.G. 59, 600.0031 World Program/101.

174. Alan Bullock, *Hitler: A Study in Tyranny* (New York: Harper and Row, 1971), pp. 234, 284–85; and Raymond J. Sontag, *A Broken World* (New York: Harper and Row, 1971), pp. 302–324, 351.

175. *Business Week*, January 28, 1939, p. 15; and February 4, 1939, p. 14.

176. George S. Messersmith to Cordell Hull, January 24, 1939, N.A., R.G. 59, 862.51/4699. See also Messersmith to Hull, Welles, Dunn, and Moffat, January 23, 1939, N.A., R.G. 59, 711.62/220 1/2.

177. Adolf A. Berle Diary, January 27, 1939.

178. Memorandum by Anthony Biddle, March 11, 1939, in Philip V. Cannistraro, Edward D. Wynet, Jr., and Theador P. Kovaleff, eds., *Poland and the Coming of the Second World War: The Diplomatic Papers of A. J. Drexel Biddle, Jr., United States Ambassador to Poland, 1937–1939* (Columbus: Ohio State University Press, 1976).

5. The Carrot and the Club

1. Robert A. Divine, *The Illusion of Neutrality* (Chicago: Quadrangle Books, 1962), pp. 162–99.

2. *The Memoirs of Cordell Hull*, vol. I (New York: Macmillan Company, 1948), pp. 563–64.

3. William L. Langer and S. Everett Gleason, *The Challenge to Isolation*, vol. I (New York: Harper and Row, 1952), pp. 50–51.

4. *Ibid.*, pp. 46–48.

5. Frank M. Andrews, Lecture Before the Army War College, October 1, 1938, Franklin D. Roosevelt Papers, P.S.F., Box 116, Roosevelt Library.

6. H. H. Arnold, Memorandum for the Chief of Staff, November 15, 1938, Franklin D. Roosevelt Papers, O.F., Box 25t.

7. *Foreign Affairs*, April 1939, p. 467.

8. Arthur Murray to Franklin D. Roosevelt, December 15, 1938, Roosevelt Papers, P.S.F., Box 53.

9. Joseph P. Lash, *Roosevelt and Churchill: The Partnership That Saved the West, 1939–1941* (New York: W. W. Norton, 1976), pp. 30–31.

10. John M. Blum, *From the Morgenthau Diaries: Years of Urgency, 1938–1941*, vol. II (Boston: Houghton Mifflin, 1964), p. 49.

11. *Foreign Policy Reports*, May 1, 1939, p. 47.

12. J. Pierrepont Moffat Diary, October 15, 1938, Houghton Library, Harvard University.

13. *Ibid.*, October 17, 1938.

14. Beatrice B. Berle and Travis B. Jacobs, eds., *Navigating the Rapids, 1918–1971: From the Papers of Adolf A. Berle* (New York: Harcourt Brace Jovanovich, 1973), p. 198.

15. *Foreign Policy Reports*, May 15, 1939, p. 60. See also March 1, 1940, p. 309.

16. J. Pierrepont Moffat Diary March 15, 1939. See also Adolf A. Berle Diary, March 16 and 17, Berle Papers, Box 210, Franklin D. Roosevelt Library.

17. *Business Week*, March 18, 1939, p. 11. See also March 25, 1939, p. 15 and May 27, 1939, p. 58.

18. *Foreign Policy Reports*, May 15, 1939, pp. 59–60. See also R. M. Stephenson, *Monthly Economic Review*, Berlin, April 12, 1939, N.A., R.G. 151; Percy G. Black, Report of the Acting Military Attaché, Berlin, April 18, 1939, National Archives, Record Group 165; and Hugh R. Wilson to Cordell Hull, May 19, 1939, Hull Papers, Library of Congress.

19. Harry Dexter White to Henry Morgenthau, April 1939, Morgenthau Diaries, Book 181, Franklin D. Roosevelt Library.

20. Adolf A. Berle, Memorandum, March 16, 1939, Berle Papers, Box 55.

21. J. Pierrepont Moffat Diary, March 15, 1939.

22. *Ibid.*

23. Berle and Jacobs, eds., *Navigating the Rapids*, pp. 199–201.

24. Blum, *From the Morgenthau Diaries*, vol. II, pp. 78–82.

25. Langer and Gleason, *The Challenge to Isolation*, vol. I, pp. 77–78.

26. J. Pierrepont Moffat Diary, March 27, 1939.

27. Langer and Gleason, *The Challenge to Isolation*, vol. I, pp. 74, 78.

28. *Barron's*, May 8, 1939, p. 10.

29. Berle and Jacobs, eds., *Navigating the Rapids*, pp. 210–13.

30. Langer and Gleason, *The Challenge to Isolation*, vol. I, p. 85.

31. Franklin D. Roosevelt to Henry Morgenthau, Telephone Conversation, April 15, 1939, Morgenthau Papers, Presidential Diaries, Book 1.

32. *Think*, May 1939, p. 12. See also John Cudahy to R. Walton Moore, August 17, 1939, Moore Papers, Box 4, Franklin D. Roosevelt Library.

33. Memorandum of a Conversation Between Robert S. Hudson, Owen Chalkley, Herbert Feis, and Francis B. Sayre, May 10, 1939, N.A., R.G. 59, 600.6217/48. See also 611.0031 Executive Committee /713/714/719.

34. *Annals of the American Academy of Political and Social Science*, July 1939, pp. 59–65. See also *Foreign Affairs*, January 1939, pp. 374–90; and *Fortune*, May 1939, p. 100.

35. Thomas J. Watson, Speech Before the Board of Trustees of the Carnegie Endowment for International Peace, May 5, 1939, Carnegie Endowment for International Peace Papers, Box 22, Butler Library, Columbia University. See also Watson to Franklin D. Roosevelt, July 5, 1939; Roosevelt Papers, O.F., Box 273.

36. Berle and Jacobs, eds., *Navigating the Rapids*, p. 229.

37. Elliot Roosevelt, ed., *F.D.R.: His Personal Letters, 1928–1945*, vol. II (New York: Duell, Sloan, and Pearce, 1950), p. 891.

38. Lash, *Roosevelt and Churchill*, pp. 31–32, 63–64.

39. *The Memoirs of Cordell Hull*, vol. I, pp. 613, 642. See also Thomas W. Lamont to Walter Lippmann, April 27, 1939, Lamont Papers, Box 105, Baker Library, Harvard Business School.

40. William C. Bullitt to Cordell Hull, May 10, 1939, Franklin D. Roosevelt Papers, P.S.F., Box 25. See also Bullitt to R. Walton Moore, May 19, 1939, Moore Papers, Box 3.

41. Divine, *The Illusion of Neutrality*, pp. 263–71.

42. J. Pierrepont Moffat Diary, May 27, 1939.

43. Arnold A. Offner, *The Origins of the Second World War* (New York: Praeger Publishers, 1975), p. 128.

44. Divine, *The Illusion of Neutrality*, p. 282.

45. Joseph E. Davies, *Mission to Moscow* (New York: Simon and Schuster, 1941), p. 452. See also pp. 168, 203, 228.

46. *Ibid.*, p. 439. See also pp. 434, 436, 440.

47. Maurice Cowling, *The Impact of Hitler: British Politics and British Policy, 1933–1940* (Chicago: University of Chicago Press, 1975), pp. 297–302.

48. Joseph P. Kennedy to Cordell Hull, February 17, 1939, Franklin D. Roosevelt Papers, P.S.F., Box 28.

49. Cowling, *The Impact of Hitler*, pp. 294, 303.

50. Joseph P. Kennedy to Cordell Hull, March 28, 1939, Franklin D. Roosevelt Papers, P.S.F., Box 28.

51. Langer and Gleason, *The Challenge to Isolation*, vol. I, pp. 94, 108.

52. William C. Bullitt to Cordell Hull, May 6, 1939, Franklin D. Roosevelt Papers, P.S.F., Box 25. See also Bullitt to Hull, June 6, and July 5, 1939, Roosevelt Papers, P.S.F., Box 25.

53. Joseph E. Davies to Franklin D. Roosevelt, June 8, 1939, Roosevelt Papers, P.S.F., Box 33.

54. Langer and Gleason, *The Challenge to Isolation*, vol. I, pp. 124–25.

55. Davies, *Mission to Moscow*, p. 450.

56. Sumner Welles to Laurence A. Steinhardt, August 4, 1939, Steinhardt Papers, Box 27, Library of Congress.

57. Alan Bullock, *Hitler: A Study in Tyranny* (New York: Harper and Row, 1962), p. 298; William L. Shirier, *The Rise and Fall of the Third Reich* (New York: Simon and Schuster, 1960), p. 542.

58. Langer and Gleason, *The Challenge to Isolation*, vol. I, pp. 165–69.

59. William C. Bullitt to Cordell Hull, August 22, 1939, Franklin D. Roosevelt Papers, P.S.F., Box 26.

60. J. Pierrepont Moffat Diary, August 24, 1939.

61. *Ibid.* See also Berle and Jacobs, eds., *Navigating the Rapids*, pp. 236, 243–44.

62. Cowling, *The Impact of Hitler*, pp. 355–360. See also Joseph P. Kennedy to Franklin D. Roosevelt and Cordell Hull, November 8, 1939, N.A., R.G. 59, 740.0019 European War 1939/133; William C. Bullitt to Roosevelt, October 4, 1939, Roosevelt Papers, P.S.F., Box 2;

and Bullitt to Roosevelt, December 11, 1939, Roosevelt Papers, P.S.F., Box 43.

63. William R. Davis to Franklin D. Roosevelt, October 11, 1939, Robert E. Wood Papers, Box 3, Herbert C. Hoover Library. See also Berle and Jacobs, eds., *Navigating the Rapids*, pp. 256, 265–66; and J. Pierrepont Moffat to Leland Harrison, November 14, 1939, Moffat Papers, Houghton Library, Harvard University.

64. Berle and Jacobs, eds., *Navigating the Rapids*, p. 264. See also J. Pierrepont Moffat Diary, October 7, 1939; and George S. Messersmith to Cordell Hull, October 8, 1939, Hull Papers.

65. Joseph E. Davies to Cordell Hull, October 15, 1939, N.A., R.G. 59, 740.0011 European War 1939/1035. See also John C. Wiley to Arthur Bliss Lane, November 27, 1939, Wiley Papers, Box 8, Franklin D. Roosevelt Library; and *Business Week*, October 21, 1939, p. 52.

66. Berle and Jacobs, eds., *Navigating the Rapids*, p. 254. See also J. Pierrepont Moffat to John C. Wiley, October 31, 1939, Wiley Papers and Moffat to Owen Norem, November 18, 1939, Moffat Papers.

67. Fred L. Israel, ed., *The War Diary of Breckinridge Long* (Lincoln: University of Nebraska Press, 1966), p. 1. See also p. 66.

68. Herbert Feis to Henry L. Stimson, October 16, 1939, Stimson Papers, Series I, Box 132, Sterling Library, Yale University.

69. Breckinridge Long Diary, December 6, 1939, Long Papers, Box 5, Library of Congress.

70. Roosevelt, ed., *F.D.R.: His Personal Letters*, vol. II, pp. 967–68.

71. William C. Bullitt to Franklin D. Roosevelt, September 13, 1939, Roosevelt Papers, P.S.F., Box 43. See also Bullitt to Roosevelt, September 16, 1939, Roosevelt Papers, P.S.F., Box 2; Bullitt to Cordell Hull, September 19, 1939, Hull Papers; George S. Messersmith to Hull, October 11, 1937, N.A., R.G. 59, 740.00/217 1/2; Messersmith to Hull, October 8, 1939, Hull Papers; Messersmith to Hull, March 26, 1940, Messersmith Papers, University of Delaware Library; and Messersmith to Breckinridge Long, March 27, 1940, Long Papers, Box 133, Library of Congress.

72. Israel, ed., *The War Diary of Breckinridge Long*, p. 72.

73. Adolf A. Berle Diary, March 4, 1940, Berle Papers, Box 211. See also Berle to Cordell Hull, March 23, 1940, Berle Papers, Box 211; Henry A. Wallace Diary, March 26, 1940, University of Iowa Library; and Josephus Daniels Diary, March 18, 1940, Daniels Papers, Box 8, Library of Congress.

74. *Proceedings of the National Foreign Trade Convention*, 1939, p. xvii. See also *Foreign Affairs*, January 1940, pp. 324–35.
75. Langer and Gleason, *The Challenge to Isolation*, vol. I, p. 277.
76. *Think*, April 1940, p. 6.
77. Langer and Gleason, *The Challenge to Isolation*, vol. I, pp. 250–88.
78. Lash, *Roosevelt and Churchill*, pp. 64–66.
79. William C. Bullitt to Franklin D. Roosevelt, September 8, 1939, Roosevelt Papers, P.S.F., Box 43. See also Bullitt to Roosevelt, September 16, 1939 and October 4, 1939, Roosevelt Papers, P.S.F., Box 2.
80. *Foreign Relations of the United States*, 1939, vol. I, p. 674.
81. Robert Dallek, *Franklin D. Roosevelt and American Foreign Policy, 1932–1945* (New York: Oxford University Press, 1979), p. 201.
82. Memorandum of a Telephone Conversation Between Thomas W. Lamont and Franklin D. Roosevelt, September 16, 1939, Lamont Papers, Box 127.
83. Langer and Gleason, *The Challenge to Isolation*, pp. 222–29.
84. Divine, *The Illusion of Neutrality*, pp. 317–35.
85. Captain William D. Puleston to Henry Morgenthau, January 9, 1940, Morgenthau Diaries, Box 298. See also Puleston to Morgenthau, May 6, 1940, Morgenthau Diaries, Book 299.
86. Lash, *Roosevelt and Churchill*, p. 87.
87. *The Secret Diary of Harold L. Ickes: The Lowering Clouds, 1939–1941*, vol. III (New York: Simon and Schuster, 1954), p. 37.
88. *Ibid.*, p. 182.
89. Israel, ed., *The War Diary of Breckinridge Long*, p. 24.
90. R. Walton Moore to Francis B. Sayre, February 28, 1940, Moore Papers, Box 25.
91. J. Pierrepont Moffat Diary, September 1, 1939. See also Moffat Diary, December 8, 1939; Joseph E. Davies to Cordell Hull, October 15, 1939, N.A., R.G. 59, 740.0011 European War/1035; John Cudahy to Missy LeHand, November 17, 1939, Franklin D. Roosevelt Papers, P.S.F., Box 56; and Alexander C. Kirk to Herbert Feis, February 12, 1940, Feis Papers, Box 20, Library of Congress.
92. *Barron's*, January 15, 1940, p. 36. See also April 8, 1940, p. 10.
93. John Foster Dulles to Harlan F. Stone, April 1, 1940, Dulles Papers, Box 19, Firestone Library, Princeton University.

94. James D. Mooney to Franklin D. Roosevelt, March 11, 1940, N.A., R.G. 59, 740.0011 European War/1824 1/2.

95. *Fortune*, January 1940, pp. 72–73.

96. *Ibid.*, April 1940, p. 96. See also *Barron's*, May 13, 1940, p. 10; and *Magazine of Wall Street*, June 15, 1940, p. 272.

97. Special Committee Memorandum Number Nine, Steps Toward a Durable Peace, February 2–4, 1940, National Policy Committee Papers, Box 19, Library of Congress.

98. *Business Week*, November 11, 1939, p. 60. See also September 30, 1939, p. 51; and October 7, 1939, p. 52.

99. *Commercial and Financial Chronicle*, January 20, 1940, p. 312.

100. *Bankers' Magazine*, January 1940, pp. 75–76. See also *Country Gentlemen*, November 1939, p. 20.

101. Thomas W. Lamont to General Jan C. Smuts, February 16, 1940, Lamont Papers, Box 131. See also Memorandum of a Conversation Between Herbert C. Hoover and W. Cameron Forbes, September 20, 1939, Forbes Papers, Confidential Letterbook, Houghton Library, Harvard University.

102. Berle and Jacobs eds. *Navigating the Rapids* p. 281. See also Henry A. Wallace Diary, January 2, 1940.

103. Hugh R. Wilson, Jr., *A Career Diplomat: The Third Chapter, The Third Reich* (New York: Vantage Press, 1960), p. 95.

104. Adolf A. Berle Diary, January 13, 1940. See also Breckinridge Long Diary, January 13, 1940, Long Papers, Box 5.

105. Leo Pasvolsky, Memorandum on the Proposed Conference of Neutrals, January 29, 1940, N.A., R.G. 59, Records of Harley A. Notter, Box 108.

106. Israel, ed., *The War Diary of Breckinridge Long*, pp. 53–54.

107. James D. Mooney to Franklin D. Roosevelt, March 12, 1940, N.A., R.G. 59, 740.0011 European War 1939/1824 1/2.

108. Myron C. Taylor to Franklin D. Roosevelt, February 27, 1940, Taylor Papers, Box 10, Franklin D. Roosevelt Library.

109. Proposal for Consultation on Postwar Economic and Disarmament Problems, February 10, 1940, N.A., R.G. 59, Records of Harley A. Notter, Box 108.

110. Sumner Welles, *The Time for Decision* (New York: Harper and Brothers, 1944), p. 74.

111. Langer and Gleason, *The Challenge to Isolation*, vol. I, p. 362.

112. Welles, *The Time for Decision*, pp. 85–86, 103–07.

113. Langer and Gleason, *The Challenge to Isolation*, vol. I. pp. 365–70.

114. Sumner Welles, The Peace Settlement, Franklin D. Roosevelt Papers, P.S.F., Box 9.

115. *The Memoirs of Cordell Hull*, vol. I, p. 735.

116. An analysis of the Replies to the Proposal for Consultation on Postwar Reconstruction, May 23, 1940, N.A., R.G. 59, Records of Harley A. Notter, Box 108.

117. Economic Subcommittee of Advisory Committee on Problems of Foreign Relations, Memorandum on America's Postwar Policy, April 2, 1940, N.A., R.G. 59, Records of Harley A. Notter, Box 108.

118. Wilson, *A Career Diplomat*, p. 100. See also Hugh R. Wilson Diary, April 16, 1940, Wilson Papers, Box 4, Herbert C. Hoover Library.

119. William C. Bullitt to Cordell Hull, January 25, 1940, Franklin D. Roosevelt Papers, P.S.F., Box 26.

120. Henry A. Wallace Diary, April 12, 1940.

121. *The Memoirs of Cordell Hull*, vol. I, 777–84.

122. Langer and Gleason, *The Challenge to Isolation*, pp. 63–65, 102–03, 147–48.

123. Berle and Jacobs, eds., *Navigating the Rapids*, p. 241.

124. Langer and Gleason, *The Challenge to Isolation*, pp. 194, 295.

125. Berle and Jacobs, eds., *Navigating the Rapids*, p. 241.

126. *The Memoirs of Cordell Hull*, vol. I, pp. 718–22.

127. Langer and Gleason, *The Challenge to Isolation*, pp. 298–300.

128. *Ibid.*, p. 305.

129. Adolf A. Berle Diary, December 11, 1939.

130. Herbert Feis, *The Road to Pearl Harbor* (Princeton: Princeton University Press, 1950), p. 44.

131. *Ibid.*, pp. 49–50.

132. *The Secret Diary of Harold L. Ickes: The Lowering Clouds, 1939–1941*, vol. III, p. 96.

133. Langer and Gleason, *The Challenge to Isolation*, p. 578–80.

134. *The Memoirs of Cordell Hull*, vol. I, p. 725.

135. *Foreign Affairs*, April 1940, p. 466.

136. Langer and Gleason, *The Challenge to Isolation*, pp. 584–88.

137. Feis, *The Road to Pearl Harbor*, pp. 56–57; Henry A. Wallace Diary, May 24, 1940.

138. Langer and Gleason, *The Challenge to Isolation*, pp. 52–53.

139. Feis, *The Road to Pearl Harbor*, p. 57.

140. Memorandum of a Meeting of the State Department Advisory Committee on Problems of Foreign Relations, May 31, 1940, Hugh R. Wilson Papers, Box 1.

141. George S. Messersmith to Breckinridge Long, March 27, 1940 Long Papers, Box 133.

6. The Nightmare of a Closed World

1. Franklin D. Roosevelt to Lewis W. Douglas, June 7, 1940, Douglas Papers, Box 261, University of Arizona Library.

2. John M. Blum, *From the Morgenthau Diaries: Years of* Urgency, 1938–1941, vol. II (Boston: Houghton Mifflin, 1964), p. 156.

3. David Reynolds, *The Creation of the Anglo-American Alliance* 1937–1941: *A Study in Competitive Co-Operation* (Chapel Hill: University of North Carolina Press, 1981), P. 78.

4. William L. Langer and S. Everett Gleason, *The Challenge to Isolation: The World Crisis of 1937–1940 and American Foreign Policy* (New York: Harper and Row, 1952), p. 414.

5. Reynolds, *The Creation of the Anglo-American Alliance*, p. 100.

6. Joseph P. Lash, *Roosevelt and Churchill: The Partnership That Saved the West, 1939–1941* (New York: W. W. Norton, 1976), p. 136.

7. *Ibid.*, p. 167.

8. Mark L. Chadwin, *The Warhawks: American Interventionists Before Pearl Harbor* (New York: W. W. Norton, 1968), pp. 32–42.

9. J. Pierrepont Moffat Diary, May 3, 1940, Houghton Library, Harvard University.

10. Frank Knox to Annie Knox, June 15, 1940, Knox Papers, Box 3, Library of Congress.

11. Langer and Gleason, *The Challenge to Isolation*, pp. 495–96, 514–15; Chadwin, *The Warhawks*, p. 9.

12. Franklin D. Roosevelt to Henry L. Stimson, May 21, 1940, Stimson Papers, Series I, Box 134, Sterling Library, Yale University.

13. Beatrice B. Berle and Travis B. Jacobs, eds., *Navigating the Rapids 1918–1971: From the Papers of Adolf A. Berle* (New York: Harcourt Brace Jovanovich, 1973), p. 314.

14. Memorandum of a Meeting of the State Department Advisory Committee on Problems of Foreign Relations, May 31, 1940, Hugh R. Wilson Papers, Box 1, Herbert C. Hoover Library.

15. Langer and Gleason, *The Challenge to Isolation*, pp. 474–76, 671–72, 676.

16. Langer and Gleason, *The Challenge to Isolation*, p. 622; Chadwin, *The Warhawks*, p. 30.

17. *Business Week*, June 29, 1940, p. 7.

18. Alexander C. Kirk, Memorandum, June 17, 1940, Franklin D. Roosevelt Papers, P.S.F., Box 44.

19. Hugh R. Wilson, *A Career Diplomat The Third Chapter: The Third Reich* (Westport, Conn.: Greenwood Press, 1960), p 105.

20. Reference Shelf, vol. 14, No. 7, p. 100.

21. Henry A. Wallace Diary, May 17, 1940, University of Iowa Library.

22. *Ibid.*, May 18, 1940.

23. Henry Morgenthau Diaries, June 17, 1940, vol. 273, p. 87, Franklin D. Roosevelt Library.

24. Fred L. Israel, ed., *The War Diary of Breckinridge Long* (Lincoln: University of Nebraska Press, 1966), p. 98. See also Summary of the First Meeting of the Interdepartmental Group to Consider Post-War Economic Problems and Policies, May 27, 1940, Hugh R. Wilson Papers, Box 1.

25. National Policy Committee, Memorandum on the Implications to the United States of a German Victory, June 8, 1940, National Archives, Record Group 59, 740.0011 European War 1939/5459. See also Harry L. Hopkins, Remarks at a Press Conference, May 23, 1940, Hopkins Papers, Box 301, Franklin D. Roosevelt Library; Harry Dexter White, Memorandum, June 15, 1940, White Papers, Mudd Library, Princeton University; and Henry A. Wallace to William F. Riley, June 17, 1940, Wallace Papers, University of Iowa Library.

26. Alexander C. Kirk, Memorandum, June 17, 1940, Franklin D. Roosevelt Papers, P.S.F., Box 44. See also Joseph E. Davies to Cordell Hull, May 23, 1940, N.A., R.G. 59, 740.0011 European War 1939/3911; and Anthony Biddle, Memorandum on the French Defeat, July 1, 1940, Franklin D. Roosevelt Papers, P.S.F., Box 41.

27. Joel C. Hudson, Memorandum on German and European Post-War Economy, August 15, 1940, N.A., R.G. 59, 840.50/184. See also Hudson to State Department, July 9, 1940, N.A., R.G. 59, 600.6215/87.

28. Bernard M. Baruch to Joseph E. Davies, May 31, 1940, Baruch Papers, Mudd Library, Princeton University. See also Baruch to Franklin D. Roosevelt, June 4, 1940; and Baruch to Sheridan Downey, June 14, 1940.

29. W. Averell Harriman, Remarks Before the Greater Omaha Association, June 1, 1940, Harry L. Hopkins Papers, Box 302.

30. Lewis W. Douglas to Carl Hayden, June 5, 1940, Douglas Papers, Box 261.

31. *Bankers' Magazine*, June 1940, p. 509. See also July 40, p. 65; and August 1940, p. 156.

32. *Magazine of Wall Street*, June 15, 1940, p. 271. See also June 29, 1940, p. 381.

33. *Business Week*, June 22, 1940, pp. 37–44. See also May 25, 1940, p. 13; and July 20, 1940, p. 52.

34. Adolf A. Berle Diary, May 25, 1940, Berle Papers, Box 211, Franklin D. Roosevelt Library.

35. Memorandum of a Meeting of the State Department Advisor Committee on Problems of Foreign Relations, May 31, 1940, Hugh R. Wilson Papers, Box 1.

36. William D. Puleston, Memorandum of a Conversation with J. W. White, June 7, 1940, Henry Morgenthau Diaries, vol. 300, p. 22.

37. *Business Week*, June 22, 1940, p. 42. See also *Commercial and Financial Chronicle*, July 27, 1940, p. 489; *Barron's*, August 5, 1940, p. 3; *Annalist*, August 15, 1940, p. 202; and *Magazine of Wall Street*, August 24, 1940, p. 562.

38. Frederick J. Dobney, ed., *Selected Papers of Will Clayton* (Baltimore: The Johns Hopkins Press, 1971), pp. 48–54.

39. George N. Peek to Chester C. Davis, June 18, 1940, Peek Papers, Box 36, University of Missouri Library. See also Peek to Charles J. Brand, May 29, 1940, Box 36; Peek to Charles McNarry, July 8, 1940, Box 37; Peek to Frank W. Murphy, July 8, 1940, Box 37; and Peek to Murphy, August 7, 1940, Box 37.

40. George N. Peek to Raymond Moley, July 4, 1940, Peek Papers, Box 37. See also Peek to Moley, June 13, 1940, Box 36.

41. Adolf A. Berle Diary, May 25, 1940, Berle Papers, Box 211. See also Duddly Wood, Memorandum, May 22, 1940, N.A., R.G. 59, Leo Pasvolsky File, Box 1; and Henry A. Wallace Diary, June 1, 3, 6, 1940.

42. Langer and Gleason, *The Challenge to Isolation*, p. 632.

43. Franklin D. Roosevelt to Henry Morgenthau, June 15, 1940, Morgenthau Diaries, Vol 273, pp. 49–53.

44. Henry A. Wallace Diary, June 19, 1940; Memorandum on Interdepartmental Conference, June 19, 1940, Henry Morgenthau Diaries, vol. 274, pp. 118–30; Henry A. Wallace to Harry L. Hopkins, June 26, 1940, Hopkins Papers, Box 301.

45. Sumner Welles, Henry Morgenthau, Henry A. Wallace, and Harry L. Hopkins to Franklin D. Roosevelt, June 20, 1940, Morgenthau Diaries, vol. 274, pp. 232–35.

46. Memorandum on White House Conference, June 27, 1940, Henry Morgenthau Diaries, vol. 276, p. 177. See also Franklin D. Roosevelt to Bernard M. Baruch, June 22, 1940, Baruch Papers.
47. Harry C. Hawkins to Henry F. Grady, June 28, 1940, N.A., R.G. 59, Dean G. Acheson File, Box 5.
48. *Barron's*, July 29, 1940, p. 10. See also *Business Week*, July 20, 1940, pp. 15–17.
49. *Reference Shelf*, vol. 14, no. 5, pp. 232–50. See also *Monthly Bulletin of the New York Chamber of Commerce*, vol. 32, no. 7 (January 1941), p. 294.
50. *Official Report of the Twenty-seventh National Foreign Trade Convention*, 1940, pp. 346–47.
51. Henry F. Grady to Edgar W. Smith, June 15, 1940, N.A., R.G., 611.0031/ 5072A.
52. *Official Report of the Twenty-seventh National Foreign Trade Convention*, 1940, pp. 384–89.
53. Eugene P. Thomas to Harry C. Hawkins, July 9, 1940, N.A., R.G. 59, 600.1115 N.F.T.C./517.
54. Charles F. Darlington to Cordell Hull, September 25, 1940, Hull Papers, Library of Congress.
55. Henry Carter to George N. Peek, May 16, 1940, Peek Papers, Box 36.
56. *The Protectionist*, October 1940, pp. 140–42. See also Mordecai Ezekiel, Memorandum on Total Defense, August 26, 1940, N.A., R.G. 59, Leo Pasvolsky File, Box 1.
57. Louis Johnson to Franklin D. Roosevelt, January 13, 1939, Roosevelt Papers, P.S.F., Box 5; *Fortune*, August 1940, p. 119.
58. Langer and Gleason, *The Challenge to Isolation*, p. 477. See also Memorandum of a Meeting of the State Department Advisory Committee on the Problems of Foreign Relations, May 31, 1940, Hugh R. Wilson Papers, Box 1.
59. *International Conciliation*, February, 1941, p. 9. See also Henry A. Wallace to Bernard M. Baruch, September 29, 1939, Baruch Papers.
60. Arthur R. Upgren, Memorandum on a Pan-American Trade Bloc, July 26, 1940, *The War and Peace Studies of the Council on Foreign Relations*. See also Upgren, A Pan-American Trade Bloc, June 7, 1940.
61. Alvin H. Hansen, "Hemisphere Solidarity: Some Economic and Strategic Consideration," *Foreign Affairs*, October 1940, pp. 17–21. See also Hanson, Memorandum on Alternative Outcomes of the

War, June 28, 1940, *The War and Peace Studies of the Council on Foreign Relations.*

62. *Official Report of the Twenty-seventh National Foreign Trade Convention,* 1940, p. 298.

63. *Ibid.,* p. 4.

64. *Foreign Policy Reports,* August 1, 1940, p. 127. See also *Barron's,* June 17, 1940, p. 10.

65. Alvin H. Hansen, Memorandum on Alternative Outcomes of the War, June 28, 1940.

66. Arthur R. Upgren, Memorandum on the War and United States Foreign Policy, October 19, 1940, *The War and Peace Studies of the Council on Foreign Relations.*

67. *Official Report of the Twenty-seventh National Foreign Trade Convention,* 1940, p. 13.

68. *Commercial and Financial Chronicle* September 21, 1940, p. 1661. See also *Vital Speeches,* December 1, 1940, pp. 120–23.

69. *Official Report of the Twenty-seventh National Foreign Trade Convention,* 1940, Final Declaration.

70. *Commercial and Financial Chronicle,* August 10, 1940, p. 783.

71. *Business Week,* August 24, 1940, p. 15.

72. Thomas W. Lamont to Lady Astor, July 10, 1940, Lamont Papers, Box 82, Baker Library, Harvard Business School.

73. *Bankers' Magazine,* July 1940, p. 40.

74. Chadwin, *The Warhawks,* pp. 43–108.

75. Langer and Gleason, *The Challenge to Isolation,* pp. 481–82, 711–12.

76. Thomas W. Lamont to Lady Astor, September 13, 1940, Lamont Papers, Box 82.

77. Reynolds, *The Creation of the Anglo-American Alliance,* p. 112.

78. Langer and Gleason, *The Challenge to Isolation,* pp. 522, 568.

79. Thomas W. Lamont to Lady Astor, July 10, 1940, Lamont Papers, Box 82.

80. Franklin D. Roosevelt to Harold L. Ickes, July 6, 1940, Roosevelt Papers, O.F., Box 4044.

81. Lash, *Roosevelt and Churchill,* pp. 212–13. See also Langer and Gleason, *The Challenge to Isolation,* pp. 715–16.

82. Memorandum of a Cabinet Discussion, August 2, 1940, Henry Morgenthau Diaries, vol. 288, pp. 159–60; *The Secret Diary of Harold*

L. Ickes: The Lowering Clouds (New York: Simon and Schuster, 1954), pp. 292–93.

83. Langer and Gleason, *The Challenge to Isolation*, pp. 750–57; Chadwin, *The Warhawks*, pp. 88–98.

84. Cordell Hull to Joseph C. Grew, May 30, 1940, N.A., R.G. 59, 711.94/1517A. See also Presidential Diaries, June 3, 1940, vol. 3, p. 568, Henry Morgenthau Diaries.

85. Langer and Gleason, *The Challenge to Isolation*, pp. 592–94.

86. Herbert Feis, *The Road to Pearl Harbor* (Princeton: Princeton University Press, 1950), pp. 61–64.

87. Langer and Gleason, *The Challenge to Isolation* pp. 597–99.

88. *The Memoirs of Cordell Hull*, vol. I (New York: Macmillian, 1948), pp. 896–97.

89. *Ibid.*, pp. 897–99.

90. Langer and Gleason, *The Challenge to Isolation*, pp. 720–21.

91. Treasury Group Discussion, July 19, 1940, Henry Morgenthau Diaries, vol. 284, pp. 214–15. See also Harry Dexter White, Memorandum for the President, July 19, 1940, Morgenthau Diaries, vol. 284, p. 122.

92. Feis, *The Road to Pearl Harbor*, pp. 89–93. See also Record of a Telephone Conversation Between Henry Morgenthau and Henry L. Stimson, July 23, 1940, Morgenthau Diaries, vol. 285, pp. 317–324.

93. Harry Dexter White, Memorandum, August 13, 1940, White Papers, Mudd Library, Princeton University.

94. Presidential Diaries, August 16, 1940, vol. 3, p. 644, Henry Morgenthau Diaries.

95. William L. Langer and S. Everett Gleason, *The Undeclared War*, 1940–1941 (New York: Harper and Brothers, 1953), pp. 9–15.

96. Record of a Telephone Conversation Between Cordell Hull and Henry Morgenthau, September 12, 1940, Morgenthau Diaries, vol. 305, p. 126.

97. Record of a Telephone Conversation Between Cordell Hull and Henry Morgenthau, September 20, 1940, Morgenthau Diaries, vol. 307, p. 142.

98. Feis, *The Road to Pearl Harbor*, pp. 101–06.

99. Henry L. Stimson Diary, September 27, 1940.

100. Henry L. Stimson, Memorandum of Japan, October 2, 1940, Henry Morgenthau Diaries, vol. 318, p. 150.

101. Henry Morgenthau Diaries, October 2, 1941, vol. 318, p. 127.

102. Feis, *The Road to Pearl Harbor*, p. 123.

103. Berle and Jacobs, eds., *Navigating the Rapids*, pp. 238–40.

104. *The Memoirs of Cordell Hull*, vol. I, p. 911.

105. Lash, *Roosevelt and Churchill*, p. 223.

106. J. Pierrepont Moffat Diary, October 6–10, 1940. See also Adolf A. Berle Diary, October 17, 1940.

107. Francis B. Sayre to R. Walton Moore, October 19, 1940, Moore Papers, Box 19, Franklin D. Roosevelt Library. See also Sayre to Moore, December 31, 1940; and Sayre to James A. Farley, October 19, 1940, Sayre Papers, Library of Congress.

108. Elliot Roosevelt, ed., *F.D.R.: His Personal Letters, 1928–1945*, vol. II (New York: Duel, Sloan, and Pearce, 1950), p. 1093.

109. Langer and Gleason, *The Undeclared War*, p. 43.

110. The Territorial Group, Memorandum on Aid to China, October 11, 1940, *War and Peace Studies of the Council on Foreign Relations*. See also the Economic and Financial Group, Memorandum on American Far Eastern Policy, January 15, 1941.

111. Langer and Gleason, *The Undeclared War*, pp. 296–301.

112. William Diebold, Memorandum, November 23, 1940, *War and Peace Studies of the Council on Foreign Relations*. See also Diebold, Memorandum, December 14, 1940.

113. Feis, *The Road to Pearl Harbor*, pp. 142–57; Langer and Gleason, *The Undeclared War*, pp. 306–07.

114. Jesse H. Jones to Franklin D. Roosevelt, June 12, 1941, Jones Papers, Box 30, Library of Congress. See also Jones to Roosevelt, June 26, 1941.

115. Herbert Feis, *Three International Episodes: Seen from E.A.* (New York: W. W. Norton, 1966), pp. 55–90.

116. Dobney, ed., *Selected Papers of Will Clayton*, pp. 59–60. See also Jesse H. Jones to Franklin D. Roosevelt, February 24, 1941, Jones Papers, Box 30.

117. Council of National Defense to Franklin D. Roosevelt, December, 1940, Roosevelt Papers, P.S.F., Box 142. See also Josephus Daniels Diary, February 6, 1941, Daniels Papers, Box 8, Library of Congress.

118. *Fortune*, December 1940, p. 154.

119. *Ibid.*, May 1941, pp. 69–120.

120. Lloyd C. Gardner, *Economic Aspects of New Deal Diplomacy* (Madison: University of Wisconsin Press 1964), p. 145.

121. Manfred Jonas, *Isolationism in America, 1935–1941* (Ithaca: Cornell University Press, 1966), pp. 70–99; John N. Schacht, ed., *Three Faces of Midwestern Isolationism* (Iowa City: The Center for the Study of Recent History of the United States, 1981), pp. 37–38.

122. Robert E. Wood to George N. Peek, April 10, 1941, Peek Papers, Box 39. See also Schacht, ed., *Three Faces of Midwestern Isolationism*, p. 13.

123. Jonas, *Isolationism in America*, pp. 100–135.

124. Robert E. Wood, Speech before the Chicago Council on Foreign Relations, October 15, 1940, Morganthau Diaries, vol. 340, p. 250.

125. *Vital Speeches*, June 1, 1941, p. 490.

126. George N. Peek to R. Douglas Stuart, Jr., May 14, 1941, Peek Papers, Box 40. See also Peek to Stuart, January 1, 1941, Box 39; and Roy O. Woodruff to Peek, July 19, 1940, Box 40.

127. George N. Peek to Roy O. Woodruff, August 18, 1941, Peek Papers, Box 40. See also Samuel Crowther to George L. Harrison, August 21, 1941, Harrison Papers, Box 2, Butler Library, Columbia University.

128. *Magazine of Wall Street*, October 19, 1940, p. 5.

129. Josephus Daniels to Bernard M. Baruch, November 18, 1940, Daniels Papers, Box 65.

130. *Fortune*, April 1941, p. 59.

131. *Ibid.*, March 1941, p. 76.

132. Adolf A. Berle Diary, March 5, 1941, Berle Papers, Box 212. See also Spruille Braden to William Braden, September 4, 1940, Braden Papers, Box 7, Butler Library, Columbia University; and Memorandum on the Nationalization of South American Airlines, November 23, 1940, *War and Peace Studies of the Council on Foreign Relations*.

133. Adolf A. Berle to Emilio Collado, October 22, 1941, N.A., R.G. 59, Hanley A. Notter Files, Box 13.

134. Jesse H. Jones to Franklin D. Roosevelt, June 26, 1941, Jones Papers, Box 30, and Cordell Hull to Jones, October 29, 1941.

135. Berle and Jacobs, eds., *Navigating the Rapids*, p. 370.

136. *Vital Speeches*, May 1, 1941, p. 433.

137. *Foreign Commerce Weekly*, May 10, 1941, p. 224.

138. *Vital Speeches*, June 1, 1941, p. 509.

139. Ibid., February 15, 1941, p. 264.

140. Thomas W. Lamont, Memorandum, May 14, 1941, Lamont Papers, Box 127.

141. Vital Speeches, April 1, 1941, p. 373.

142. *Annals of the American Academy of Political and Social Science*, July 1941, pp. 50–51.

143. *Barron's*, January 6, 1941, p. 8.

144. *Ibid.*, June 16, 1941, p. 10.

145. Fortune, June 1941, p. 59.

146. *Vital Speeches*, February 15, 1941, p. 270.
147. Harley A. Notter, Memorandum on the Menace to the United States Through Other American Republics of a German Victory, January 24, 1941, N.A., R.G. 59, Notter File, Box 8.
148. William Phillips Diary, January 31, 1941, Houghton Library, Harvard University.
149. Herbert Feis to Bruce Bliven, January 31, 1941, Feis Papers, Box 11, Library of Congress.
150. Lynn R. Edminster, Memorandum on Foreign Trade and the World Crisis, May 21, 1941, Harry L. Hopkins Papers, Box 158.
151. Percy W. Bidwell and Arthur R. Upgren, "A Trade Policy for National Defense," *Foreign Affairs*, January 1941, p. 295. See also Eugene Stanley, "The Myth of the Continents," *Foreign Affairs*, April 1941, p. 492.
152. *Banker's Magazine*, September 1941, p. 210.
153. Percy W. Bidwell, "Self-Containment and Hemisphere Defense," August 12, 1941, reprinted in *Annals of the American Academy of Political and Social Science*, November 1941, pp. 184–85.

7. Roosevelt's Dilemma

1. Adolf A. Berle Diary, October 10, 1940, Berle Papers, Box 212, Franklin A. Roosevelt Library.
2. Ibid., October 11, 1940.
3. Beatrice B. Berle and Travis B. Jacobs, eds., *Navigating the Rapids: From the Papers of Adolf A. Berle, 1918–1971* (New York: Harcourt Brace Jovanovich, 1973), p. 336.
4. J. Pierrepont Moffat Diary, October 6–10, 1940, Houghton Library, Harvard University.
5. Thomas W. Lamont to Lord Bicester, October 11, 1940, Lamont Papers, Baker Library, Harvard Business School.
6. Henry L. Stimson Diary, December 13, 1940, Sterling Library, Yale University.
7. Berle and Jacobs, eds., *Navigating the Rapids*, p. 340. See also J. Pierrepont Moffat Diary, October 10, 1940.
8. Henry Morgenthau Diaries, October 29, 1940, vol. 326, p. 59, Franklin D. Roosevelt Library. See also Breckinridge Long Diary, November 12, 1940, Long Papers, Box 5, Library of Congress; Henry L. Stimson Diary, November 12, 1940; and Leon Henderson Diary, December 16, 1940, Henderson Papers, Box 36, Franklin D. Roosevelt Library.

9. William L. Langer and S. Everett Gleason, *The Undeclared War, 1940–1941* (New York: Harper and Brothers, 1953), p. 202.

10. *Ibid.*, pp. 204–09.

11. Admiral Harold R. Stark, Memorandum for the Secretary of the Navy, November 12, 1940, Franklin D. Roosevelt Papers, P.S.F., Box 5, Roosevelt Library.

12. Robert E. Sherwood, *Roosevelt and Hopkins: An Intimate History* (New York: Harper and Brothers, 1948), pp. 272–73; Langer and Gleason, *The Undeclared War*, pp. 222–23, 285–88; and Joseph P. Lash, *Roosevelt and Churchill: The Partnership That Saved the West, 1939–1941* (New York: W. W. Norton, 1976), pp. 266–67.

13. Robert Dallek, *Franklin D. Roosevelt and American Foreign Policy, 1932–1945* (New York: Oxford University Press, 1979), pp. 256–57.

14. Langer and Gleason, *The Undeclared War*, pp. 239, 254:56.

15. Russell C. Leffingwell to Franklin D. Roosevelt, January 9, 1941, Roosevelt Papers, P.S.F., Box 156.

16. Langer and Gleason, *The Undeclared War*, pp. 259–67.

17. Berle and Jacobs, eds., *Naviating the Rapids*, p. 362.

18. Langer and Gleason, *The Undeclared War*, pp. 421–22.

19. Henry L. Stimson Diary, December 16, 1940. See also December 19, 1940.

20. Lash, *Roosevelt and Churchill*, p. 298.

21. Presidential Diary, April 2, 1941, vol. 4, p. 280, Henry Morgenthau Diaries.

22. Henry L. Stimson Diary, April 10, 1941.

23. Langer and Gleason, *The Undeclared War*, pp. 446–451.

24. J. Pierrepont Moffat Diary, April 9, 1941.

25. Fred L. Israel, ed., *The War Diary of Breckinridge Long* (Lincoln: University of Nebraska Press, 1966), pp. 185–86, 195–96.

26. *Ibid.*, p. 196.

27. Leon Henderson Diary Notes, April 28, 1941, Henderson Papers, Box 36.

28. Henry Morgenthau Diaries, May 14, 1941, vol. 397, p. 301.

29. Frank Knox Diary, May 13, 1941, Knox Papers, Box 1, Library of Congress. See also Henry L. Stimson Diary, April 22, 1941, May 24, 1941; Stimson to Franklin D. Roosevelt, May 24, 1941, Stimson Papers, Series I, Box 137; and Jesse H. Jones to Roosevelt, May 27, 1941, Jones Papers, Box 29, Library of Congress.

30. Henry L. Stimson Diary, April 24, 1941.

31. *Ibid.*, May 23, 1941.

32. Orville H. Bullitt, ed., *For the President Personal and Secret*:

Correspondence Between Franklin A. Roosevelt and William C. Bullitt (Boston: Houghton Mifflin, 1972), p. 512.

33. Presidential Diary, May 17, 1941, vol. 4, p. 929, Henry Morgenthau Diaries.

34. Langer and Gleason, *The Undeclared War*, pp. 459–61.

35. Berle and Jacobs, eds., *Navigating the Rapids*, p. 369.

36. Breckinridge Long Diary, April 17, 1941, Long Papers, Box 5. See also April 25, 1941.

37. Langer and Gleason, *The Undeclared War*, pp. 476–77.

38. *Ibid.*, pp. 311–59.

39. *Ibid.*, pp. 122, 337, 342; William L. Shirer, *The Rise and Fall of the Third Reich* (New York: Simon and Schuster, 1960), pp. 798–821.

40. Laurence Steinhardt to Cordell Hull, June 12, 1941, Franklin D. Roosevelt Papers, P.S.F., Box 31. See also William C. Bullitt to Franklin D. Roosevelt, July 1, 1941, Roosevelt Papers, P.S.F., Box 1124; and Donald R. Heath to Henry Morgenthau, May 27, 1941, National Archives, Record Group 59, 862.50/1156.

41. Adolf A. Berle Diary, June 19, 1941, Berle Papers, Box 212; and J. Pierrepont Moffat Diary, June 26, 1941.

42. Langer and Gleason, *The Undeclared War*, pp. 537–38.

43. Joseph E. Davies, *Mission to Moscow* (New York: Simon and Schuster, 1941), pp. 475–97.

44. Langer and Gleason, *The Undeclared War*, p. 546.

45. Harry L. Hopkins to Franklin D. Roosevelt, August 20, 1941, Roosevelt Papers, P.S.F., Box 7. See also Sherwood, *Roosevelt and Hopkins*, pp. 317–44.

46. Langer and Gleason, *The Undeclared War*, pp. 792–97, 816–19.

47. *Ibid.*, p. 538.

48. Lash, *Roosevelt and Churchill*, p. 363.

49. Henry L. Stimson and McGeorge Bundy, *On Active Service in Peace and War* (New York: Harper and Brothers, 1947), p. 373; and Langer and Gleason, *The Undeclared War*, pp. 576–77.

50. Thomas W. Lamont to William North Duane, July 9, 1941, Lamont Papers, Box 92.

51. Henry L. Stimson Diary, July 9. 1941.

52. Lash, *Roosevelt and Churchill*, p. 372.

53. Henry L. Stimson Diary, July 21, 1941.

54. Langer and Gleason, *The Undeclared War*, pp. 570–74.

55. Roy C. Woodruff to George N. Peck, August 19, 1941, Peck Papers, Box 40.

56. Lash, *Roosevelt and Churchill*, pp. 401–02.
57. Shirer, *The Rise and Fall of the Third Reich*, pp. 879–82. See also Herbert Feis, *The Road to Pearl Harbor.* (Princeton: Princeton University Press, 1950), p. 214.
58. Captain John R. Beardall to Franklin D. Roosevelt, September 9, 1941, Roosevelt Papers, P.S.F., Box 5.
59. Langer and Gleason, *The Undeclared War*, pp. 743–47; and Lash, *Roosevelt and Churchill*, pp. 417–21.
60. Langer and Gleason, *The Undeclared War*, p. 738.
61. Henry L. Stimson Diary, August 28, 1941.
62. *Ibid.*, August 29, 1941. See also August 19, 1941; and September 25, 1941.
63. Joint Board Estimate of United States Over-All Production Requirements, September 11, 1941, Franklin D. Roosevelt Papers, P.S.F., Box 1. See also, for a published copy of the report, Sherwood, *Roosevelt and Hopkins*, pp. 410–18.
64. George C. Marshall to Franklin D. Roosevelt, September 22, 1941, Roosevelt Papers, P.S.F., Box 103. See also Henry L. Stimson to Roosevelt, September 23, 1941. Roosevelt Papers, P.S.F., Box 106.
65. Harold R. Stark to Cordell Hull, October 8, 1941, Harry L. Hopkins Papers, Box 298. See also, for published excerpts of the memorandum, Sherwood, *Roosevelt and Hopkins*, pp. 379–80.
66. Franklin D. Roosevelt to Mackenzie King, September 27, 1941, Roosevelt Papers, P.S.F., Box 35.
67. Lash, *Roosevelt and Churchill*, p. 422.
68. Thomas W. Lamont to General Jan C. Smuts, October 10, 1941, Lamont Papers, Box 131.
69. Thomas W. Lamont to John Foster Dulles, October 8, 1941, Lamont Papers, Box 20.
70. *Proceedings of the Twenty-eighth National Foreign Trade Convention*, 1941.
71. Langer and Gleason, *The Undeclared War*, pp. 595, 753–58. See also Bruce M. Russell, *No Clear and Present Danger: A Skeptical View of the U.S. Entry into World War II* (New York: Harper and Row. 1972), p. 80.
72. Franklin D. Roosevelt to William D. Leahy, November 1, 1941, Leahy Diaries, Library of Congress.
73. Harry L. Hopkins to James Norman Hall, November 12, 1941, Hopkins Papers, Box 308. See also Hopkins to John G. Winat, September 5, 1941, Box 306; J. Pierrepont Moffat Diary, September 24, 1941; and Henry L. Stimson Diary, October 21, 1941.

74. Henry A. Wallace to Harry L. Hopkins, November 21, 1941, Hopkins Papers, Box 298. See also Hopkins to Franklin D. Roosevelt, November 28, 1941, Box 312.

75. Israel, ed., *The War Diary of Breckinridge Long*, p. 221. See also Feis, *The Road to Pearl Harbor*, p. 200.

76. Herbert Feis, *The Road to Pearl Harbor*, pp. 209–18; and Langer and Gleason, *The Undeclared War*, pp. 625–31, 661–62.

77. Stanley K. Hornbeck to Thomas W. Lamont, June 25, 1941, Lamont Papers, Box 209.

78. Thomas W. Lamont to Stanley K. Hornbeck, June 30, 1941, Lamont Papers, Box 209.

79. Elliot Roosevelt, ed., *F.D.R.: His Personal Letters, 1928–1945*, vol. II (New York: Duell, Sloan, and Pearce, 1950). p. 1173.

80. *Ibid.*

81. *Ibid.*, p. 1174.

82. Feis, *The Road to Pearl Harbor*, pp. 215–19, 227.

83. *Ibid.*, pp. 224–29.

84. Notes on the Cabinet Meeting of July 18, 1941, Henry Morgenthau Papers, Presidential Diary, vol. 4, pp. 946–47.

85. Daniel W. Bell, Memorandum on the Cabinet Meeting of July 24, 1941, Henry Morgenthau Diaries, vol. 424, pp. 145–46.

86. *The Secret Diary of Harold L. Ickes: The Lowering Clouds, 1939–1941*, vol. III (New York: Simon and Schuster, 1954), p. 588.

87. Langer and Gleason, *The Undeclared War*, p. 653.

88. Feis, *The Road to Pearl Harbor*, pp. 245–52.

89. Langer and Gleason, *The Undeclared War*, pp. 654, 659.

90. *Ibid.*, pp. 657–58, 660.

91. Memorandum of a Conversation Between Sumner Welles and Alexander Cadogan August 9, 1941, N.A., R.G. 59, John D. Hickerson Files, Box 14.

92. J. Pierrepont Moffat Diary, August 20, 1941.

93. Sumner Welles, Memorandum on the Atlantic Conference, August 11, 1941, N.A., R.G. 59, John D. Hickerson Files, Box 14.

94. Langer and Gleason, *The Undeclared War*, pp. 694–97.

95. Lash, *Roosevelt and Churchill*, p. 410.

96. Langer and Gleason, *The Undeclared War*, pp. 700–02.

97. Lash, *Roosevelt and Churchill*, pp. 412–13.

98. Langer and Gleason, *The Undeclared War*, pp. 705–14; and Feis, *The Road to Pearl Harbor*, pp. 267–68.

99. Langer and Gleason, *The Undeclared War*, pp. 713–21; and Feis, *The Road to Pearl Harbor*, pp. 272–78.

100. Feis, *The Road to Pearl Harbor*, pp. 286–97; and Langer and Gleason, *The Undeclared War*, pp. 849–56.

101. Henry L. Stimson and McGeorge Bundy, *On Active Service in Peace and* War (New York: Harper and Brothers, 1947), p. 388.

102. Henry L. Stimson Diary, October 6, 1941.

103. Henry L. Stimson to Franklin D. Roosevelt, October 21, 1941, Roosevelt Papers, P.S.F., Box 106.

104. Lash, *Roosevelt and Churchill*, pp. 458–59. See also Dallek, *Franklin D. Roosevelt and American Foreign Policy*, p. 303.

105. Langer and Gleason, *The Undeclared War*, pp. 844–46.

106. *Ibid.*, p. 860.

107. Feis, *The Road to Pearl Harbor*, pp. 303–11; Langer and Gleason, *The Undeclared War*, pp. 858, 865–66.

108. J. Pierrepont Moffat Diary, Notes on a Visit to Washington, December 1–4, 1941; Memorandum of a Conversation Between Henry Morgenthau and J. V. Snoog, November 27, 1941, Morgenthau Papers, Presidential Diary, vol. 4, p. 1031.

109. Feis, *The Road to Pearl Harbor*, pp. 312–14. See also Memorandum of a Telephone Conversation Between Henry Morgenthau and Franklin D. Roosevelt, November 22, 1941, Morgenthau Papers, Presidential Diary, vol. 4, p. 1028.

110. Henry L. Stimson Diary, November 25, 1941.

111. Langer and Gleason, *The Undeclared War*, pp. 885–87; and Lash, *Roosevelt and Churchill*, p. 470.

112. Langer and Gleason, *The Undeclared War*, pp. 884, 888–91. See also Chiang Kai-shek to T. V. Snoog, November 25, 1941, Henry Morgenthau Papers, Presidential Diary, vol. 4, p. 1029.

113. Langer and Gleason, *The Undeclared War*, pp. 892–99.

114. Lash, *Roosevelt and Churchill*, pp. 474–83.

115. *Ibid.*, pp. 927–35.

116. Arnold A. Offner, *The Origins of the Second World War: American Foreign Policy and World Politics, 1917–1941* (New York: Praeger Publishers, 1975), p. 242.

117. Eleanor Roosevelt, *This I Remember* (New York: Harper and Row, 1949), p. 233.

118. Henry L. Stimson Diary, December 7, 1941.

119. Sherwood, *Roosevelt and Hopkins*, p. 431.

120. Langer and Gleason, *The Undeclared War*, pp. 937–41. See also Mark L. Chadwin, *The Warhawks: American Interventionists Before Pearl Harbor* (New York: W. W. Norton, 1968), pp. 264–66.

8. The Dream of a Pax Americana

1. *Commercial and Financial Chronicle,* January 6, 1940, p. 26.

2. *Vital Speeches,* April 1940, p. 394. See also *Think,* May 1940, p. 5.

3. Business Advisory Council, Report on the Reciprocal Trade Agreements Program, January 12, 1940, Harry L. Hopkins Papers, Box 109, Franklin D. Roosevelt Library. See also Edgar W. Smith to Cordell Hull, January 5, 1940, National Archives, Record Group 59, 611.0031/ 4599.

4. U. S. Congress, Senate, Extension of Reciprocal Trade Agreements Act: Hearings Before the Committee on Finance, 76th Congress, 3rd Session, 1940, p. 12.

5. *Foreign Affairs,* January 1940, p. 330. See also Fred L. Israel, ed., *The War Diaries of Breckinridge Long* (Lincoln: University of Nebraska Press, 1966), p. 38.

6. George N. Peek to Burton F. Peek, November 25, 1939, Peek Papers, Box 34, University of Missouri Library.

7. *Commercial and Financial Chronicle,* January 20, 1940, p. 363. See also Henry A. Wallace to Dan Wallace, January 16, 1940, Wallace Papers, University of Iowa.

8. Henry A. Wallace, *The American Choice* (New York: Reynal and Hitchcock, 1940), p. 27.

9. Cordell Hull to Edward A. O'Neal, January 26, 1940, Hull Papers, Library of Congress.

10. Beatrice B. Berle and Travis B. Jacobs, eds., *Navigating the Rapids: 1918–1971, From the Papers of Adolf A. Berle* (New York: Harcourt Brace Jovanovich, 1973), p. 301. See also Francis B. Sayre to R. Walton Moore, May 21, 1940, Moore Papers, Box 19, Franklin D. Roosevelt Library.

11. *Commercial and Financial Chronicle,* April 13, 1940, p. 2346.

12. *Ibid.,* May 25, 1940, p. 3295.

13. *Proceedings of the Export Managers' Club of New York,* March 26, 1940, pp. 3–11.

14. Russell C. Leffingwell to Thomas W. Lamont, April 4, 1940, Lamont Papers, Box 103, Baker Library, Harvard Business School.

15. Russell C. Leffingwell to Thomas W. Lamont, September 11, 1940, Lamont Papers, Box 103.

16. Thomas J. Watson, Speech Before the Board of Trustees of the

Carnegie Endowment for International Peace, December 11, 1939, Carnegie Endowment for International Peace Papers, Box 22, Butler Library, Columbia University.

17. Sumner Welles, The Peace Settlement, Franklin D. Roosevelt Papers, P.S.F., Box 9, Roosevelt Library.

18. Henry L. Stimson Diary, December 18, 1940, Sterling Library, Yale University. See also Hugh R. Wilson, Memorandum on World Order, January 22, 1940, R. Walton Moore Papers, Box 15.

19. *Business Week*, February 8, 1941, p. 64. See also March 1, 1941, p. 64; and May 3, 1941, p. 72.

20. *Fortune*, May 1941, pp. 54–55. See also July 1941, p. 35; and November 1941, p. 19.

21. *Bankers' Magazine*, September 1941, pp. 207–11. See also *Iron Age*, April 17, 1941, p. 21.

22. George N. Peek to Bernard M. Baruch, October 15, 1941, Baruch Papers, Mudd Library, Princeton University.

23. William Diebold, Memorandum, June 22, 1941, *The War and Peace Studies of the Council on Foreign Relations*.

24. Alvin H. Hansen, Memorandum on Altumative Outcomes of the War, June 28, 1940, *The War and Peace Studies of the Council on Foreign Relations*.

25. Leo Pasvolsky, Memorandum on the Proposed Neutrals Conference, January 29, 1940, N.A., R.G. 59, Harley A. Notter Files, Box 108.

26. Sumner Welles, The Peace Settlement, Franklin D. Roosevelt Papers, P.S.F., Box 9.

27. *Fortune*, November 1939, p. 121.

28. John Foster Dulles to William A. Irwin, November 17, 1941, Dulles Papers, Box 21, Firestone Library, Princeton University.

29. Thomas W. Lamont to Jan C. Smuts, February 16, 1940, Lamont Papers, Box 131. See also Lamont to Julian Huxley, January 2, 1940, Box 99.

30. Henry A. Wallace to Franklin D. Roosevelt, March 30, 1940, Roosevelt Papers, P.S.F., Box 73. See also Wallace to Roosevelt, April 1, 1940, P.S.F., Box 73.

31. Henry A. Wallace to Franklin D. Roosevelt, April 25, 1940, Henry Morgenthau Diaries, vol. 257, pp. 236–40, Roosevelt Library; and Thomas W. Lamont to Wallace, April 17, 1941, Wallace Papers.

32. *Foreign Policy Reports*, May 15, 1941, p. 63.

33. *Proceedings of the Export Managers' Club of New York*, March 25, 1941, pp. 22–30. See also *Business Week*, April 5, 1941, p. 68.

34. *Annals of the American Academy of Political and Social Science,* July 1941, p. 50.

35. Thomas W. Lamont to Jan C. Smuts, June 20, 1941, Lamont Papers, Box 131.

36. Adolf A. Berle Diary, July 31, 1941, Berle Papers, Box 213, Franklin D. Roosevelt Library.

37. J. Pierrepont Moffat Diary, September 24, 1941, Houghton Library, Harvard University. See also entries for December 1–4, 1941.

38. John D. Hickerson to J. Pierrepont Moffat, October 15, 1941, N.A., R.G. 59, Hickerson Files, Box 5. See also James C. Dunn to Cordell Hull, October 2, 1941, N.A., R.G. 59, 611.0031/5162.

39. Berle and Jacobs, eds., *Navigating the Rapids,* p. 378.

40. Harley A. Notter to Leo Pasvolsky, September 24, 1941, N.A., R.G. 59, Notter File, Box 8.

41. Henry Morgenthau Diaries, June 16, 1941, vol. 409, p. 69.

42. Franklin D. Roosevelt to Adolf A. Berle, June 26, 1941, Berle Papers, Box 212.

43. Mr. Stinebower, Memorandum on Surplus Commodity Agreements, June 5, 1941, N.A., R.G. 59, Dean G. Acheson Files, Box 5. See also Acheson to Fredrick Leith-Ross, July 22, 1941, N.A., R.G. 59, Leo Pasvolsky Files, Box 2.

44. Memorandum of a Conversation Between Harley A. Notter and Mr. Rothwell, August 30, 1941, N.A., R.G. 59, Notter Files, Box 8.

45. Adolf A. Berle to Franklin D. Roosevelt, July 9, 1941, Roosevelt Papers, P.S.F., Box 7. See also Berle Diary, September 25, 1941.

46. Mr. Fuqua to Dean G. Acheson, May 12, 1941, N.A., R.G. 59, 611.4131/2556½.

47. *The Memoirs of Cordell Hull,* vol. I (New York: Macmillian, 1948), pp. 748–49. See also pp. 734–35.

48. J. Pierrepont Moffat Diary, January 24, 1940.

49. *Ibid.,* February 2, 1940.

50. Leo Pasvolsky to Cordell Hull, March 12, 1940, N.A., R.G. 59, 600.0031 World Program/386½.

51. *Commercial and Financial Chronicle,* January 13, 1940, p. 58. See also William Allen White to Henry L. Stimson, November 27, 1939, Stimson Papers, Series I, Box 132, Sterling Library, Yale University; and Thomas W. Lamont to Quincy Wright, December 29, 1939, Lamont Papers, Box 20.

52. *Fortune,* January 1940, pp. 71–72.

53. Ibid., April 1940, pp. 90–100.

54. J. Pierrepont Moffat Diary, March 31, 1941. See also Henry Morgenthau Diaries, April 28, 1941, vol. 392, p. 86.

55. Memorandum for the President, June 9, 1941, Harry L. Hopkins Papers, Box 307.

56. Henry Morgenthau Diaries, June 4, 1941, vol. 404, pp. 272–73. See also Adolf A. Berle Diary, April 15, 1941.

57. Christopher Thorne, *Allies of a Kind: The United States, Britain and the War Against Japan, 1941–1945* (New York: Oxford University Press, 1978), p. 104.

58. Lloyd C. Gardner, *Economic Aspects of New Deal Diplomacy* (Madison: University of Wisconsin Press, 1964), pp. 276–77.

59. J. Pierrepont Moffat Diary, July 14, 1941.

60. Adolf A. Berle Diary, July 17, 1941.

61. Memorandum of a Conversation Between Dean G. Acheson and John Maynard Keynes, July 28, 1941, Franklin D. Roosevelt Papers, P.S.F. Box 16.

62. John Maynard Keynes to Dean G. Acheson, July 29, 1941, N.A., R.G. 59, Leo Pasvolsky Files, Box 2.

63. Harry C. Hawkins, Memorandum, August 4, 1941, Franklin D. Roosevelt Papers, P.S.F., Box 90. See also Hawkins to Dean G. Acheson, August 1, 1941, N.A., R.G. 59, Leo Pasvolsky Files, Box 2.

64. Sumner Welles, Memorandum, August 11, 1941, N.A., R.G. 59, John D. Hickerson Files, Box 14.

65. *Ibid.*

66. J. Pierrepont Moffat Diary, August 20, 1941.

67. Sumner Welles, Memorandum, August 11, 1941, N.A., R.G. 59, John D. Hickerson Files, Box 14.

68. Cordell Hull to American Embassy in London, August 23, 1941, N.A., R.G. 59, 740.0011 European War 1939/14454.

69. William L. Langer and S. Everett Gleason, *The Undeclared War, 1940–1941* (New York: Harper and Brothers, 1953), p. 689.

70. J. Pierrepont Moffat Diary, September 25, 1941.

71. *Official Report of the Twenty-eighth National Foreign Trade Convention,* 1941. See also Cordell Hull to Eugene P. Thomas, September 29, 1941, N.A., R.G. 59, 600.1115 N.F.T.C./549.

72. Dean G. Acheson to Cordell Hull, October 28, 1941, N.A., R.G. 59, Leo Pasvolsky Files, Box 2.

73. Harry C. Hawkins to Dean G. Acheson, October 10, 1941, N.A., R.G. 59, Harley A. Notter Files, Box 14.

74. Cordell Hull to Franklin D. Roosevelt, November 19, 1941, Roosevelt Papers, P.S.F., Box 16; and Memorandum of a Conversation

Between Dean G. Acheson, Herbert Feis, and Lord Halifax, December 2, 1941, N.A., R.G. 59, Harley A. Notter Files, Box 14.

75. John G. Winant, *Letters From Grosvenor Square* (Boston: Houghton Mifflin, 1947), p. 156.

76. William L. Langer and S. Everett Gleason, *The Challenge to Isolation: The World Crisis of 1937–1940 and American Foreign Policy* (New York: Harper and Row, 1952), pp. 644–46.

77. *Foreign Relations of the United States*, 1940, vol. I, p. 390.

78. Langer and Gleason, *The Undeclared War*, p. 125.

79. *Foreign Relations of the United States*, 1940, vol. I, p. 623.

80. Langer and Gleason, *The Undeclared War*, p. 529.

81. Joseph P. Lash, *Roosevelt and Churchill: The Partnership That Saved the West, 1939–1941* (New York: W. W. Norton, 1976), p. 366.

82. Langer and Gleason, *The Undeclared War*, p. 535.

83. *Ibid.*, pp. 551–53.

84. Adolf A. Berle to Franklin D. Roosevelt, July 8, 1941, Roosevelt Papers, P.S.F., Box 52. See also Berle to Sumner Welles, July 7, 1941, Berle Papers, Box 54; and John D. Hickerson to Berle, July 21, 1941, N.A., R.G. 59, Hickerson Files, Box 1.

85. Robert E. Sherwood, *Roosevelt and Hopkins: An Intimate History* (New York: Harper and Brothers, 1948), p. 311.

86. Franklin D. Roosevelt to Winston Churchill, July 14, 1941, Roosevelt Papers, P.S.F., Box 52.

87. Memorandum of a Conversation in the Office of Adolf A. Berle to Consider Eastern European Questions, August 1, 1941, N.A., R.G. 59, 740.00/ 2148 2/10; and Memorandum of a Conversation Between Berle and Ralph C. S. Stevenson, September 15, 1941, N.A., R.G. 59, 840.50/248.

88. Langer and Gleason, *The Undeclared War*, pp. 545–55; and Lash, *Roosevelt and Churchill*, p. 367.

89. James C. Dunn to Cordell Hull, August 2, 1941, N.A., R.G. 59, 740.00/ 2148 2/10; and Berle and Jacobs, eds., *Navigating the Rapids*, p. 375.

90. Adolf A. Berle to Cordell Hull, August 4, 1941, Berle Papers, Box 58.

91. Memorandum of a Conversation Between Sumner Welles and Alexander Cadogan, August 9, 1941, N.A., R.G. 59, John D. Hickerson Files, Box 14.

92. Sherwood, *Roosevelt and Hopkins*, pp. 401–02. See also William C. Bullitt to Franklin D. Roosevelt, December 5, 1941, Roosevelt Papers, P.P.F., Box 1124.

93. Herbert Feis, *Churchill, Roosevelt, Stalin: The War They Waged and the Peace They Sought* (Princeton: Princeton University Press, 1957), pp. 26–27.

94. Arthur Sweetser, Memorandum on Approaches to Postwar International Organization, September 17, 1941, *War and Peace Studies of the Council on Foreign Relations.*

95. Martin J. Sherwin, *A World Destroyed: The Atomic Bomb and the Grand Alliance* (New York: Random House, 1977), p. 38.

96. Langer and Gleason, *The Undeclared War*, pp. 685–88.

97. James B. Conant to Lewis W. Douglas, October 4, 1940, Douglas Papers, Box 261, University of Arizona Library.

98. Lewis W. Douglas to James B. Conant, October 9, 1940, Douglas Papers, Box 261. See also Douglas to F. P. Koppel, November 12, 1941, Box 262.

99. Hugh R. Wilson Diary, March 1, 1940, Wilson Papers, Box 4, Herbert C. Hoover Library.

100. Hugh R. Wilson, Memorandum of a Meeting of the State Department Advisory Committee on the Problems of Foreign Relations, May 31, 1940, Wilson Papers, Box 1.

101. Adolf A. Berle Diary, September 5, 1940. See also entry for March 22, 1940.

102. *Ibid.*, October 11, 1940. See also entry for October 17, 1940.

103. J. Pierrepont Moffat Diary, October 6–10, 1940.

Bibliography of Primary Sources

National Archives of the United States
Record Groups: 59, 151, 165, 353

Manuscript Collections
Library of Congress, Washington, D.C.:
  Robert W. Bingham
  Josephus Daniels
  Norman H. Davis
  William E. Dodd
  Herbert Feis
  Cordell Hull
  Jesse H. Jones
  Frank Knox
  William D. Leahy
  Breckinridge Long
  National Policy Committee
  Leo Pasvolsky
  Francis B. Sayre
  Laurence A. Steinhardt
Franklin D. Roosevelt Library, Hyde Park, N.Y.:
  Adolf A. Berle
  Leon Henderson
  Harry L. Hopkins
  R. Walton Moore
  Henry Morgenthau
  Franklin D. Roosevelt

Bibliography

Myron C. Taylor
John C. Wiley
Harvard University Houghton Library, Cambridge, Mass.:
    W. Cameron Forbes
    J. Pierrepont Moffat
    William Phillips
Harvard Business School Baker Library, Boston, Mass.:
    Winthrop W. Aldrich
    Thomas W. Lamont
Columbia University Butler Library, New York, N.Y.:
    Nicholas Murray Butler
    Spruille Braden
    Carnegie Endowment for International Peace
    George L. Harrison
Princeton University Mudd Library, Princeton, N.J.:
    Bernard M. Baruch
    Fred I. Kent
    Harry Dexter White
Princeton University Firestone Library, Princeton, N.J.:
    John Foster Dulles
Yale University Sterling Library, New Haven, Conn.:
    Edward M. House
    Henry L. Stimson
Herbert C. Hoover Library, West Branch, Iowa:
    Hugh R. Wilson
    Robert E. Wood
University of Delaware Library, Newark, Del.:
    George S. Messersmith
University of Iowa Library, Iowa City, Iowa:
    Henry A. Wallace
University of Arizona Library, Tucson, Arizona:
    Lewis W. Douglas
University of Missouri Library, Columbia, Mo.:
    George N. Peek

Government Publications

Foreign Commerce Weekly
Foreign Relations of the United States

Periodicals and Pamphlets

Annalist
Annals of the American Academy of Political and Social Science
Bankers' Magazine
Barron's
Business Week
Commercial and Financial Chronicle
Foreign Affairs
Foreign Policy Reports
Fortune
Iron Age
Magazine of Wall Street
Official Reports of the National Foreign Trade Conventions
Proceedings of the Export Managers' Club of New York
Proceedings of the World Affairs Institute
The Protectionist
Reference Shelf
Think
Vital Speeches
War and Peace Studies of the Council on Foreign Relations

Published Papers and Diaries

Berle, Beatrice B., and Jacobs, Travis B., eds. *Navigating the Rapids: From The Papers of Adolf A. Berle, 1918–1971.* New York: Harcourt Brace Jovanovich, 1973.

Blum, John M. *From the Morgenthau Diaries: Years of Crisis, 1925–1938.* Boston: Houghton Mifflin, 1959.

Blum, John M. *From the Morgenthau Diaries: Years of Urgency, 1938–1941.* Boston: Houghton Mifflin, 1964.

Bullitt, Orville H., ed. *For the President Personal and Secret: Correspondence Between Franklin D. Roosevelt and William C. Bullitt.* Boston: Houghton Mifflin, 1972.

Cannistraro, Philip V., Wynet, Edward D., and Kovoleff, Theodore P., eds. *Poland and the Coming of the Second World War: The Diplomatic Papers of A. J. Drexel Biddle, Jr., United States Ambassador to Poland, 1937–1939.* Columbus: Ohio State University Press, 1976.

Davies, Joseph E. *Mission to Moscow.* New York: Simon and Schuster, 1941.

Bibliography

Dobney, Fredrick J., ed. *Selected Papers of Will Clayton*. Baltimore: The Johns Hopkins Press, 1971.

Dodd, William E., Jr., and Dodd, Martha, eds. *Ambassador Dodd's Diary*. New York: Harcourt, Brace, and Co., 1941.

Israel, Fred L., ed. *The War Diary of Breckinridge Long*. Lincoln: University of Nebraska Press, 1966.

Nixon, Edgar B., ed. *Franklin D. Roosevelt and Foreign Affairs*. Cambridge: Harvard University Press, 1969.

Roosevelt, Elliot, ed. *F.D.R.: His Personal Letters, 1925–1945*. New York: Duel, Sloan, and Pearce, 1950.

The Secret Diary of Harold L. Ickes: The First Thousand Days, 1933–1936. New York: Simon and Schuster, 1953.

The Secret Diary of Harold L. Ickes: The Lowering Clouds, 1939–1941. New York: Simon and Schuster, 1954.

Index

Index

321